PRAISE FOR
THE METAVERSE ECONOMY

"It is clear that the metaverse is going to be a *big* thing and, for many in finance, it is a development that clearly needs financial services. Arun and Theo have pre-empted this development with an essential guide to how to navigate this thing. I thoroughly recommend it."
Chris Skinner, CEO, The Finanser

"No one knows what the future will hold. Kudos to Theo and Arun for their bold attempt to lay out a vision of the future in *The Metaverse Economy*, with innovation and community in mind. I highly recommend this book to gain valuable insights from the renowned authors."
Spiros Margaris, global fintech, finance and AI influencer

"*The Metaverse Economy* emerges just as artificial intelligence bursts into public awareness. Are the metaverse and web3 heading in the same direction? Exploring this question from multiple angles, this book provides a balanced perspective on the possibilities, the headwinds and the potential for advancing our human development. This is essential reading for those who wish to understand this possible future."
Frank Diana, Managing Partner and Futurist, TCS

"Web2, web3, DeFi, metaverse, hype cycles? If you are in finance and trying to look to the future, you need to read this book. Yes, you will get the technical details, but you also get a rational view of how this is really just history repeating itself. Just as social media has become a critical part of our daily lives, the metaverse is coming. Will you be ready, or will you be a bystander?"
Curt Queyrouze, President, Coastal Community Bank

"As I read *The Metaverse Economy*, I couldn't help but feel a surge of excitement and inspiration. The possibilities that lie before us are boundless, and our journey into this digital frontier is one that holds transformative potential in every aspect of our lives. In this digital realm, diverse minds converge, ideas collide and creativity thrives. Thanks to Theodora Lau and Arun Krishnakumar, people will be motivated to embark on this transformative journey with open hearts and open minds."

Martha Boeckenfeld, Meta-Host, Choice LGBTQIA+

"Whether you're new or 'early' to web3, you need to read this book. Theo and Arun provide a solid foundation to understand and make sense of this fast-evolving digital world. The book's thoughtful construction makes it easy to follow with relevant context and expert insight without overwhelming you with jargon. When you've finished *The Metaverse Economy*, you'll be ready to explore for yourself how this technology can change how we connect, collaborate and create together."

Patrick Rivenbark, Principal, The Rivenbark Group

"As we move towards web3, it is imperative that we all participate. Consider this book as a captivating invitation to explore the present iteration of the metaverse, allowing you to form your own perspectives of the future with the guidance of the authors who share their thoughts on the challenges and opportunities that lie ahead."

Efi Pylarinou, global fintech and tech influencer

"What a wonderful read and Herculean effort! *The Metaverse Economy* provides the reader with accessible, tangible points and connections to real-world brands and experiences, making the content digestible and accessible."

Liat Shetret, Director of Global Policy & Regulation, Elliptic

"The metaverse must be one of the most difficult concepts to describe, dissect, analyze and philosophize. Theodora Lau and Arun Krishnakumar have done it masterfully. This is a very helpful book for those that are new to the industry."

Jenn Tesch, Senior Director, Enterprise Business Development, Elliptic

"*The Metaverse Economy* is a must-read for finance professionals seeking to stay ahead of the curve and harness the opportunities presented by web3. Arun and Theodora's expertise and forward-thinking approach shine through as they explore the potential impact of blockchain, decentralized finance, and virtual worlds on the financial industry."

Medhy Souidi, Head of Transformation & Ecosystems, DBS HK

"On the cusp of a revolution in AR, VR, Digital Assets and the metaverse in general, Theo and Arun step into the fray with *The Metaverse Economy*. If you are in financial services, you need a plan. This book will get you on the road to success."

Brett King, Bestselling author of *The Rise of Technosocialism*

The Metaverse Economy

How Finance Professionals
Can Make Sense of Web3

Arun Krishnakumar
Theodora Lau

KoganPage

First published in Great Britain and the United States in 2023 by Kogan Page Limited

2nd Floor, 45 Gee Street	8 W 38th Street, Suite 902	4737/23 Ansari Road
London	New York, NY 10018	Daryaganj
EC1V 3RS	USA	New Delhi 110002
United Kingdom		India
www.koganpage.com		

© Arun Krishnakumar and Theodora Lau 2023

ISBNs

Hardback   9781398610583
Paperback   9781398610538
Ebook   9781398610576

British Library Cataloguing-in-Publication Data
A CIP record for this book is available from the British Library.

Library of Congress Control Number
2023940516

Typeset by Hong Kong FIVE Workshop, Hong Kong
Print production managed by Jellyfish
Printed and bound by CPI Group (UK) Ltd, Croydon CR0 4YY

Kogan Page books are printed on paper from sustainable forests.

CONTENTS

FOREWORD

Growing up, I had always wanted to be an architect—a creative quant that combines the beauty of art with the mathematics of construction. There is something profound about architecture, weaving together such opposite disciplines, and creating spaces and structures for people to inhabit. We are so used to our buildings and landmarks that we no longer see them, their accomplishment and storytelling is invisible to us. And yet the architect is a poet across time, anchored in the now of the space where people live, and in the future of the cities to come.

Life took a different turn, and pulled me through the digital transformation of financial services. From the bankruptcy of Lehman Brothers, to the rise of digital investing in New York City, to the neobanks of London, and eventually the global web3 movement powered by computational blockchains, I had flowed along the river of money and economics as entrepreneur, strategist, and builder. It is in these waters that I met Theo and Arunkumar, passionate about innovation and excited about the explosive potential of this moment. They too sit at the intersection of these novel trends, parsing them and understanding the direction of travel.

And what a strange moment it is! What we had thought of as dry, boring spreadsheets and financial plumbing has transformed into digital assets, non-fungible tokens (NFTs), and popular culture. Social media is ablaze with the markets for collectible digital art. Gaming companies talk about creating new worlds and economies of virtual items and avatars. The world's largest brands and enterprises race to offer digital goods to fans and communities.

The architects are back—concerned not with just the physical world, but with the magical world of our digital environment. As people spend more and more time in this unfolding universe, as augmented and virtual reality hardware and infrastructure mature, as blockchains become more performant and scalable, we all become builders of infinite potential. You can see the big tech companies grasping for position—Meta working on the social layer, Epic on rendering, and others on blockchain technology.

But the metaverse will not be owned or shackled by companies, regardless of the growing pains of regulation and attempts at control. It is a broad-based public good, comprised of imagination, creativity, and economic potential. Where the internet failed, beholden to the walled gardens of endless content, the metaverse promises to reset our digital lives to human scale. There, we will find the missing pieces of a sane online world—identity, ownership, privacy, transparency, and economy. There, we will not just be entertained, but build businesses and become architects of our own digital experience.

It is a beautiful, utopian vision. The hard part is connecting the dots to make the whole coherent amongst the many constituent parts. I am thrilled to see the publication of this book to tackle the challenging question of *how*. Artificial intelligence, mixed reality, and web3 are all rich, difficult trends to understand. How will they weave together and create a new space that we inhabit? Tokens, NFTs, and cryptoeconomic design are all emergent and new. How will they be used to power a metaverse of digital avatars and their inventories? Large companies struggle with innovation, and often collapse as the world goes through technological platform shifts. How will enterprises adopt not just blockchain and web3, but the broader promise of the metaverse?

These are difficult questions to ask, and even harder questions to answer. The book you hold sets out on this monumental task, and opens up the answers to make up your own mind. While the future remains unknown, it is up to us to learn about the possibilities, and then to shape it, to architect the future that benefits humanity the most. While nobody knows the outcome, I am excited to be going on this journey along with you.

Lex Sokolin

ConsenSys Chief Economist and founder of Fintech Blueprint

FOREWORD

When one of the world's largest firms catering to two billion people decides to rename themselves based on a technology concept, the world has to stand up and take notice. In October of 2021 Facebook changed the name of their parent company to "Meta," as a mark of the company's strategic dive into the emerging world of metaverse. Mark Zuckerberg stated that they would become "metaverse-first," and "hoped that within the next decade, the metaverse will reach a billion people, host hundreds of billions of dollars of digital commerce, and support jobs for millions of creators and developers."[1] With plans to spend tens of billions of dollars and recruit over 10,000 engineers, it showed a big commitment towards a phenomenon that was crossing multiple worlds—from gaming to virtual reality to blockchain and the future of money. The phenomenon has advanced significantly from Neal Stephenson's sci-fi novel *Snow Crash* (1992), referring to a virtual world that parallels our physical one, where people may collaborate, socialize, and entertain themselves to the reality of Steven Spielberg's *Ready Player One*.

The fundamental elements and technological breakthroughs that have allowed this vision to become a reality include the advances in virtual reality (VR), underpinned by increased computational power of graphic cards and other hardware, progression in connectivity with 5G, and the emergence of blockchain technology and digital assets. With access to VR through sleeker and high-quality headsets, consumers have the ability to navigate a virtual space with relative ease, giving individuals an immersive experience that mimics the real world. Achieving full-scale immersion will probably take a few more years, and we will continue to see desktop-based metaverse platforms co-existing with VR-enhanced metaverse platforms to cater to the different end users and experiences.

The emergence of blockchain technology furthers the infrastructural development of current metaverse projects, refining the notion of ownership in a digital context as cryptographically constructed digital items in the virtual world. With provenance and traceability of ownership, one can solve for challenges regarding the ownership of digital properties with the ownership of virtual items, such as virtual property, skins, points, and tokens, in non-blockchain-based platforms being largely unsecured. The immutability and traceability features of blockchain technologies has also given rise to new types of metaverse platforms which enable full digital control over items for owners—achieved via the use of NFTs.

While the metaverse is still a virtual world running parallel to our physical reality, the metaverse economy is evolving rapidly with the involvement of a host of organizations from governments, regulators, and traditional economy firms at one end, to large technology firms, startups, and luxury brands at the other. In many senses, the metaverse is a new form of digital real estate akin to a webpage, providing companies and individuals with another avenue to connect and market themselves. It builds on the closed-loop in-game economy that has existed for quite some time now in many games. Varying transactions of game items take place amongst gamers on these online platforms. These transactions, done through bartering, in-game transactions, or offline trades with monetary terms, were precursors of what we expect the metaverse's new economic system to look like or resemble.

Without a reliable and trustworthy mechanism for the movement of digital assets on the metaverse, digital assets owners would have less incentive to trade/exchange their assets with each other. In closed-loop platforms/games, it is difficult for players to transfer their items out of the platforms, and, when feasible, their gaming valuables may not have much outside value. Further, most of these transactions are essentially an internal movement of items. As the metaverse matures, we are witnessing engagement of both TradeFi as well as web3 financial firms to cater primarily to Millennials and Gen Zs.

While e-commerce was also transformative, and dare one say revolutionized how we shop, there haven't been any substantial improvements to the online shopping experience over the last five years or so. Within the metaverse, retail is a sector which possesses one of the largest business potentials through the power of augmented and mixed reality. Metaverse-based shopping can greatly revolutionize the shopping experience of viewing and purchasing products virtually; for instance, customers will be able to "try out" the latest collections of goods through an immersive experience.

Many companies have begun creating showrooms and developing designs specially for metaverses, with other tech startups providing the service to build such showrooms for a three-dimensional experience. In December 2021, fashion brand Ralph Lauren opened its virtual stores in the Roblox metaverse, while Gucci launched a virtual project in Roblox dubbed Gucci Garden. We are also seeing the major e-commerce players, such as Alibaba, providing a mixed reality experience for their users to purchase goods online.

Taking this a step further, one can view financial services in the metaverse as the new, evolved version of electronic or internet banking. During Web1 and 2, internet-based banking services, online shopping, and email composition have all been accessed through web browsers such as Netscape, Microsoft IE, Firefox, and finally Google Chrome. The experience has not been highly interactive, with platforms typically providing a standard two-dimensional feel, lacking the quality to make these mundane activities more engaging. The metaverse, however, is going to add a new layer to "surfing the internet," applying to all forms of internet or web-based activities. Fintech and the blockchain will have a big role to play in the metaverse as experience enhancers, which further promote business and commercial activities in the virtual world.

As an extension, there is significant potential to transform one of the oldest professional services: Banking. The metaverse allows enhancement of existing functionality in a three-dimensional and immersive manner, making customer engagement exciting while enabling the development and emergence of new products and markets. While the last decade was driven by the true integration of finance and technology, via fintech and techfin, driven by electronic payment, the emergence of Bitcoin and other digital assets is an evolutionary step in technology being embedded in everything we do.

While e-payments overcame the inefficiencies of a manually cleared money ledger and provided digitized and automated clearance, web3 payments and their authorizations can be instant and seamless. With metaverse platforms having the ability to embed digital wallet, not only are payments easier and faster to make, but virtual gaming assets are also easier to manage and save. Further, as stated by J P Morgan,[2] one of the keys to enabling a gaming ecosystem on the metaverse is to create custom payment solutions with embedded and interoperable virtual wallets that allow flexible single pay or multiple pay options, and a fast, secure checkout in multiple currencies, both fiat-based and digital.

Users have already begun transacting in digital assets over the metaverse, and we witness a host of banks, ranging from banks in Korea to global giants, working towards offering a broader range of financial capabilities and services in the near future. The aim is to make the experience more accessible, streamlined, and enjoyable even when one is looking to transact through the assistance of a relationship manager (in his or her avatar form, or for that matter a fully virtual relationship manager). The whole banking experience will therefore become a gaming-like journey that Millennials and Gen Z clients are familiar with.

In February 2022, for example, J P Morgan became the world's first major bank to set up a presence in the metaverse. The Onyx venture of J P Morgan opened a virtual lounge in the Metajuku District inside Decentraland to showcase the bank's services and fintech propositions. This was followed by the likes of HSBC Group and Standard Chartered announcing partnerships with The Sandbox, a blockchain metaverse platform owned by the Hong Kong-based Animoca Brands, to create innovative experiences for their clients and the community. This is a clear indication that crypto-linked metaverses were no longer irrelevant to traditional banks or banking services. It further showed the possibility of conventional banks being able to organically integrate into new virtual spaces. In parallel, we are also witnessing the drive from decentralized finance institutions being keen to also provide financial services within the metaverse and sense that they have a leg-up on TradeFi institutions given they are digital (and, in this case, crypto) native.

While the concept of the metaverse is new to many, speculative behaviors are not uncommon. We have seen both the rise and significant decline in value of in-platform metaverse tokens over the past year, in line with the broader markets. Those entering the space for speculation would have been adversely affected by the fall in the value of the native tokens, as also the fall in the price of virtual properties. Secondly, with new technologies come new challenges. While there is still a continuous trend of international financial institutions providing financial services in the metaverse, legal and regulatory treatment is evolving and not yet solidified globally. In particular, challenges that come with the process of "know your customer" and anti-money laundering on platforms that may not have strong governance.

Challenges also present themselves when it comes to moderating and eliminating abusive behavior and digital harassment. We still have questions to be addressed regarding the protection of both intellectual property and individual rights in the virtual world. Will regulators be able to apply pre-existing legal systems built for the physical world, and will we be able to see changes to existing laws to cater to the metaverse, in line with the treatment of the online economy?

Then there are the challenges typically faced by online platforms, ranging from cybersecurity risk given the nascency of the industry, to the issues with scams. Any digital platform can be subject to hackers; therefore, it is important for both platform operators as well as users to be vigilant at all times. Other cybersecurity risks include platform engineering attacks, network credential theft, the security risks of virtual reality itself (for example, biometric data in fingerprints, retina scans, voiceprints, and facial geometry), and identity theft. Custody of metaverse assets, especially digital assets, needs to be robust and well governed with transparency to avoid theft, misappropriation, and phishing. Scammers may also use various methods to falsely represent any fake metaverse projects to create some sort of hype around prevailing popular business ideas such as virtual real estate. These illicit activities may involve offline monetary transactions that could potentially lead to serious crimes.

As the crypto world emerges from a prolonged winter, driven by large-scale collapses and fraudulent activities, the pace of growth of the metaverse industry has tempered. However, with stronger regulations, more educated users, and the development of experiential metaverses over speculative platforms, the next five years will be the making of the industry. The metaverse brings together the rise of the multi-billion-dollar gaming industry with the digital-first habits of digital natives. As with the internet, for this potential to be realized it will take substantial development in experience, connectivity, reliability, and regulations. Traction will only increase once users find the metaverse to be part of their day-to-day lives. Facebook, nay, Meta, made an existential bet on the industry and if the industry matures, the bet originating from a snow crash can take us all to a galaxy far, far away.

Syed Musheer Ahmed
Founder, FinStep Asia

PREFACE

Musings from Theodora Lau

Being able to spend time with children is one of the most fulfilling things. The expressions on their faces, especially when they uncover something new, is priceless. The insatiable thirst for knowledge sometimes makes me wonder, when do we, as adults, stop asking "Why?" How did we lose that sense of curiosity?

It was with that sense of quest that I began the journey of writing *The Metaverse Economy*.

Diving deep into a space that evolves so quickly is like writing while standing on top of quicksand. You can feel a sense of excitement and giddiness that comes with such a nascent paradigm; and you can also feel a sense of uncertainty, doubting, and wondering what might go wrong. And you will be forgiven if you feel like a chicken running around with its head cut off. Because it is exactly that. Look, here is a new use case! And look, here is another application! And for every positive news story, there are always a few more negative ones. As with everything in life, there are always bad actors that are trying to exploit and game the system.

But just because something isn't perfect, doesn't mean we stop pursuing it. Think back to your children, and what it took to get them to take the first step, to say the first word, and to write that very first sentence. Every step was a journey unto itself. Every step was a milestone. Even though the journey might be bumpy, even though we might fall along the way, we never stop. We learn from our mistakes. We get back up and we keep going. Because every failure helps get us one step closer to where we need to be.

And we must not forget—the ecosystem is still incredibly new compared to the tech paradigm that we have. Just as when the World Wide Web was launched no one could have predicted how it is being used today, let alone the business models that have evolved along the way. I remember how my father taught me the first line of code:

"Hello World" with a Macintosh back in 1990. I remember the clunky Compaq laptop and portable ink computer that my parents bought me for college. I remember doing my school projects in the beautiful Voorhees Computing Center (VCC) in my undergrad alma mater, Rensselaer Polytechnic Institute (RPI) in upstate New York. The VCC was previously a library that was converted from a chapel and it was one of multiple computer labs on campus that housed Unix machines. Many late nights were spent there, compiling code and debugging. My entertainment was playing Minesweeper and Solitaire on Windows 3.1 on my Compaq machine back in my dorm room. I got my first mobile phone, a Motorola MicroTac, in 1994, which was mostly used for safety and emergency purposes as the limit for the cellular plan back then was only 30 minutes. Long-distance phone calls via the landline were still expensive then.

A few years after I graduated from college came the height of the dot-com boom. Working for internet startups became the "it" thing to do. Companies offered lavish incentives, including free BMW Z4, in order to compete for talent. A "grow at all cost" mentality took over sound business models and cash flow fundamentals as the industry raced to capitalize on the internet craze. Even I built a static webpage with the url idunnowhy.com, because truly, why not? The valuations of startups continued to climb as venture capital kept the champagne flowing.

Until it didn't.

In 2000, the dot-com bubble burst and many startups, along with a few telecommunications companies, went out of business. But that was not the end of the story; rather, it was the wake-up call that the industry needed. New companies were formed during the downturn, having tested out new business models and survived. The internet continued to thrive and consumers and businesses alike benefited from more affordable high-speed connectivity and mobility, bringing about even more disruptive use cases and sustainable economic models. How we live, work, and connect with each other has never been the same since then.

In many ways, what the tech industry is going through reminds me of our dot-com days. If there was one thing we learned, it is that communities matter. At the end of the day, technology is a means towards the end. For any innovation to get to mass adoption, it must serve a true purpose, regardless of how cool the technology may seem.

As you walk through the enchanted forest of the metaverse, I hope that you will find not only what you are looking for, but also the *raison d'être*. For that will be the North Star that we will need to steer us on our journey. And that, when you look back at the roads you have traveled, you will remember not only the blood, sweat, and tears, but also what you have overcome.

Musings from Arunkumar Krishnakumar

It was a few years ago, during one of my holidays to my hometown, I was on my mobile playing Clash of Clans. It was a little routine of mine, where I used to play it for a few minutes every day, just to feel I was making some progress. My mother observed me for a few days and asked me what it was. I explained that I was building a castle and upgrading it by accumulating gold from the mines. Her comment was in my native tongue, Tamil, and it meant "How does it add any commercial value to your life?" She had a point, she most often does.

It's been less than half a decade since that conversation. My routine hasn't changed. but the game has, and this time the game does add commercial value to my life. Whether this is just a game that is unsustainable is for time and the markets to decide. But we have found a business model, and it will take a few years for it to turn into something that can scale for the world to come and play. The app may want me to sprint to make the money, but I know it's a marathon, not a sprint. It will take time for the model to prove that it can be a routine for a large user base who can have some fun with it and earn along the way. We are not too far away from a world where my mom may be wrong, and that would be a rarity.

In 2019, I was watching the Netflix documentary *The Great Hack*. The Cambridge Analytica episode happened and passed. But the reasons and implications had hardly sunk in. Watching the story on Netflix, with perhaps some embellishments, got me thinking. Gone were the days where we paid for good-quality products. I realized that the new world is specifically set up to get us addicted to dopamine, make us the product, and earn revenues from that process. Books have been written on how to keep an audience hooked and several of them have gone on to become bestsellers.

The world needs a reset, a detox; we will need our lives back and where we do indeed need these apps that make us the product, they had better share the revenues they make from us, with us. Ninety-nine percent of data created has been created in the last decade. It takes 70 million servers to manage that quantity of data we produce, and those servers add two tons of CO_2 into the atmosphere just for the manufacturing process.[1] Data wasn't called "the new oil" for just its utility.

Therefore, it is critical that we hold ourselves, and the firms we entrust our data with, responsible for how our data is used and stored. The firms of the dot-com era haven't shown any respite in amassing the data. We wouldn't have seen amazing AI products such as ChatGPT and Bard if not for those volumes of data. Yet, it is time we know precisely where our data sits, who is holding on to it, who is using it, and how the data is getting monetized. It's high time we moved onto solutions that respect their users, acknowledge what users own on their platform, and the value users add, and compensate users for that. Users must have complete transparency of their data footprint that leads to the carbon footprint. We deserve better.

Through my career as a venture capital investor, I pitched to limited partners (LPs—investors who deploy capital into virtual currency funds), who understood the exponential returns this asset class offered but were put off by the illiquid nature of their investments. Often LPs of virtual currency funds have to wait a decade if not more to get their monies back. It was such a pain point that we have tried to overcome it by thinking through various options to provide better liquidity to LPs without many compromises. Not until the "Initial Coin Offering" structures became famous in 2017 did I see a better alternative.

Tokenization could now allow investors to invest in a high returns asset class, with low liquidity risks. The model had merit but initial coin offerings (ICOs) did come crashing down, thanks to human greed. The model hasn't died, but many firms that have used it without a good product and a business model have not seen the next Bitcoin cycle.

Are we suggesting that the alternatives are perfect? Theo has used the baby-steps analogy, so I am going to resort to another to answer that question. In life we often compare one generation with another. The actors of one generation to the previous one, the sportspeople of one generation to the previous one, and in this book the technology of one generation is being compared to the previous one. But we must remind ourselves that the new generation often stands on the shoulders of the previous one. They are supposed to be able to scale greater heights and look much further into the future from those heights. They don't necessarily have to be better because of what they are, but also because of what came before them. The new alternatives are just finding their feet, and they should tower greater heights.

Through my web3 journeys as an investor, an author, and an entrepreneur, I have come across several technology and business paradigms that have shown excellent promise. The promise attracts new investors, and as more capital arrives, so do illicit actors. It's important to tap into the promise and channelize capital while building a controls framework to mitigate illicit activities and identify Ponzi schemes and shut them down more proactively.

Yet, the focus must be on tapping into the promise, hand-holding the baby, and helping the next generation realize the dream.

ACKNOWLEDGMENTS

This book is not meant to be a dictation or a prediction of what the metaverse is supposed to be like. After all, it is hard to define something that is so early in its lifecycle. Rather, it is a vision of what we think it could, and should, be. And it is a glimpse of what it might be, if we are willing to build it together.

The future at times may seem uncertain and the road that we still need to travel is bumpy. But we can't create a different future if we are not willing to take the first step and change what is not working. And we are not even at the opening act yet: the next page of the story is yet to be written.

To the dreamers and creators, the believers and the rebels, we see you.

To our families, we cannot say thank you enough. Without you, this book would not have existed. Our words live to see the day because of your unconditional support.

To our friends near and far, thank you for your invaluable advice. Writing about a tech space that evolves as quickly as web3 and metaverse is like writing while standing on quicksand. Your input throughout our writing journey helps to keep us grounded.

To our amazing team at Kogan Page, especially Bronwyn Geyer, thank you for your encouragement and advice, and for keeping us on track as we navigate through the maze of time zones and commitments.

And last but not least, a massive thank you to all our wonderful readers. We hope this book can serve as your loyal companion for the journey that you are on.

Let's write the next chapter—together.

Background 01

True financial empowerment considers the benefits to our community as a whole instead of the needs of the few.

Ever since the stone age, humans have been able to thrive as we have continuously reinvented ourselves and reconfigured our social setup. From stone tool innovation like Acheulean hand axes over 500,000 years ago, to the invention of the wheel in Mesopotamia in the 4th millennium BC or more recently the Industrial Revolution itself, we have always strived for more.

The desire has often been for a better and easier lifestyle, or just simply a more prosperous life. That quest has allowed us to create leapfrog moments throughout the history of the species. One such moment was the Neolithic Revolution, which enabled the transition from small, nomadic bands of hunter-gatherer lifestyles to larger, permanent agricultural settlements with a reliable food supply. With farming and agriculture, people started living together in communities and civilizations grew as a result, leading to more modern-day advancements.

As we got more efficient as a society, we have most certainly come closer to each other as we built the rails for sharing information more effectively. In particular, the last hundred years have seen the development of better communication and technology that has allowed the world to function as one interconnected innovation ecosystem. That has certainly helped us break physical barriers such as national borders. But, most importantly, it has allowed us to innovate at breakneck speed at scale.

The invention of the personal computer, the internet, social media, and the smartphone are four significant milestones of the last 100 years of innovation. Sprinkle technology paradigms like artificial intelligence (AI), quantum computing and blockchain across this timeline, and it shows how restless we have been as a species.

If we were to draw a timeline of all these amazing paradigms, we would notice that over the past 50 years the distance between these key milestones has been drastically reduced. Not only do we see breakthrough innovation being introduced more frequently than ever before, user adoption as well as the time to reach market saturation have accelerated.

On the other hand, our survival instincts still make us conscious and cautious of new things. Every time we see innovation, most of us look at the risks of embracing it. We even see experts of incumbent approaches criticize disruptive trends while they are still taking baby steps. Multi-generational inventions are those that see through multiple winters, and in the end prove early critics wrong.

It is this continuous tension between the want for more, and the fear of the less known, that keeps us on our toes. In this book, we are going to explore one such paradigm that is in motion—the metaverse and the economic models around it.

The last generation of innovation brought to us web2 and several applications and economies that thrived on this. We are now witnessing web3 models like the metaverse emerge as alternatives and they introduce applications and economics that seem better, at least in theory.

In this chapter we will study the evolution of web2 business models and key areas where they fall short. In doing so, we will set the foundations for the rest of this book as we explore the design principles of metaverses and other web3 models that could potentially address these shortfalls of web2 models.

The Birth of Web2

The rise of the personal computer (PC) and the World Wide Web really set the scene for a thriving web2 ecosystem through the 1990s and 2000s. These two elements fulfilled the infrastructure requirement needed for web2 to scale globally. This coincided with the phenomenal rise in venture capital led by the Silicon Valley ecosystem.

As venture capital met an influx of high-quality human capital that was capable of non-stop innovation, exciting business models and applications emerged. This was suitably supported by a consumer base excited about the applications that allowed social connections, seamless content access, and digital e-commerce. As the supply and demand converged at scale, digital adoption skyrocketed.

The first spurt of growth in this market came from developed markets due to better penetration of PCs and the internet. However, over the course of the last 20 years, many emerging economies have seen digital transformation at scale. This was particularly the case after the emergence of smartphones over the last decade. Several emerging economies invested in their telecommunication and digital infrastructure during this period that catalyzed internet adoption across billions of people.

The billions of internet users became potential customers to these web2 applications. Facebook, Google, and Amazon were all models that tapped into this growth to become trillion-dollar empires. There were similar models in the east too, particularly in China and India. Led by Alibaba, Tencent, Flipkart, and Paytm, these web2 models scaled across Asia. The US technology giants also penetrated some of these markets. For instance, India became the largest user base for WhatsApp.

The user base that these apps attracted led to an explosion in data generated and processed. Facebook generates 4 million gigabytes (4 petabytes) of data per day,[1] and Google attracted over 88 billion of visits in the three months ending 2022.[2] In most cases, users of these apps didn't have to pay to use their basic services. Facebook, Google, WhatsApp, and YouTube were all offering their services for free to these customers.

The world got closer, more entertained, and better informed using these technologies and mostly without spending a penny. So, what could go wrong? It's just that, if it's a free lunch, you are the lunch.

Web2 showed us how to scale digital businesses globally using the right composition of capital through business cycles. It demonstrated how powerful data could be, when it is used the right way in augmenting business models. As controversial as it may be, web2 also showed us why taking the market through a growth-focused strategy could potentially lead to sustainable businesses.

Firms like Amazon showed us that these businesses can scale without turning profits, and eventually the scale would allow them to accelerate revenue-making opportunities leading to profits.

Yet, web2 was built on the rails of traditional capital markets, exploited user data, breached data privacy, was centrally governed, and used the community rather than serving it. In doing so, a very small subset of people profited from the growth of web2 as these businesses largely acted in the interest of maximizing their returns.

Another key aspect of traditional capital markets and web2 is that several middlemen were created. There were layers of incremental value addition across value chains, increasing the distance between the creator of value and the consumer of value. This has led to a large portion of value accrued to the middlemen, and very little for the creator of value.

Let us now go deeper into each of these aspects in greater detail and demonstrate why web2 could soon be obsolete as a model unless it addresses some of the fundamental flaws in its approach. We will also highlight web3 models that already address most of these design flaws yet are a long way from demonstrating scalability and sustainability.

Web2 Business Models

The ethos of web2 business models has its roots in the Silicon Valley venture capital (VC) ecosystem. Several innovative firms at a very early stage would compete for a pot of capital from early-stage VC funds. Once they get funded, they follow a rigorous regime of tracking growth metrics of the business and reporting them back to their investors on a periodic basis.

As these businesses scale, their growth metrics, often termed as unit economics, should improve. The firms with the best unit economics often win the next pot of capital from growth stage investors. This cycle of growth metrics-based funding eventually creates a category winner within a sub-cluster of a domain.

For instance, if we are looking at fintech lending in the US, the VCs typically focus on identifying the winner within fintech in the region based on growth metrics. As a few winners emerge, late-stage capital chooses the winner with a hope to take them into the public markets. Generally, by the time businesses enter public markets, they must have cracked a business model. This means they are not just a growth-focused company that keeps sucking capital but have a profitable business in place.

That is the ideal journey of a web2 company that goes through several market cycles to finally make it. While this model has been successful through a "winner takes all" approach, it still serves a selected few who are able to navigate this system.

Often, the best VCs get access to the top entrepreneurs who can execute the growth strategy well. This is also because these founders are looking for the top VCs for their brand and ecosystem connections. In doing so, these VCs build their portfolios with the top names, and these firms build their cap table with these VCs. Therefore, over the years the system has become an exclusive club that delivers alpha to those that are in it.

Ideally this pool of venture capital must be accessible to a wider set of founders, and top investment opportunities should be available to a wider spectrum of investors who understand the risks. Unfortunately, web2 failed in creating such an inclusive model, enabling only a small subset of investors and founders to benefit.

The rest of the world did gain from this model, but more so on the other side of the transaction. These consumers neither had a slice of the upside as these firms grew, nor did they have the power to make decisions as customers or shareholders, exacerbating the trend of the rich getting richer and the poor getting poorer.

Let us take a closer look at the stakeholders involved in making these models work.

The Stakeholders' Incentives

The founders and the management team of the firms are the first set of stakeholders. Investors from seed, growth to late-stage investment rounds are the next set of stakeholders. The third set of stakeholders are the customers who use these products. Without customers, the efforts from founders and investors would be in vain.

Therefore, from the value that these web2 models generate, a good slice should be shared with the customers. But web2 has not been that inclusive and even after seeing more inclusive models emerge in recent years, it is hard for them to pivot as they are largely reliant on traditional capital markets for funding and will need to stick to the ethos set by these market forces.

The counter to this argument could be that customers are attracted by a specific service offered by the platform at a price that they are willing to pay. Therefore, it is unnecessary to share any further incentives with these customers. This could be true if a web2 app is selling a book, a customer buys the book and the relationship between the app and the customer ends there.

It doesn't end there in most web2 apps, as they keep mining transaction data of the customer to not just serve that customer better, but also serve other customers more effectively. In effect, the transaction made by the customer has helped the platform to get more intelligent and bring in more revenues at a lower cost. The platform therefore makes recurring revenues based on the intelligence from the customer's transaction data.

Therefore, the intelligence generated from the customer's transaction must be partially credited to the customer. This effectively means that any revenue upside from this intelligence must be shared with the customer too. Yet, web2 models are relentlessly focused on maximizing the upside for the first two stakeholders—the founders and the investors.

In the process, the well-being of the customers becomes an afterthought.

Let us now look at the key business models that have helped the growth culture scale.

Digital Advertising

In 2022, Facebook's total advertising revenue was $113 billion.[3] This business model has helped validate the "growth first, profitability next" approach. Firms like Google, Twitter, and Facebook were able to attract capital based on the user base they commanded.

The pitch to investors was that the user base could eventually lead to ancillary revenues which was primarily advertising. With the growth they achieve in offering free services, they have also pioneered the "winner takes all" model, which has become a template to scale technology businesses.

Digital advertising continues to be a key revenue stream for many of these web2 applications. These apps have also built the intelligence that bridges the identity gap between a digital user and their real-life self. As those two identities were linked, advertisements have become a lot more contextual. The fact that Alexa could be listening to your whispers is essentially to tap into even that data to provide relevant advertisements. This model could extend to the metaverse future too.

Understanding user preferences through their content, interactions with content, and search history allows these platforms to build intelligence about the user. This eventually helps platforms build echo chambers around the user and effectively feed them with relevant content and advertisements. Such targeted advertisements are now driven by data analytics, which is built on petabytes of data. This helps maximize the performance of these ads and increases platform revenues.

As the quantity and quality of user data on web2 platforms increases, so will their advertisement revenues. In 2021, the percentage of advertising revenue at Google, Facebook, and Amazon was 28.6 percent, 23.7 percent, and 5.8 percent respectively.[4] The cost to achieve this revenue will also go down due to the data analytics employed with mining users. Despite data owned and created by users being used to generate these revenues, they very rarely get compensated for their content. They do not get credit for their efforts in being part of the community and the resulting network effects that help growth and revenues on these platforms.

In essence, the digital advertising business model has proven to be successful for web2 platforms. They attract users by generating content designed to play with dopamine levels and hang on to them by getting users to invest into the platform—acting as a digital drug of sorts. With each swipe, like, tweet, or reshare, our brains are constantly being stimulated and we can become easily obsessed with instant gratification, which we can easily find with the click of a button. Those who have benefitted from this exercise are the founders and shareholders, thus the stakeholders of these businesses.

E-Commerce

Over 8,000 years ago, in Mesopotamia, people used the barter system to exchange cattle, produce, and goods. Producers, creators, and owners would bring their products for sale and look for products they needed. If 10 bags of rice were equal to a cow or a sheep, the transaction was agreed. The barter system even involved art being exchanged for food products. But one of the fundamental traits of the barter system was that people conducted transactions based on credibility, trust, and relationships.

This kind of peer-to-peer commerce happened across businesses and even countries. Yet, with the advent of money, all things had to be given a dollar value before commerce took place. The dollar value was decided by supply and demand for the product. This extra layer of adding money to commerce added intermediaries to the value chain. These intermediaries provided the capability to assess the supply and demand and come up with a market price for the products on sale.

This model of commerce was largely prevalent across the globe until the advent of the internet. As social media platforms scaled, it gave an opportunity for the next set of business lines to thrive on the internet. E-commerce is arguably one of the largest business lines on the internet. In 2021, global e-commerce sales were approximately $5.2 trillion. Researchers expect this number to grow to $8.1 trillion by 2026.[5]

While the rise of e-commerce models has certainly globalized trade, it has also given rise to several stakeholders and platforms that act as middlemen. Let us take the process of selling/buying organic bananas on Amazon.com. The bananas could be produced by a farmer in Puerto Rico, sold to the logistics provider, who then sells them to a large wholesale buyer or a warehouse in the US. A small business or a grocery chain buys this inventory of bananas and offers online shelf space to its consumers. If the bananas were sold to the consumer for $5 for a dozen, they most likely were bought off the farmer for a tenth of the price.

Looking at this model, the farmer, who is the value creator, gets 10 percent of the value that they created. The logistics provider, the wholesaler, the grocer or the small business and the digital platform (Amazon), who have all provided a service to the farmer, enjoy the larger percentage of the value created. The logistics provider offered the service to ship the bananas to the US, the wholesaler provided inventory services, and the grocer and the online store provided the digital shelf space as a service to the farmer. Yet, in the process of creating a huge distance between the value creator and the consumer, value accrual is largely skewed towards web2 firms and away from creators.

The new world will not only involve peer-to-peer value exchange, but also squash middlemen and economic actors in the value chain. Any economic actor who doesn't seem to add value will be automatically purged from the value chain through transparency. Not only could this provide a model for the future of trade and commerce, but also the future of several other highly intermediated industries like financial services and logistics.

Monetizing Users

When it comes to technology innovation, the progress in the past few decades is indisputable. Enormous wealth has been generated, albeit unevenly.

To scale any innovation requires more than good ideas. Beyond availability of resources (talent and capital) and an innovation environment supportive of creativity and collaboration, government policy and regulatory frameworks also play an important role. If we compare North America, Asia, and Europe, the latter can sometimes be perceived as a tech follower instead of a leader, mainly due to the lack of big technology ecosystems and unicorns compared to their counterparts, as well as the relatively smaller pool of venture capital.

As we look at regulations between the regions, the differences cannot be more pronounced.

Government Funding and Policy as Enabler

It is worth traveling back in time a bit to look at what has enabled the massive capital market that has been the signature of Silicon Valley. And it all started right before World War II with Federick Terman, a pioneer who has greatly influenced the Silicon Valley that we know today. Terman was best known for being the mentor to William Hewlett and David Packard, the founders of Hewlett-Packard (HP). At the time, Terman dedicated some of the unused land on the Stanford campus in Palo Alto, California, to build the Stanford Industrial Park, which was the first of its kind, and convinced William and David to start their company there. HP was founded in 1939, and one of their first customers was Walt Disney.[6] Over time, the Park thrived as more companies moved to Palo Alto, including William Shockley, who moved to the Bay Area to become the Director of the Shockley Semiconductor Laboratory of Beckman Instruments in 1955.[7] The Lab was the first company for research development as well as production of new silicon semiconductor devices in what is now called the Silicon Valley.

To spur venture capital investment, the Small Business Administration created a 2:1 fund-matching program in 1958. And in 1978, the government drastically reduced Capital Gains Tax and allowed pension funds to invest in venture funds. With bountiful private capital and favorable economic conditions, along with an abundance of talent, the stage was set for technology innovation to thrive in Silicon Valley.

It is no surprise that many of the big technology companies today found their roots in the Bay Area, from Cisco, HP, Intel, Oracle, and Western Digital, to Apple, Adobe, Facebook, Google, and PayPal.

Similar policies are being enacted in recent years to spur innovation and development activities for the digital economy. Specifically, the CHIPS and Science Act of 2022 includes $52.7 billion in funding to strengthen manufacturing, supply chains, and national security, and invest in research and development (R&D), science and technology, and the workforce of the future in areas including nanotechnology, clean energy, quantum computing, and artificial intelligence.[8] Such targeted focus on key areas, especially the semiconductor industry, will play a crucial role in stimulating private investments and technology innovation for the future world, just as it did back in the 1960s and 1970s.

> The US CHIPS and Science Act of 2022 establishes and provides funding to boost domestic research and support domestic production of semiconductors, with the goal of revitalizing domestic manufacturing, creating jobs, strengthening American supply chains, and accelerating the industries of the future. It was enacted by the 117th United States Congress and signed into law by President Joe Biden in 2022.

Beyond encouraging venture investing, the US has, until recently, had a more laissez-faire approach towards technology policy as compared to their counterparts in Europe and Asia. Antitrust regulation in the country often focuses on cases of demonstrable harm to consumers (e.g., predatory pricing) rather than harm to competitors, and has not evolved much with the digital ecosystems. For years, big technology platforms flourished without much intervention from the federal government.

Big Tech's Growing Dominance

From Facebook's $1 billion deal to buy Instagram and $22 billion deal for WhatsApp, and Salesforce's $15.7 billion acquisition of Tableau to create an end-to-end enterprise software ecosystem, to Amazon's $13.7 billion deal to buy Whole Foods supermarkets in order to create a massive shopping operation from brick-and-mortar to e-commerce, and Oracle's takeover of Sun Microsystems for $7.4 billion (one of the largest tech acquisitions at the time),[9] these acquisitions represented just a sliver of the mergers and acquisitions activities in the technology space that have been left unchecked for years.

This has left consumers with little choice other than products and services offered by only a handful of companies. With limited regulatory oversight, unfettered data collection has become a hallmark of this digital era, fueling the growth of many of these tech giants, including Amazon, Facebook, and Google, all of whom have faced allegations of exploiting their access to consumer data for their own gain, squeezing out competition in the digital economy by leveraging their outsized market power to their own advantage, and buying up the smaller competitors at dizzying pace.

With the recent unveiling of the American Data Privacy and Protection Act, however, there are signs that the landscape in the US is finally shifting, and the country is taking a much-needed step closer towards instituting a framework of privacy legislation.

While the US sits largely on the sideline, China and the European Union, in contrast, have been actively pursuing legislation to limit the tech giants' market power and to protect consumers' interests. Chinese regulators, for example, have attempted to curtail the influence of its big technology companies such as Tencent, Alibaba, Didi, and Meituan by imposing heavy fines on anticompetitive practices and data privacy issues.

Meanwhile, General Data Protection Regulation (GDPR) is the EU's data privacy and security law that came into effect in May 2018, imposing "obligations onto organizations anywhere, so long as they target or collect data related to people in the EU."[10] Such regulation was established to safeguard consumer data rights as digital becomes more prevalent in our daily lives, forcing providers and operators of services to secure user buy-in for collecting and sharing their data.

However, some contend that the introduction of GDPR negatively impacted innovation due to the heavy compliance cost, leading to fewer apps being created and introduced into the ecosystem. The barrier thus results in fewer choices for consumers, and reduced market power. As of July 2022, EU regulators have levied more than €1.67 billion in fines to rule-breakers.[11]

One of the more recent and most sweeping EU regulations to date is the Digital Markets Act (DMA). The goal of the policy is to promote fair competition by limiting the market power of big online platforms to promote fairer competition, more innovation, and more choices for consumers. The DMA targets large companies providing so-called "core platform services" most prone to unfair business practices, such as social networks or search engines, with a market capitalization of at least €75 billion or an annual turnover of €7.5 billion. To be designated as "gatekeepers," these companies must also provide certain services such as browsers, messengers, or social media, which have at least 45 million monthly end users in the EU and 10,000 annual business users.[12]

Alphabet, Amazon, Apple, Meta, and Microsoft will all be subjected to the rules when implemented. Under the DMA, the largest messaging services, which include the likes of WhatsApp and Facebook Messenger (both owned by Meta), as well as iMessage (owned by Apple), will be required to be interoperable with smaller rival messaging platforms, allowing users to exchange messages, send files, and make video calls across the messaging apps.

In addition, users will be able to choose their browser, virtual assistants, and search engines. Currently, Apple and Google make the operating systems that run on almost all the smartphones, which include specific apps imposed by the two companies that users cannot remove. And Apple will also be forced to open up its App Store to accept third-party payment options.

Larger sellers of online advertising, including Meta and Google, will also face restrictions with combining user personal data for targeted ads, which will be prohibited unless explicit consent is received.

Given the dependency that big technology platforms have on data to enhance their ecosystem, and how their activities are increasingly intertwined with those of financial institutions, how such interdependencies with financial services will play out in the evolving regulatory landscape and the roles they play in the emerging metaverse economy remain to be seen.

The Role of Community

Raghuram Rajan, the former Governor of the Reserve Bank of India, in his book *The Third Pillar* (2019) highlights the role of community in any fundamental transformation that the world must go through. From climate change, to gender equality, to social identity, the state and markets can only help up to a point. The role of community is paramount in achieving transformation at scale.

The three pillars of transformation are:

1 The state—the governments, central banks, or regulators.

2 The markets—large private businesses that make up the markets.

3 The community—the people, the citizens, or just members of an ecosystem.

Any change is incomplete and is made increasingly difficult by not including and incentivizing all these stakeholders. Therefore, business models of the future must ensure that all economic actors that add value in the form of governance, capital, or consumption and growth, will need to be incentivized as part of the ecosystem.

In web2 business models, the biggest winner from an incentives perspective has been the market operators. The state has largely been a silent spectator allowing for outsized growth, and only intervening to either mitigate or recover from a crisis. There have been few incentives for the governance actor to be proactive in the ecosystem.

Coming to the community aspect, in web2 the community pillar has been largely exploited by the markets. This has led to very little progress in critical initiatives like climate change, poverty, and food supply chains. It is essential that all actors involved in making the model work feel incentivized.

Take climate change as an example. While there is a movement for more and more businesses to declare themselves climate neutral or climate negative, such efforts are largely driven and incentivized by tangible (e.g., long-term viability) and intangible (e.g., brand image) benefits. Meanwhile, for governments in the developed world, their policy actions are typically driven by a political agenda, such as putting the country in a leadership position in the new green economy.

Yet, the same isn't always true for the average consumer, who is often left in the dark when it comes to one's environmental footprint due to lack of data, or lack of understanding on climate change and the circular economy. After all, how much can the action of *one person* contribute to a challenge so immense?

The lack of immediate tangible incentives to drive sustained behavioral change can also play a role; although as with most transformations, it is more of a business and policy decision, rather than a technological limitation.

But what if we could create a carbon label, like what we have for nutrition? Not only would consumers be more aware of the impact of their purchase decisions, but they would also be able to see a *sustainability score* reflecting their own environmental footprint, in addition to a credit score. And what if we took it one step further by *gamifying* the process of going green and offering upsides such as money back from the merchants or tax rebates from the government?

As the saying goes, money makes the world go round; incentives can drive long-term behavioral change and ultimately create a win–win situation for all.

If the community sees gains from its behavior by sharing the upside with the market and the state across industries, we will be able to effect change more seamlessly. Highly centralized web2 models are ill suited for this purpose. When Meta announced that the creators in their metaverse would receive 47.5 percent of the value they create on their platform, the web3 world saw them as "out of touch," largely because creators in web3 receive more than 90 percent of the value they create in an ecosystem.

While the provision of incentives to the community is part of the key issue in web2, another aspect worth considering is that of governance: very rarely does the community get a voice in the direction of the business. For example, while Facebook has over two billion users, most of the strategic decisions are made by the board and the management team, and users have very little say in the way the firm is run. One might wonder if Facebook's partnership with Cambridge Analytica would have gone ahead if the community had been made aware of its implications and had the right to vote on the decision.

How, then, can we create a new digital future that is more aligned with consumer and public interests? Perhaps the key lies in who gets a voice at the table. "Who are you building the product for?" and "Who do you serve?" are non-trivial questions that businesses grapple with. And this is where *community* comes into play. Done properly, communities can become a crucial business driver, enabling better products to be built. Communications become more open and multi-directional, and deeper, more committed relationships are formed.

On the other hand, when incentives are structured to maximize shareholder value first and foremost, the community's wants and needs come second. Later in the book, we will dive deeper into the crucial roles that communities play in the emerging ecosystems, and how the decentralized governance structure helps to fuel the development of new economic models, in favor of the communities that support them.

Digital and Economic Identity

As reported by the World Bank Global Findex Database, account ownership via financial institutions and mobile money accounts both grew and spread around the world in the past few years, and the Covid-19 pandemic has driven a further increase in mobile money adoption as more people embraced the ease of using mobile devices for financial transactions. Such progress is crucial, as the movement of money can help spur innovation and entrepreneurship; and both are critical for the economic well-being of individuals as well as society at large.

However, while the account access gaps are narrowing, the gains are not equally felt across all demographics, especially for women, the poor, and the less educated. In developing economies, 145 million people, representing 11 percent of unbanked adults, received agricultural payments in cash, according to the World Bank. Among them were about 65 million women and 70 million adults with incomes in the poorest 40 percent of households in their economy.[13] And nearly half of the 145 million people came from Sub-Saharan Africa.

A closer look at the data would reveal that multiple factors contribute to the gap in account ownership, including lack of money, lack of necessary documentation, and lack of access to mobile phones.

In Sub-Saharan Africa, for example, 35 percent of unbanked adults in the territory reported lack of a mobile phone as one of the reasons for lack of mobile money account ownership. And this figure increases for unbanked women across the same territory, where they are 7 percentage points more likely than unbanked men to cite lack of a mobile phone as the reason they do not have an account. The gender gap doubles to 14 percentage points in Nigeria, where women are almost twice as likely as men to cite lack of a mobile phone as a barrier to account ownership.

Similar challenges exist in other geographies including South Asia, which has one of the world's largest digital gender gaps, due to social, economic, and structural limitations.[14]

Beyond mobile access, the lack of formal identification adds to the challenges faced by those who are already marginalized, with 30 percent of unbanked adults in the Sub-Saharan region reporting that they lack the documentation needed to open a mobile money account.[15]

Ample opportunities exist to provide better financial services for more of the population, via better access to mobile services and formal identity, while acknowledging the critical role that women play in fueling the economic engine in our society. When we lift up women and those who are disadvantaged, we lift everyone up.

Even when women conduct trade and transactions in their businesses, they are often socially suppressed and are considered unworthy of credit and other types of financial services, since their economic transactions are often not recorded and do not contribute to their identity.

On the topic of identity, there are over 89 million people who have been forcibly displaced worldwide, according to the United Nations High Commissioner for Refugees (UNHCR). Out of which, over 27 million are refugees and over 4.3 million are stateless. Having a state-issued national identity is one thing; being able to maintain an identity across borders and attain economic self-sufficiency is another. While the current system caters for national identities through passports, they are insufficient in supporting people displaced and hurt by a crisis.

In a world where seamless mobility across borders and economic contexts is expected, identities must be redefined and revamped. Any citizen who is economically active and is contributing to the country's GDP must be identified and have their identities linked to their contribution. In our example, an African woman farmer who is constantly producing and shipping crops every season must have her transactions added to her credibility.

And this will be the ultimate state of inclusion—one where financial and digital inclusion goes beyond access, one where a person is truly included in the economic engine of the society, and whose identity transcends borders. A system that identifies and supports rural communities in terms of the value they add to local economies.

Yet, we are so far away from achieving these simple infrastructural upgrades to the way we have designed our social and economic infrastructure.

One More Thing

Before we dive into the next chapter, it might be helpful to review the high-level differences between the different evolutions of the web.

UTable 1.1

	Web1	Web2	Web3
Content	Mostly read-only static content connected by hyperlinks (Yahoo, Wiki)	Read–write web with more interactive content targeted to gain user attention (Facebook, YouTube)	Read, write and own the content generated, prove ownership, and get paid royalties as content is monetized (OpenSea, Magic Eden)
Monetization	Protocols such as TCP/IP couldn't be monetized directly. Applications could be monetized	Monetization possible at the application layer (Amazon, Google)	Both protocol and application layers can be monetized by the community (Ethereum, Uniswap)

UTable 1.1   *continued*

	Web1	**Web2**	**Web3**
Data Ownership	Platforms; data typically stored in centralized locations	Platforms; data typically stored in centralized locations	Content creators; data stored in decentralized locations
Data Storage	On disk	On net	On chain
Incentivization of Economic Actors	Centralized ownership leads to value accrual to a few actors	Centralized ownership leads to value accrual to a few actors	Decentralized and inclusive incentives for all relevant economic actors
Governance	Centralized governance within economies and businesses	Centralized governance within economies and businesses	Decentralized governance
Nature of Economic Actors	Separate actors play the role of governance (state), markets, and community	Separate actors play the role of governance (state), markets, and community	Communities can play the role of the state and markets
Role of Networks	Data store	Data store and exchange	Data and value exchange

In the next few chapters, we will go deeper into the different elements and explore the future economic models of the new paradigm.

The Future is Web3

02

"This is for everyone."

TIM BERNERS-LEE

The world's first web page (http://info.cern.ch) was launched on August 6, 1991 by British scientist Tim Berners-Lee while working at CERN.[1] The page was dedicated to the World Wide Web project itself and was hosted on Berners-Lee's NeXT computer, describing the web and showing users how to create web pages as a means to share information between devices.

It is hard to believe that it has been more than 30 years since then and the internet, as we know it, has evolved from a static web serving up information to a more collaborative environment that we have come to depend on, socialize on, and exchange information on.

The emergence of social networks, blogs, and other content platforms has also enabled the creation of a new category of stakeholders: content creators. Long gone are the days when we were merely passive users of the internet. With one click of a button, we now have the power to not only create content but also to share it with people from around the world.

The power of the web to overcome physical barriers and connect people from around the world was in full display during the Covid-19 pandemic when we were all forced to socially distance ourselves from one another. The collaborative web became the lifeline for many as we shifted to full remote working and learning environments.

But something unexpected has happened as well.

Along the process, we have created massive data infrastructures, where providers' business models are built on the extraction and exploitation of endless streams of personal data. Each time we search for information on Google, buy a book on Amazon, or order delivery from Amazon Fresh, we *pay* with our data, leaving behind a trail of digital exhaust that is being used to enrich profiles of who we are and what we like as consumers, in exchange for more personalized experiences. But such convenience comes at a cost. Whether knowingly or unknowingly, we are fueling a growing data economy that is dominated by a few, who increasingly control every aspect of our lives. It is certainly not by accident that the top three digital ad-selling companies worldwide are Google, Meta, and Amazon, with Google being projected to generate US $168 billion in global online advertising revenue.[2] Together, these three top tech giants accounted for more than $7 in $10 (74 percent) of global digital ad spending in 2021.[3]

As more and more data is generated from different sources and as computing power increases exponentially, our data also becomes a more valuable resource that can be used to train different models, to predict not only our behavior, but that of larger demographics. In turn, the tech companies that these digital services run on become even more powerful due to their sheer scale and control. Unfortunately, under the current paradigm, we don't truly *own* our data; rather, it is controlled by the companies that collect it—including social networks, healthcare apps, and Internet of Things (IoT) device manufacturers. Not only are we at their disposal when it comes to safeguarding the data, we also need to ask for permission to use our own data (e.g., think application programming interfaces, APIs).

When social media giants exploit users' engagement on the network to fuel their advertising business at all costs, at the expense of social discourse, and without regard to the well-being of the users, one can't help but wonder, isn't there a better way? Can we envision a future that tilts the balance of power back to the users and creators of the data economy?

"*Who owns our data?*" is more than a philosophical or trust question. One might question whether we truly have a choice or a say-so in the future trajectory of the digital economy. But if we don't *demand* change, the next evolution will simply become a replicator of the economic and social inequalities that exist today.

And history will continue to repeat itself.

What Kind of Web Do We Want?

How many times do you have to enter your name and address in various websites and service providers? And when you relocate, how many times do you have to update the same information? Can you recall all the sites and providers who have your contact information? And do you know what they are doing with your data? How much do you, or can you, trust them to keep your data safe?

What if you can take your data with you, freely grant permission of your data to different providers, and manipulate different data sets in any way *you* want, instead of being at the mercy of the tech over-lords? What, then, will a fairer data economy look like?

Data interoperability, decentralization, and universality should have been the basic tenet of today's digital economy. Yet, the reality is far from it.

Trust at the Core

Perhaps we can take inspiration from the Web3 Foundation's mission statement.[4]

> The Web3 Foundation supports web3 teams and open-source projects through funding, advocacy, research, and collaboration. Its flagship protocol is Polkadot—a scalable shared chain and the first protocol that provides a secure environment for cross-chain composability.

At its core, the Web3 Foundation believes in an internet where:

- users own their own data, not corporations
- global digital transactions are secure
- online exchanges of information and value are decentralized

One of the biggest shortcomings of web2 is lack of data ownership and rights; where our destiny and privacy are determined by the entities that collect the data, and we have virtually no say in what they do with it. One where we *pay* with our personal data.

Now imagine a world where we own our data, set permissions on what data can be used for, and by whom; one where creators are compensated by what they produce, without intermediaries. A paradigm where we can unlock the full potential of a data-driven economy, and facilitate trusted and fair data sharing, with privacy built into the core; one where we can achieve better outcomes for more, where technology becomes an enabler for common good.

Here are a few characteristics of this new paradigm of web3 that are worth exploring further in the coming sections:

- economic value—where data can be optimized for different use cases.

- data permissioning—where users have explicit and clear power and ownership over their own data, and can set permissions for different uses.

- data provenance—where data can be identified throughout the chain to allow appropriate reward to be allocated appropriately.

- portability and verifiability—where credentials are owned and controlled by your wallet and private keys, and portable and verifiable from one community to the next

We are still at the infancy stage of the web3 movement, which aims to make the web and the internet more decentralized, verifiable, and secure. The road ahead represents an exciting new frontier, for not only how we view data and identity, but also the value exchange and economic models in the new ecosystem.

A CONVERSATION WITH
Kevin Rose and Justin Mezzell, Proof Collective

Kevin Rose on web2 and web3:
With web3, we have a chance to completely realign incentive models and the way that products are built and rolled out in web2. The previous generation of products focused on growth at all costs, locking in eyeballs, and on relentless iteration. It would be about more or less tricking the user into spending more time on the product, because the

longer you could hold their attention, the more money you could make. I think it's now clear that selling out the users in a way that makes them an asset to be monetized is damaging. That has led to unhealthy behaviors like addiction to social media. It has also led to consumerism that is unhealthy. Web2 products have been really good at getting the right information in front of the right eyeballs at the right time to make purchases.

With web3 we have a chance to flip the idea of ownership. We have a chance to flip the idea of value accrual to the individual users. We have a chance to transform advertising from the way it is done today. We see a lot of blue ocean there. It is a chance for us to go out and build new products and ways of doing business.

Justin Mezzell on generative art:

Generative art is one category that I am insanely excited about. The acceleration of AI technology as applied to art is mindblowing and cool. Anyone that has just played around with these tools over the last year can see that it's an exponential ramp of improvement in terms of quality. Just see what Art Blocks has done with generative art.

I believe that AI art is going to unlock creativity of a new type, and it is thinkers and creatives that have wild imaginations but may not have the pen to paper or mouse to pixel wherewithal to take what's in their brain and actually produce a visual, but they still have a creative aspect to the way that they think about things. We're going to see the emergence of prompt artists where people are really good at describing what they'd like to see and then using further descriptions to refine aspects of the art. You may describe a scene that produces something but want to tweak five or six different visual elements inside of that scene, which will lead to some really creative new types of pictures that we've just never seen before and new types of art that we've never seen before. That would unlock a massive flood of new artists entering the space.

Kevin Rose on tokenomics:

I was a member very early in the Dogecoin community, and something that I really appreciated was we had a group of people that came together, that freely exchanged tokens to do amazing things, all for the collective betterment of the meme and the community. There was a fantastic tipping culture and a charity aspect to it. Unfortunately, then the developer stepped away and didn't continue any further product work.

When I think about the positive things that we would like to encourage within the PROOF Collective, it is all about collecting art and empowering artists. There's a lot of really interesting connective tissue that we think a token can bridge across all the different things that we do from members of PROOF Collective to future products that we're building. That would be a very powerful thing to boot up and watch what happens.

Justin Mezzell on the High-Rise and Moonbirds' metaverse ambitions:
Our take on the metaverse is that it was too closely tied to leveling up experiences, gaining abilities, traversing around a virtual world awkwardly, standing in a room with the speech bubble above your head. We don't rule out that you may have an avatar representing the user in a digital space. However, unless it is an additive element to that journey, it is not very useful.

When it came to the idea of displaying art, displaying who you are as an artist or a collector telling that story, we did explore some options. For our use case, the user experience may not need the gimmick today, and the metaverse may hurt user experience more than help it. However, we're not saying anything is off limits. Maybe one day there will be a way we could set up a perceptual world around an art lover that makes sense. But as of right now, anytime that I have to load a 3D gallery view and awkwardly click forward and right to look at art on the wall, I just think, why am I doing this? And so, until we get to see better user experiences from the metaverse, it's not going to be a part of our journey.

Economic Model Implications

When we study the foundational principles of economic models on web3, we should look into them from the perspectives of both the consumer and the business owner. This will help set the foundations for subsequent chapters where we will go into detail about economic model constructs and the key takeaways.

Creator Economy

During the times when the barter system was a prevalent mode of trade, the creators of a product could get a big slice of the market value of their product. The value was decided by the demand that the market had for a specific product and largely accrued to its creator. This was, however, upended by the concept of money and intermediated capital markets. Thanks to the rise in capitalism, the creator is now more removed from the consumer than ever before.

This can be better illustrated by an example in the agriculture value chain, where the farmer is the creator of value in the form of crops. By the time the food reaches the consumer shopping at a grocery store, a logistics provider, a wholesaler, an inventory provider, and the retailer are all actors involved in activities that bring the drops from the field to the consumer, through stages such as processing, packaging, and distribution.

It can be argued that all of these economic actors are adding value along the way, albeit incrementally: the logistics provider helps the farmer take their product to different locations; the wholesaler and the inventory provider provide excellent storage facilities to extend the value of the crops until they are sold in the market; and the retailer provides access to a wide range of consumers who will buy the crops.

While the farmer will need to pay to use the services of these actors to help them sell their crops in different locations, in most instances the bigger slice of the pie goes to the carriers of value rather than the creator of value. These carriers of value, namely the logistics provider, the inventory provider, the wholesaler, and the retailer are all capital market participants. To exist, they need to create value for their shareholders by commanding a larger portion of the value that would have belonged rightfully to the creator, in this scenario the farmer.

A similar scenario played out in recent years with on-demand delivery services. In the early days of the Covid-19 lockdown when many of us were avoiding visits to stores and restaurants, workers of the gig economy platforms (e.g., Uber Eats, Deliveroo, Seamless, Postmates) became the essential frontline workers connecting the demand (consumers) and supply (restaurant meals). Unfortunately, jobs in the gig economy are often offered by platforms that do not play by the rules and instead use the business model to squeeze as much profit as they can from the value chain. As a result, they often employ workers who lack opportunities in the labor market and are afraid to speak up about their working conditions. Restaurant owners are also exploited by the platform companies, since they are reliant on them to reach the mass market and to move the product (in this case, the meals). Similar to the prior agricultural example, the intermediary ends up capturing more than their fair share of value.

How can web3 change it? Just looking at the agriculture supply chain, the farmer remains the owner of the crop until it's sold to the consumer. There are multiple economic actors who participate in the process of value transfer between the creator and consumer and get compensated based on the incremental value they add. All this happens in a transparent and traceable process. Thinking ahead, as this model becomes more mainstream, farmers should be able to choose the precise set of actors they would like to work with. For instance, if a farmer in Indonesia feels that they benefit more in selling their coffee to consumers in Singapore, they can choose the set of service providers to get their crops there, instead of selling it to consumers in London. The cost incurred by the farmer in choosing the service providers would be transparent and allow them to choose what they want to do with their crops.

From a consumer's perspective, they can see where the crops have come from and who the farmer is. Today, when we walk into a supermarket and buy grapes, for instance, we have little transparency on which farm the grapes come from. If we see that grapes from a specific farm in France are consistently of a high quality, we can request more. Service providers can see the increase in demand and help the farmers in the region accordingly to get their grapes to the consumer. Therefore, the future of trade will be driven by the creator and consumer of value, rather than the middlemen.

A Native Web3 Example

The above are examples from conventional markets. Now, we can look at a native web3 example and see how that can contribute to the creator economy. The rise of non-fungible tokens (NFTs) is an excellent example of how the creator economy can thrive on web3 rails.

An NFT is a data element that is created on a blockchain and acts as the proof of ownership of a specific product; the metadata of the

NFT describes the essential properties of the product, including its name, description, and other qualities deemed important by the creator. This data is also used by the market to ascertain the value of the NFT. This technology paradigm has become the bedrock of a market with a capitalization that is expected to expand to be over $80 billion for 2025 and has offered an opportunity to several forms of content creators from artists to musicians and game creators to monetize their work.[5]

Artists can create digital art or digitize their art and get it on a blockchain to be displayed across various forums. There are several marketplaces that offer shelf space for this art at a small fee upon successful sale of the art. More importantly, as the provenance of the art is on blockchain, each time the art is sold, the royalty gets paid to the creator of the art piece.

While this is a simple description of the business model, the role of community in this ecosystem is paramount. Artists that are highly successful can create a community before launching their product. This community can also be growth hacked from other NFT collections or projects where the artist sees collaboration opportunities.

Social media platforms like Twitter, Instagram, and Discord are used by creators to get an inspired audience together. They then roll out community-building exercises like little competitions, auctions, raffles, and real-life events. As the euphoria around the community peaks, they announce the date for the launch of an art collection. This helps to achieve high prices for the art collection.

Creators can launch multiple collections to tap into a loyal and sticky community if their first collection was successful. The most loyal community members often get preferential access to new art collections. This incentivizes the community to stay together as they realize they are in for a long haul with the creators that they follow and admire passionately.

The web3 way of building businesses not only bridges the commercial and economic gap between creators and consumers, but it also creates an emotional connection between the two. Many creators can identify their top contributing community members through their social handles and value their participation. For outsiders looking to assess a community before they join it, such emotional connections provide validation that the creator is close to the community.

Speaking of which, should we ask Mark Zuckerberg who is the most loyal user in his massive social network?

Inclusive Incentives

In conventional capital markets, the term inclusion is often viewed with skepticism. While immense wealth has been created, it has not been done in an equitable manner, resulting in growing income inequality and opportunity gaps, especially for underrepresented demographics including women, those who live in rural communities, as well as those who have less access to education and digital connectivity.

While there isn't a singular approach to solving inequality, and much of that will require efforts from both public and private sectors, there are opportunities for us to rethink how we incentivize and encourage a different distribution of wealth. For example:

- where we need a large user base to behave in a certain way where the benefits of the behavior can be only reaped in the long term
- where we need a large user base to transition from one way of doing things to another
- where we need data from a large user base to sustain a business model

Long-Term Benefits

Anyone who has raised young children can attest to how difficult it can be to get kids to save their dessert till after dinner. "I want this, and I want this now." In fact, instant gratification is not restricted to children; this is something that is hardwired into all of us. And with the urge to act and get fulfillment right away, our ability to consistently embrace a behavior for the greater and longer-term good can prove to be difficult, especially in the absence of incentive to nudge us in the right direction.

A great example is how sustainability can become a key considera-
tion for a variety of consumer segments. As mentioned in Chapter 1,
while some consumers might have become more aware of the need
to lead a sustainable lifestyle, they might not always have the
data needed to help them act accordingly. And without nudges and
incentives, consumers are also less inclined to change their behavior,
especially if they lack the interest to do so.

It is therefore not surprising that sustainability applications that
have tried to shift consumer attitude and behavior to more sustainable ways on web2 rails have struggled to scale, especially in a highly
competitive startup environment where companies are dependent on
a limited pool of venture capital to gain traction and grow.

Whereas in the web3 way of building a new business, instead of
incentivizing a selected few, we can onboard consumers as investors
into the application. This is achieved through token economics (tokenomics), where participants can be not only consumers but also
investors and ambassadors of the application. They will receive
incentives as investors in the form of returns, incentives as consumers
when they behave sustainably, and as ambassadors where they help
onboard other stakeholders into the ecosystem. Therefore, even as
just a user of the platform, consumers have more than one way to
monetize their value addition. On top of that, they benefit by being
part of the community that often drives the initiative in the right
direction, creating a resonance frequency. This community of consumers, investors, and ambassadors can help retain the user base
and create value for everyone in a more inclusive fashion.

Transitioning into a New World

Change is hard, and sometimes that hardest part about change is to
act. In a scenario where a large user base must change platforms or
ways of doing things, incentivizing them into the new world can help
the transition. The world of gaming is an excellent example here. The
total video games revenue (excluding e-sports) reached $214.2
billion in 2021, and it is expected to rise to over $321 billion in
2026.[6] At the time of writing this book, the web3 gaming market
represents only a fraction of the overall gaming market.

As described in the prior section, the gaming industry is looking
to transition to web3 and metaverse to better reward the creators

of games. Web2 gaming platforms are often set up by large game studios who have the technology and the funding to create games. Since they are typically centrally owned organizations with business models designed to maximize shareholder profits, having community-created games on such platforms does not provide an attractive economic model for the creators.

But gaming, like art, is a creative industry and needs community contribution to thrive and scale. This can happen more seamlessly in a web3 context as incentives can be more inclusive and distributed. A community member can be a player of the game, creator of a game, or just own an asset within the game to be compensated for their participation in the ecosystem.

When such community-based models are rolled out, these incentives are extremely helpful in moving gamers from web2 into web3 and retaining them. The initial entrants into web3 may come on for the incentives, but as they stay and bring more users on, the system will start to provide for itself by virtue of network effects created across gamers, asset holders, and creators. This helps retain value within the economy and hence scale sustainably.

Incentives for Data

As described at the beginning of the chapter, data ownership and privacy have been controversial subjects of discussion in web2 business models. Every action we do leaves a trail of data, which the web2 giants tap into to nudge us towards the next action. The actions are often dopamine drivers, and that's generally what a user gets.

Web3 has the potential to change that paradigm. Not only can users control what they share about themselves, they are also incentivized for sharing their data as part of the business model. In fact, this is one of the building blocks for web3 social media, or SocialFi, where incentivizing data is, again, just the beginning of the journey. We expect newer models to be developed, including ones that promote social equity or brand equity on social media. For instance, if Gary Vee uses a SocialFi platform to send tweets, users of the platform can only engage with his content if they are of the Gary Vee economy. In other words, to retweet, respond, or like a Gary Vee tweet in a web3 world, his community members should hold some $Vee coins in their crypto wallet. That holding shows how committed someone's community is to their brand on the platform. The more the demand for an influencer's coin, the higher the value of the coin, reflecting the social swag that the influencer has.

Inclusive incentives can be a great way to celebrate creators and motivate consumers to do the right thing to let people share data securely and help monetize abstract value elements like brand equity. Yet, it must be noted that web3 as a concept is still evolving. Most of the models are in the theoretical stage, while some of them are still experimental, with varying degrees of success. Proving out the models is a journey unto itself. While these models can scale when the community is in support of a specific business model and it is compensated as it scales, the reverse is also true. If the community does not see the value, or starts seeing diminishing returns as the model scales, it can hurt growth.

The same token economy that helps accrue value to all the key stakeholders can have the reverse effect and bleed value for all stakeholders. This can also happen in a market crisis; when the economy goes through a downturn and the tokens lose value at a fast pace, the community can start exiting the economy, resulting in further downside to the token value.

Another key challenge with these token models is that they are often seen as Ponzi schemes by conventional investors. But let's think back to Amazon's journey in 1994. In two years, by the end of 1996, Amazon had racked up $15.7 million in revenues. One year later, Jeff Bezos took the company public with an IPO that raised $54 million.[7] Despite the traction and the potential, there was no lack of critics, including those who thought Amazon "is at best a complete sham and at worst an explicit fraud."[8] In those days, not being profitable for that long, particularly as a listed firm, was considered unhealthy. Amazon finally posted its first profit in 2003, and the rest, as they say, is history.

These token models are still finding their feet through various experiments. There are prone to be failures in the process, but it is a journey worth taking if it could help us create community-driven business models that can help us achieve greater things over the longer term.

In later chapters of the book, we will review more detailed case studies of these models.

Digital Ownership and Value Permanence

Earlier in this chapter, we discussed how creators can monetize their art and music using NFTs. Thanks to the power of web3, artists can generate royalty incomes from their digital creations, and consumers are able to see the provenance of the art and can prove ownership of the art through NFTs.

This model of ownership is now starting to see adoption for real-world assets as well. Several apparel businesses, including Adidas and Nike, are exploring NFTs as a way to prove real-world ownership. Consumers buying Adidas products can connect their wallets and get an NFT dropped into their wallets. This model would only scale well if there are robust ways of creating a link between real-world goods and NFTs, for example, for luxury items like watches where creating traceability of ownership becomes critical. In recent years, for example, Breitling introduced the Breitling NFT for all Breitling watches, to offer proof of ownership of the watch and lifecycle transparency. The digital passport currently supports features such as the ability to transfer watch ownership, extend warranty, and obtain insurance. New services and perks can be added to enrich the experience of a community of loyal Breitling watch owners, beyond the standard care.

Digital ownership and value permanence are a lot more important in the gaming industry. There are an estimated three billion gamers in the world.[9] In the process they buy in-game assets like gems, weapons, land, and properties to build their gaming environment, and complete quests and profiles, creating an in-game asset market capitalization of $250 billion. Yet, these assets that the gamers have invested in do not hold much value in the real world, nor across gaming platforms. For instance, a gun that you purchase to fight with in Call of Duty cannot be reused in Doom.

These pain points are directly addressed in the web3 world through NFTs. Most in-game assets can be bought and sold on digital marketplaces. That has huge implications for the gaming industry. In web2, when a weapon is bought by a gamer within the game, it goes in as revenues to the game studio and essentially the value accrues to the shareholders of the game studio.

In the web3 world, the weapon is a digital asset. When it is bought by gamer A (as an NFT), the value still accrues to the shareholders of the game studio. In addition to that, the weapon can be sold to other gamers and therefore is an asset to gamer A. Gamer A can also choose to buy a weapon, use it in the game and record wins, in order to gain the ability to upgrade the weapon. Now the weapon is not just an asset, it is an appreciating asset, where gamer A can turn a profit by selling the upgraded weapon.

There are a couple more economic actors who participate in the web3 gaming industry as well. One is an asset owner and the other is an asset creator. In-game assets can appreciate in price quickly as gamers upgrade their game play abilities, making these assets unaffordable for a huge majority of gamers.

As a result, there is a role for asset owners, who focus on acquiring these in-game assets in search of appreciation of value and for passive income. Web3 games allow asset owners to rent their assets to gamers. Therefore, if a gamer cannot afford a weapon, they can rent it from an asset owner, play the game, win a bounty, and pay the rent to the asset owner.

The other stakeholder in the gaming ecosystem is the asset creator. Bringing the gaming and creator economic models together, an asset creator can create a weapon that can be used in the game. Alongside a rental marketplace, most web3 games also have an asset marketplace. This is where creators can list their weapons or any other in-game assets they have designed for the game. Gamers and asset owners can buy these assets and use them in the game or choose to make passive income by renting these assets. The proceeds of the sale will largely go to the asset creators, and, more importantly, as these assets get re-sold within the ecosystem, the creators of these assets will also receive royalties for their creation.

One last dimension that web3 gaming brings is interoperability of value. Not only are these digital assets valued within the game but they would also hold their value in other gaming ecosystems as interoperability is created across gaming metaverses and ecosystems.

Economic Identity

One of the key challenges we see with the web2 way of creating identities is that it is contextual to national borders. In Chapter 1, we discussed how an African woman farmer struggles to get a bank account due to social constraints. We also mentioned how, in a war-torn world, refugees would need their economic identity and wealth transferable across borders.

Web3 models can potentially address both scenarios. We live in a world where developers are assessed by their GitHub profiles more than their résumé. The same could apply to the common citizen, where their value addition to any ecosystem is assessed by on-chain activities that are transparent and can be used as evidence of economic activity in any part of the world.

These models are already being tested by organizations like the World Bank in the food industry. But even within the creator economy or the gaming economy, someone who has contributed to these economies as a credible actor, even anonymously, can have their credibility verified through on-chain activity. An artist who has sold their collection and raised a few million will have their track record visible for the whole world to see. A gamer who is a superstar in a particular gaming ecosystem can transfer their credibility over to other gaming ecosystems. In fact, these gaming influencers will be welcomed by other gaming platforms as they will draw crowds along with them.

We are slowly moving into a world where all of us could have an economic identity depending on the ecosystem that we are a part of. These identities are on-chain and will allow us to demonstrate our credibility using these activities.

So, Do We Need Web2?

If web3 is so superior to its predecessor in so many ways, is it a web2 replacement? As we delve into that inevitable question, we must be realistic about where we are on the journey. Web2 is the incumbent, but it is here and now. While web3 is forthcoming at the time of writing, there is still a lot of work to be done so it can become part of the mainstream.

Web3 has proven itself as a robust infrastructure and economic model layer, at least within a few key use cases in Bitcoin and Ethereum. Both these chains have proven themselves over several market cycles, and survived and thrived through them. Even institutional investors are starting to consider these two chains as potential candidates for their portfolio. But apart from being an economic model and infrastructure layers, web3 is lacking in so many ways.

To start with, web3 still struggles with user experience issues. Largely driven by deeptech enthusiasts over the past decade, web3 projects haven't really made much effort to simplify user journeys. For instance, the process of buying an NFT involves the following steps:

1 First, the user needs to understand the chain the NFT is created on.

2 Next, the user needs to create a digital wallet and safely store the private key and recovery phrase of the wallet.

3 Next, the user needs to buy Ethereum (ETH), Solana (SOL) or any digital token that is required to purchase the NFT, either from an exchange or from the wallet itself using integrated payment plugins like MoonPay.

4 Next, the user needs to find a marketplace where the NFT is listed and connect the wallet to the platform.

5 And, finally, the user can buy or bid for the NFT.

There are several on-ramp solutions that seek to improve the user experience. But for a web2 user who is used to a seamless, frictionless experience, web3 can feel like the Wild West.

Improving web3 access and functionality on mobile is also what Solana had in mind when they announced the upcoming launch of Saga, an Android web3 mobile phone, with a web3 decentralized app store, an integrated "Solana Pay" to facilitate QR code-based on-chain payments, a mobile wallet adapter, and a "seed vault" for private keys.[10]

The other key shortcoming within web3 is the lack of data intelligence, since this is still a fairly new paradigm. Unlike web2 applications, most transactions are on-chain, offering data-mining opportunities to those who want to build the intelligence around this data. Apart from that, data transfer across chains has also been a risky proposition. The Wormhole hack on Solana in February 2022— where the hacker managed to get away with 120,000 ETH—is an example of how cross-chain interactions remain a risky proposition.

We discussed how web3 offers an inclusive economic model for the gaming industry. But most games in this space are more focused on tokenomics and less focused on gaming experience. Hardcore gamers in web2 who are used to immersive experiences will find web3 extremely lacking. There are pockets of web3 game studios that are looking to improve the experience, but it will likely take a few years before this is resolved.

The last pain point is quantum proof cryptography, or the lack thereof. In Vitalik Buterin's speech at the Paris ETH CC event, he mentioned that one of the key milestones in Ethereum's roadmap was to make it quantum proof.[11]

Web3, unlike its predecessor, is not just a network that stores data. It is a value network and therefore needs a lot more protection as people lose real money every time there is an attack. With the threat that quantum computing poses, in the event of an attack, it would not be sporadic little attacks on one chain or project; instead, it would be a much bigger threat. Therefore, it is critical that, over the next few years, most of these blockchain infrastructures move to quantum proof cryptography.

Web3 is not perfect. But over time, and with improvements to address some of the challenges described here, it can be a better version of web2, and a more inclusive version for more participants across the world. Web2 is the land we live in, web3 is the sky and the future. It could be a fine balance between how far we go for the skies while staying grounded. We are fortunate to be witnessing this evolution and the rest of this book will take a deep dive across those blue skies.

Non-Fungible Tokens (NFTs) and the Ownership Economy

03

We can shape the future with our actions of today.

NFT, the abbreviation for non-fungible token, became Collins Dictionary's word of the year for 2021, and metaverse and crypto made Collins' longer list of ten words of the year. Collins describes NFT as "Non-fungible token: A unique digital certificate, registered in a blockchain, that is used to record ownership of an asset such as an artwork or a collectible".

Although NFTs are a type of cryptocurrency token, they differ from fungible tokens such as Bitcoin in that they are entirely unique and not mutually interchangeable. They can be created by anyone and require little to no coding skills to create. They are most commonly applied to digital art, but their utility goes beyond the digital collectibles that they are known for and associated with, including event tickets, game items, contracts, and even diplomas.[1]

An NFT represents proof of ownership of a blockchain record: When someone sells an NFT that represents their work, the buyer does not necessarily receive the copyright to the work and the seller can create additional NFT copies of the same work, unless the intellectual property rights of the individual images are explicitly assigned to their respective owners.

While we have seen the usage of the term increase by 11,000 percent in 2021 and the buzz is remarkable, have you ever wondered when the first NFT started?[2] In this chapter, we will explore the past, present, and future of non-fungible tokens, and their potential impact on the future of the community. We will revisit the topic of community and ownership later in the chapter.

Let's talk a walk down the memory lane to see how this all got started.

A Brief History

Could Colored Coins be the first NFTs?

Yoni Assia, the CEO of eToro, was the first to mention Colored Coins in his blog published in 2012, describing the technology and Colored Coins as unique and identifiable from regular Bitcoin transactions.[3] The idea was examined further in subsequent white papers written by Meni Rosenfeld as well as by Assia himself, where the merits of using Colored Coins in different use cases were explored, from smart property, company stock, contracts, and bonds, to demand deposits, emergent currencies, and decentralized digital representation of physical assets.[4]

The year 2014 saw the founding of Counterplay, a peer-to-peer financial platform and open-source, distributed internet protocol constructed on top of the Bitcoin blockchain. It provided a means for users to create their own tradeable digital currencies. And in 2015, Spells of Genesis (SoG) was launched, combining trading card game functionalities with point-and-shoot aspects of arcade games. It was among the first in issuing in-game assets onto a blockchain.

Two gamechanging events came about in 2017, first with the launch of CryptoPunks, where Watkinson and Hall, the technologists behind the NFT project, opted to let anyone with an Ethereum wallet claim a CryptoPunk for free. The influence of the CryptoPunks project helped inspire the NFT ERC-721 standard and establish the current crypto art movement. All 10,000 CryptoPunks were rapidly claimed and traded online, kicking off a thriving secondary marketplace. In that same year, NFTs hit the mainstream with CryptoKitties, a blockchain-based virtual game that allowed players to adopt, raise, and trade digital cats. It was widely covered in the mainstream media, with some virtual cats selling for over $100,000. The project was eventually spun out as a $12.5 million venture dollars-attracting startup called Dapper Labs, and it set the standard for NFT projects to come.

The NFT ecosystem has experienced massive growth since then, with the likes of NFT marketplaces such as OpenSea and SuperRare.

We have also seen more NFT games and projects collaborating with each other to promote interoperability, which is crucial for the growth of the ecosystem.

Collectibles

Collectibles are one of the earliest forms of NFTs launched. Imagine Pokémon cards and vintage toys in digital forms. Minted in 2017, Curio Cards is viewed as the first collectible digital art on the Ethereum blockchain, while Bored Ape Yacht Club (BAYC) has turned out to be the most valuable digital collectible out there.

Speaking of collectibles, collecting sports memorabilia goes a long way in the physical world. Signed posters, baseballs from baseball games, and game-used items such as worn jerseys are all popular items among collectors. Could this passion translate to the virtual world as well? Golden State Warriors, the championship-winning National Basketball Association (NBA) team, became the first professional sports team to experiment with NFT, with the release of their first NFT collection in April 2021 to commemorate the team's six NBA championships and other moments in their franchise history.[5] The team subsequently released a second collection that programmatically responded to the team's on-court performance, rewarding holders as the Warriors advanced through the NBA playoffs, and gamifying fandom by turning their fans into speculators invested in the team's future.

Can you imagine a future where you will receive a special edition collectible NFT as a season ticket holder, and your authenticated digital stub can be displayed in your digital hangout? Perhaps virtual access tokens could be the key to unlock the future of sports, beyond the boundaries of a physical game.

Digital Art

As mentioned, digital art is one of the most common use cases for NFTs. In fact, one of the most expensive NFTs sold as of the end of January 2023 was a series of NFTs called "The Merge," created by digital artist Pak, with an auction price of $91.8 million. It was bought by 28,983 people who pitched in to get a total of 312,000 shares, with each being an NFT.[6]

Other interesting pieces include:

- "Everydays: The First 5,000 Days"—A collage of 5,000 pictures made each day over more than 13 years by digital artist Mike Beeple Winkelmann, and sold at Christie's first-ever digital art auction in March 2021 for $69.3 million.

- HUMAN ONE—A kinetic video sculpture with a corresponding dynamic NFT, also created by Mike Beeple Winkelmann and sold for $28.9 million at Christie's auction. It is a hybrid of physical and digital technology, and has a smart contract coded into it so Beeple could maintain control over the display remotely, making the artwork one of the most expensive NFTs and a forever-in-progress piece of digital art.

Apart from auction houses, NFTs are also bought and sold via NFT platforms, such as OpenSea, which was one of the first marketplaces to host different types of NFTs.

Fashion

Whether it be digital or "phygital" (buying and selling real-world physical goods through digital collectibles), fashion brands seem to be eager to embrace the new virtual world. This is hardly surprising as it is an industry that rarely misses a beat.

Take Dolce & Gabbana for example. Their record-breaking Collezione Genesi was the first luxury NFT collection to include digital and physical products, collecting $5.7 million at auction. The winning bidders received both a virtual version as well as a physical product that they could touch and wear.

Fashion powerhouse Gucci takes the effort one step further. Its collection features an array of NFT projects as well as presence in Sandbox and Roblox. SUPERGUCCI, for example, is a collaboration between Gucci and Superplastic, which includes two drops of 500 NFTs co-created by Gucci's Creative Director Alessandro Michele and synthetic artists Janky & Guggimon, accompanied by an exclusive 8-inch tall ceramic SUPERGUCCI sculpture, hand-crafted by ceramicists in Italy.

Another interesting example is Adidas, who launched their first NFT project, Into The Metaverse, in collaboration with BAYC, PUNKS Comic, and gmoney. Separately, the sporting goods brand also launched "Adidas for Prada," a community-contributed NFT art project in collaboration with digital artist Zach Lieberman, designed to enable new creators to play a part in a largescale artwork.

From digital twins to virtual goods, it will be interesting to watch the creativity brands can bring to develop more engaging and immersive experiences.

Gaming

In the gaming world, NFTs represent different in-game assets, such as digital plots of land, and are often traded on third-party marketplaces without permission from the game developer. Examples include the aforementioned CryptoKitties, where players adopt and trade virtual cats, and Axie Infinity, one of the most popular NFT-based online games where users collect fantasy monsters to breed or trade.

We will explore this topic further in the GameFi sections later in the book.

Music and Film

A growing number of artists, musicians, and directors are turning to NFTs as a way to mint and preserve digital music, album art, movie scenes, memorabilia, and concert tickets on the blockchain. These represent new and unique ways to monetize content, while allowing the artists to be free of constraints brought on by royalty agreements, thereby retaining a greater share of royalty rights and creative control of their work.

Beyond commercialization, such technology also provides a more intimate way for creators to connect with their fanbase. Take the Lennon Connection for example, which features Beatles memorabilia from Julian Lennon's personal collection. Julian, the elder son of John Lennon and his first wife, Cynthia, also minted an audio narration explaining the significance of these items as part of the NFT collection.[7] Together, the Collection, which included visual artwork, video footage, and two digital recordings, served as a reflection of his own personal journey, as well as a vehicle to help him raise funds for the White Feather Foundation, a social and environmental nonprofit that Lennon runs.

NFT music is much more than just music, after all.

Virtual Land

Buying real estate as an investment has long been one of the ways to generate wealth. Beyond generating ongoing passive income, it can also be a good long-term investment when the value increases over time.

But what about virtual real estate?

While the topic is still evolving, it is worth noting that the concept of virtual land is not new. Remember The Sims, one of the best-selling video games series of all time? The Sims, the first in the series, was launched in 2000, featuring an open-ended simulation of the daily activities of the people near SimCity. Players can create virtual characters to buy land, construct homes, and live through different life stages digitally.

Alternatively, Second Life, which was launched in 2003, was an online multimedia platform where players could create avatars and interact with others online, build, create, and trade virtual property. Interestingly, Second Life also has its own virtual currency called the Linden Dollar, a closed-loop virtual currency that can be used within the Second Life platform only. Players, however, can also buy Linden Dollar through the Lindex Exchange, and they can also buy and sell land, much like a real-world real estate market.

In the new web3 environment, virtual land is sold as NFTs, with proof of ownership recorded on the blockchain. These NFTs can be minted from the primary land sale, or via a marketplace such as OpenSea and Magic Eden. Some of the popular NFT land projects include Decentraland, The Sandbox, and Axie Infinity. And theoretically, beyond the right to sell, users should also be able to migrate the virtual land between metaverses. We will explore the interoperability issue in later chapters.

But, more importantly, what would a digital landlord do, you might wonder. Apart from speculation purposes, what would be some real use case, if any, of virtual property? An obvious one is advertising in the metaverse. Imagine having NFT billboards built with different themes. After purchasing the NFT, the owner can then install that billboard in any metaverse of their choosing (e.g., Decentraland), available for brands to advertise on, and gain a cut of the revenue generated, together with the NFT owner and asset creator.

Beyond advertising, landowners can also host events and showcase more immersive experiences with users, such as the Gucci Garden Experience on Roblox, as a means to "combine the past with the present to tell stories of the future."[8]

Yuga Labs launched an innovative model with their land NFTs, the Otherdeed. Otherdeed represent ownership of land within their metaverse "Otherside." Yuga approached the metaverse narrative differently to some of the previous land sale strategies. Instead of launching virtual lands where one can host events, grow metaverse props, etc., Yuga made Otherdeed part of a game.

As a result, Otherdeed's metadata was defined such that the attributes could contribute to the gaming experience. While most other metaverses have simply just created land NFTs without such tightly coupled features, Otherdeed came up with a closely knit model for their NFTs. When the land becomes part of a game, it would increase retention of the land as gamers would feel invested into the land through their game play.

However, Yuga's strategy for Otherside is at a very nascent state, and over the years we should see it mature and pave the way for more innovative virtual land models.

A CONVERSATION WITH Robbie Ferguson, Co-Founder and President of Immutable

I grew up playing a lot of video games. One of the stories that I remember is James (Ferguson) and I used to play a lot of RuneScape games. One day I went into the wilderness with all of his dragon armor, which was worth a lot, and I foolishly died and lost all of it. And I felt so bad that the next day I actually went on an illicit gold buying website to buy it back with my pocket money. The next day, the account was banned. A few months later, RuneScape rolled out bonds where you could actually buy gold.

So, pretty early on, I thought it was rubbish that games could operate on their economy with centralized impunity, and that there were no real guarantees of our property rights for the people who mattered most in playing them. My brother and I then spent probably the better half of a decade building startups together. We built a few different experiences such as a Shopify competitor. We built a League of Legends betting platform where you could raise your own matches. When Ethereum came out in 2015, we became truly obsessed because we could build the smart contracts ourselves.

There was a Dapp called Ether Roll, which is where you can roll a die and get a probabilistic reward based on the roll. I'm not excited about gambling in particular, but the fact that someone in a couple of hundred lines of code made a program that governments spend hundreds of billions of dollars every year around the world enforcing, which is enforcing transparent probabilities, and enforced payouts on slot machines, was to me a sign that this would take over the world.

In particular, because they did something that these companies could never do, which was they took the profit stream from this machine and they gave it to everyone who played this game. So, suddenly, they had figured out how to make every single person who uses this application an evangelist and effectively a shareholder, which was an incredibly powerful incentive. When Ethereum had its first NFT built in the middle of 2017, which is a CryptoPunk, we saw that and we said NFTs will be massive because they will help people own digital property, and the one sector we were really excited about was games.

We actually started out by building our own video game, which was called Ether Bots. It was a fully on-chain battling game, where you could win NFTs via having your robots, which were made out of NFTs, battle each other. It had an on-chain trustless randomness via a commit reveal scheme. It was woefully gas inefficient. I think running a match today will cost you thousands of dollars to learn pretty early on what architecture should stay on chain versus off chain. I think that really formed the basis for a lot of our thoughts around game design, economics, and technical architecture. We always wanted to build a platform that would enable other people to build successful games that gave gamers property rights. So we decided to build a game in much the same way that Epic built Fortnite. That was a trading card game where you could own your cards in much the same way you do Pokémon cards. It has several hundred thousand players and over 25 million NFTs. We've always been at the coalface of scaling on Ethereum. I think that really informed a lot of the tactical architecture choices we made when we designed our layer two Immutable X.

The reason we focus on gaming is I think it's the most exciting opportunity for web3 right now. The next 100 million users of web3 will come from a game, and that will triple the total user base of web3 overnight. If you look at the economic opportunity, gaming is a $100 billion-a-year industry built off in-game assets alone. If you take that 100 billion dollars and transform it from being an exploitive rental model into open composable assets that are tradable with real scarcity and real property rights—overnight, you've transformed an enormous chunk of value.

More importantly, you've opened up a trillion dollars' worth of secondary financial markets and opportunities where people can build loans or index markets or sophisticated derivatives and options on top of these fundamental assets. Economically, it's extremely interesting, but the most important thing is just that, philosophically, people should own property that they have, whether it's tangible or intangible, there's no real reason gaming rights should be any different from when you go and buy an item of clothing.

Therefore, I think gaming is the place to start. But Immutable's mission is much more than that. We see the entire world being tokenized into unique NFTs. So, really, all unique value is going to be transferred via

NFTs and this will be the way people trade stuff. If you solve for the use case of gaming, so that you can bring liquidity to hundreds of billions of assets that are highly heterogeneous and differentiated, you've solved the core problems that allow us to empower digital property rights now for finance, or for real estate, or for intellectual property.

Economic Model Elements

The NFT paradigm began with a digital art and ownership narrative, yet it has seen several business models being experimented within a short span of time through 2021 and 2022. Needless to say, this is a very nascent space and requires several cycles to mature, though we have seen signs of early promise. Perhaps the biggest success stories of this NFT cycle have been those of BAYC and CryptoPunks. The rise of these two NFT collections is a case study and has created a benchmark for other NFT collections to follow. Then came the dawn of the profile picture (PFP) craze.

"I am my ape and my ape is me" became a slogan on Twitter. You have probably seen a BAYC, even though you might not realize you are looking at one. Holders of PFP NFTs identified themselves with the NFTs they held and created an emotional connection with these NFTs. These emotional connections were so strong that, when an NFT holder sold their NFT for 10 times the purchase price, some would still feel an emotional void while doing so.

Let us look at the qualitative elements behind NFTs that make them a critical building block to web3 business models of the future.

Digital Ownership

The first NFT minted in 2014 was digital art. Generative art has been a key asset that has used NFT rails in the past few years. While the first NFT-based digital art was sold for $4, this space has grown in market capitalization since then. As mentioned earlier in the chapter, at the time of writing this chapter, "The Merge" by artist Pak is the most expensive art and sold for $91.8 million, followed by "Everydays: The First 5,000 Days", sold for $69.3 million.

Art remains a bedrock use case for NFTs primarily because it allows digital ownership of content. The proof of ownership is emotionally important, but it can also act as a critical lever to new business model opportunities. For instance, an artist who has sold 10 of their art collection pieces might want to give their art holders "the first rights of refusal" for their next art collection. This effectively leads to the creation of alpha communities that get early access to content creators and their work.

Digital ownership can extend far beyond art. With web3 games, players can buy assets within the games like guns or weapons. Unlike web2 games, where these purchases are just revenue sources for the gaming studios, in web3 NFTs are used to identify these assets and the gamer who purchases the asset owns it.

Luxury groups from LMVH's luxury jewelry brand Tiffany & Co., to Gucci, Dolce & Gabbana, and Burberry have joined in the NFT craze. For such brands, NFTs not only act as proof of ownership, but also can be redeemable tokens as resale of these real-world assets happens. In August 2022, Tiffany rolled out 250 units of limited-edition NFTiff pendants offered exclusively to owners of CryptoPunks, a collection of 10,000 eight-bit-inspired characters on the Ethereum blockchain. Sold out immediately and at a cost of $50,000 each, the NFTiff was redeemable for a custom Tiffany pendant in the physical world.

The Boson Protocol has been leading efforts in bridging the gap between digital NFTs and real-world assets. They offer a mechanism where NFTs can be tagged to a real-world item like a hoodie and when the hoodie is sold or resold the NFT changes hands.

They have created a handshake mechanism that protects the buyer and the seller from spurious actors exploiting the system and offer a dispute mechanism to address any issues too. As this application of NFTs becomes more mainstream, we may see them integrated with marketplaces like eBay where there is a need for trustless transactions.

This feature of NFTs, despite showing promise, is still a work in progress. The legal implications of digital ownership are often misunderstood by founders of NFT-based businesses and their communities. There is a lack of clarity on what levels of ownership NFT holders gain by buying them. Since a substantial percentage of NFT holders are more interested in the speculative nature of their collections, they are less concerned about ownership implications. This, however, is slowly changing as top NFT collections like Moonbirds look to educate their communities on the implications of digital ownership.

Provenance (Digital and Real-Life)

As a logical continuation to proof of ownership, being able to see the provenance of an expensive real-world asset is another use case that NFTs address. We see firms in the luxury retail segment like Breitling offering NFTs as "proof of ownership" to those who buy their watches. Other brands such as Tag Heuer and Lamborghini have also started to explore similar use cases as well.

Purchasers of expensive goods and luxury products need to be able to track the provenance of these items. This is particularly true in the art segment, where buyers would like to see how a piece of art has changed hands before coming to them. Ability to trace ownership of art back to the artist also proves its authenticity.

Identity

Blockchain and the decentralized, self-sovereign world have been focused on solving the challenge of digital identity for a long time. Blockchain-based solutions are being tested in refugee-affected parts of the world to provide them with identities. However, with the emergence of paradigms like NFTs and SocialFi, identities in a web3 ecosystem can have multiple layers. The different layers of identities that web3 contributes to are:

- digital identity
- economic identity
- emotional identity

Digital Identity

Digital identities are a simple self-sovereign method of identifying a citizen or a user digitally. Here the user owns their identity and the ability to decide what they share to establish their identities.

Cryptographic solutions like zero-knowledge proof allow users to establish that they hold the identity credentials without having to reveal the credentials to third parties. However, this layer of identity is an operational and utilitarian way of looking at identities.

Economic Identity

Economic identities will be driven by a user's activities within an ecosystem. As a gamer in a web3 ecosystem, all key wins, activities, and in-game asset purchases are logged on-chain. This allows gaming ecosystems to spot top contributors and help them grow within the ecosystem through tools like "soulbound tokens." Soulbound tokens are similar to credit scores in the financial market. The better your score, the higher your chance of access to finance. Similarly, these tokens identify the credentials of a user within the economy that they are contributing to.

This is also true in layer 1 blockchain protocols like Solana and Avalanche. Hedge funds that assess these blockchain for investments look at their GitHub activities, developers' code updates, and, importantly, the quality of developers involved in these protocol layers. The higher the quality of the developers, the higher the rating that the hedge funds provide to the chain under review. Therefore, the participants of gaming, financial, and even infrastructure platforms within web3 are critical to the whole ecosystem gaining traction, and therefore will be economically identified and incentivized for their contributions.

Emotional Identity

Emotional identity in web3 is largely driven by NFTs. While digital ownership is a clear utilitarian aspect of NFTs, digital identity is more of an emotion-led use case that is particularly relevant to PFP NFTs. PFP NFTs derive their name from being used as social media profile pictures. CryptoPunks are perhaps the first PFP NFTs that have taken the world by storm since their mint in 2017. Of the 10 most expensive NFTs, four are CryptoPunks, and a couple more are inspired derivatives of CryptoPunks. At the time of writing, CryptoPunks' market capitalization stands at $2.2 billion.

Through 2021, BAYC rose in stature and became one of the top NFT collections by market capitalization. At the time of writing, the total market capitalization of NFT is about $1.7 billion, with BAYC and CryptoPunks leading most of the growth of PFP NFTs.

But why are PFP NFTs so highly valued? Are they just overpriced JPEGs?

There are a couple of key reasons. PFP NFTs created an element of *perceived* value by limiting the number of NFTs minted. For example, BAYC NFTs are limited to 10,000 cartoon apes only, each with varying attributes from fur types and clothing to facial expressions and more. Limited supply combined with demand due to community engagement and loyalty drove prices to exponential highs.

Celebrities joining the community also added to the upside pressure in prices of these collections. Justin Bieber made headlines with his collection of BAYC NFTs in 2022.[9] Holding these NFTs and sporting them as PFPs is becoming a status symbol, with their value coming from perception and branding, just as how expensive suits and yachts are to ultra-high-net-worth (UHNW) individuals. When Bullieverse was fundraising in December 2021, we used a Bored Ape owned by their CEO, Srini Anala, as a profile picture to approach key investors on Twitter. We saw remarkable success even in the cold approach, and even had a few investors commit to the funding round.

Through 2021 and 2022 there were several quick followers within the PFP NFT space, namely DeGods, Okay Bears, Moonbirds, and Bullieverse. PFPs soon became such an emotional identity of the holders that there was inertia to selling them in the secondary market, a practice known as flipping. To add to the stickiness, several decentralized applications (Dapps) started to emerge to allow users to link their wallets and use their NFTs as PFPs.

Bullieverse and Yuga Labs (BAYC's parent company) have gone one step further to bring these two-dimensional images to life, by providing a three-dimensional (3D) avatar on a metaverse-like virtual experience. Gamers started identifying the 3D avatars of their apes and bulls as their digital self playing the games. Some hardcore community members of these NFTs even tattooed their logos. Thus, PFP NFTs have created an emotional connection with their holders and have become their emotional identities in the digital world.

Web3-driven identities will continue to have multiple layers to them. A section of web3-driven identities will be compliant and in line with the expectations of traditional financial services. This type of identity, which is more in line with traditional financial services, will be a digital identity.

This type of identity should support the roll-out of custodial wallets that the main street banks are offering. In a world with central bank digital currencies (CBDC), these wallets could be used by central banks and tax officials to calculate taxes in real time, aligning web3 to the conventional use cases of identities.

WHAT IS A CENTRAL BANK DIGITAL CURRENCY?

CBDC is a currency that is issued by a country's central bank. Implementations that are being discussed should allow central banks to see the state of transactions within their economy in near real time.

However, for economic and emotional identity types, NFTs drive ecosystem-specific identities. They should become the norm as DeFi, GameFi, and SocialFi applications scale. These identities will rely largely on NFT rails for tracking on-chain activities of a user and incentivizing them when they behave in a way that would benefit the ecosystem. An example could be an NFT community incentivizing their members to participate in global meetups to help build communities, thereby creating an ecosystem-specific identity through NFTs.

Value Permanence in the Creator Economy

The world is slowly but surely moving towards a creator economy. This will largely rely on web3 to make sure the incentive structures are skewed towards those who create value in any economy. If it is an economy of art, then artists should receive the largest slice of the pie. If it is an agricultural economy, farmers must get the largest slice of the pie.

The creator economy is a $104 billion market and is projected to increase over the next few years. This has unsurprisingly coincided with the rise of the metaverse narrative. The metaverse market cap is expected to be several trillion dollars in size over the next 10 years. In today's social media-dominated world, the term "creator economy" largely refers to bloggers, micro bloggers, and influencers who have a strong social media presence. To appreciate the scale of the creator economy, it would help to visualize social media as just one instance of the creator economy. There are several more like art, games, and metaverses in just a virtual context. If we are able to link the real-world creator economy to digital worlds, this narrative can see limitless possibilities.

Without dealing too much in hypotheticals, let us focus on how NFTs help creators create and retain value in these virtual worlds. As of 2022, the in-game assets market capitalization is about $75 billion. These are assets bought by web2 gamers within the games they play. They may be any playable characters, fashion products, game weapons, or environments that the gamers buy from the gaming studios.

Despite purchasing these in-game assets, they don't own them. There have been instances where games upgrade to a new level, and game players have lost all their in-game assets and need to start from scratch. You may have built a digital world on Roblox with several months and years of effort, and it may still mean very little in the real world. These are challenges that NFTs are already addressing.

Needless to say, NFT is a new paradigm and can be a volatile and sometimes illiquid asset. Yet, when a gamer buys an in-game asset that is an NFT, they own the asset and can sell it in a marketplace. These assets can also be created by a user and sold to another on a marketplace. Therefore, gaming platforms only offer the environment, experience, and mechanism for these transactions to happen. The game play experience instigates users to participate more actively and stay invested through in-game asset creation and ownership.

These assets, unlike in web2, are owned by creators and buyers. When the assets change hands within the economy, creators are rewarded with a royalty. The gaming platforms are incentivized through a small slice of the entire value. But in a web3 context, they are offering the platforms and experience and get incentivized just for that. They do not own assets created on their platform by a creator, and they definitely don't own assets that a user has purchased from a creator. These skewed incentive models are already being transformed through NFTs.

Brand Loyalty

Bitcoin, Ethereum, and the entire world of cryptos have struggled to gain mainstream and institutional adoption. While some of their use cases have shown promise, they have largely been confined within the world of web3. For the first time, NFTs, a web3 paradigm, have started to show relevance and application in a web2 context. How is that?

Customer loyalty and retention is a key performance indicator for businesses in web2. When a venture capital-backed firm scales, they look to grow aggressively through clever customer acquisition strategies. They use different strategies to monetize their customer base. Yet, the critical indicator for the health of a business is how well they retain their customer base. A business with very high user acquisition and low retention is perceived as a leaky bucket.

Coming back to the NFT value proposition, several web3 and web2 brands are able to acquire and retain customers through NFTs. This is due to the inherent emotional connection that holders have with their NFTs and a sense of belonging users feel due to the community interactions. Every NFT community has holders who look to sell their NFTs for a quick upside. Yet, most good NFT communities have a healthy percentage of holders that hang on to their NFTs. These community members buy their NFTs because they see a strategic upside over the medium and long term. They believe in the brand, their business model, the founding team, and, most of all, the quality of the community they are part of. As a result, they become long-term brand loyalists. Through 2021 and 2022, this feature of NFTs became more and more obvious and several traditional businesses like Nike, Adidas, Gucci, and Tiffany started experimenting with various NFT-based models to build their communities. All these brands most definitely have a group of loyal users, but these users haven't had a medium to connect with each other, and identify themselves as loyal to Adidas or Nike. The subtle value that NFTs bring to their communities makes a big difference to the brand equity of these large organizations.

Web2 social media organizations are starting to use NFTs, too. Facebook and Instagram are integrating NFTs into their user experiences. Telegram is exploring ways to turn user handles to mintable tokens. Starbucks is rolling out NFTs for their customer loyalty initiatives. Even Salesforce is looking at avenues to integrate NFTs into their platform, so that all their business clients can roll out an NFT-based experience for their customer relationship management processes. While most of these initiatives are still just experiments, we did not see the same level of involvement from such large organizations in cryptocurrencies or other paradigms of web3 at a similarly early stage. Web3 brings together elements of mathematics, engineering, marketing, and finance into a holistic business model, and NFTs are a bridge between the traditional world and this new way of doing business.

Gated Communities

Amongst several NFT features, one of the less inclusive aspects is the ability they offer to create gated alpha communities. However, this remains a key economic use case that the technology has opened up. Some of the top NFT collections have created Discord channels with access only for their NFT holders.

Often these channels have tiers of access and alpha provisioning, for instance, NFT communities like the Proof Collective that have Proof NFTs, Moonbirds and Oddities holders that have channels that are exclusively accessible for the holders of these NFTs. To add to that, when there are free drops of art or early access to an art collection, Proof holders get the top preference, followed by Moonbirds and then Oddities.

Therefore, even when the founding teams of the collection create partnerships to provide alpha to their communities, they often find tiers of alpha with the pecking order in mind. Even with the Yuga Labs' historic land minting event, the more expensive and feature-rich virtual land plots were assigned to the Bored Ape holders, followed by Mutant Ape holders. Public minting that followed for those who didn't hold ape NFTs didn't offer lands with as many features. Therefore, the pecking order was followed in provisioning land even when they were purchased at a price. This also meant that those who held the more expensive NFTs were on a continuous trajectory to acquire better digital assets.

Gated communities may sound like the traditional capital markets set-up where the rich keep getting richer. But it does serve the use case of paid membership in a traditional business model, where platinum holders get better access to products and services versus gold and silver holders.

The primary difference between the web2 membership models and NFT-based gated models is that the latter offers the ability for community members to identify with each other and feel the camaraderie of being part of a larger group.

This tiered model can be extended where those who contribute more to the community and economy grow their credentials and as a result earn an expensive NFT and become part of the alpha club. Therefore, growing up the pecking order doesn't just need to be bought, but can also be earned.

A CONVERSATION WITH Dan Romero,
Co-Founder of Farcaster

What are some of the aspects about web2 social platforms that drive you to create a web3 alternative?

I've always been interested in permissionless protocols like the web and RSS. I was also an early developer on the Twitter API. After leaving Coinbase in 2019, I thought it was the right time to build a sufficiently decentralized social networking protocol that guaranteed two things: users can maintain a direct relationship with their audience and developers can have direct access to the underlying data and APIs for the protocol. Contrasting this to traditional social networks where if you spend 10 years building an audience and the platform decides to turn off your account, there's no exporting of your followers. Similarly, developers on the original Facebook and Twitter APIs were later hurt by strategic changes from those companies.

How do you think web3 solutions should address those shortcomings in a scalable fashion?

The two key principles for making the decentralized social network scalable in the long run are: use a minimal amount of the Ethereum blockchain; and iterate new features at the client level first (and make sure they have usage/are working) before pushing them down to the decentralized protocol-level.

How do you think SocialFi and credentialing a contributor/creator on a platform helps the broader ecosystem?
I'm excited for what skin-in-the-game verified on-chain activity can enable for social networks. Whereas on web2 you can claim you did X or Y, web3 social networks that have deep integrations with cryptocurrency blockchains and wallets can prove what you did within the native user interface for that social network.

Final thoughts on the future of SocialFi?
I am bullish on NFT and digital collectibles as a way for people with an audience to identify and design new experiences for their biggest fans. As an aside, I don't think social networks are zero sum. You can see this in web2—there are multiple social networks, and news ones come along every so often.

More Than Just Digital Art

What makes an NFT valuable? Are we witnessing the downfall of a hype or the beginning of a new paradigm? While the answer might be somewhat subjective, it is helpful to remember that the value of NFTs is dependent on multiple factors: community, culture, and utility. The dramatic rise of BAYC is testament to the power of community, while CryptoPunks, inspired by the London punk scenes, the cyberpunk movement, and electronic music artists Daft Punk, are credited with starting the NFT craze and helping establish the modern cryptoart movement.

In March 2022, Yuga Labs released Ape Coin, a BAYC-themed cryptocurrency governed by the ApeCoin DAO. All Bored Ape NFT holders were airdropped over 10,000 Ape Coins at launch—which will act as the main currency for Otherside, a new metaverse connected to the BAYC ecosystem. Beyond the digital universe, the BAYC brand is very visible in the real world as well, including mobile games and fashion brands.

Access to VIP events and exclusive promotions are great starter use cases. Going forward, we expect to see continued development around the utility aspects, offering more seamless experiences between metaverses and beyond the realms of our physical world.

While we often link NFTs to art and PFPs, they are, and can be, much more. They represent a community's identity, and individual identities within a community. They offer value permanence in a GameFi ecosystem and help retain customers through the emotional connect they bring.

NFTs are arguably the first web3 paradigm to affect the lifestyle of everyday users. Over the next few years, we expect to see more businesses from web2 e-commerce to social media to roll out NFTs at a more significant scale.

Decentralized Finance (DeFi)

04

We often talk about the globalization of our world, referring to our world as a global village. Too often those descriptions refer solely to the free movement of goods and capital across the traditional barriers of national boundaries. Not often enough do we emphasize the globalization of responsibility.

NELSON MANDELA

Banking as a concept has been around for thousands of years, even before currencies emerged. Regardless of what form money takes, throughout history money has enabled the development of social and economic systems in different civilizations. It allows us to trade goods and services, and enables us to make plans and save for the future.

Decentralized finance (DeFi) refers to the financial applications run by smart contracts on a permissionless blockchain. Advocates of crypto assets have long championed such a system that would allow people to conduct transactions including lending, investing, and trading without relying on centralized intermediaries. Beyond cost efficiency, such a setup also provides users with greater anonymity and full transparency on the financial flows, propelling heightened interest in adoption in recent years.

WHAT IS A SMART CONTRACT?

A smart contract is a self-executing contract where the terms of agreement between the buyer and the seller are written into the lines of code. Such transactions are traceable, transparent, and irreversible.

Before we dive into DeFi and the potential benefits and challenges, it is important to take a look at the pros and cons of the modern financial services system.

As the old adage goes, "With great power comes great responsibility." This is especially true when it comes to money, with trust at the center of it all. From depositors to borrowers, from buyers to sellers, guided by rules and regulations, a centralized financial system has enabled the movement of money and provides the guarantee that promises will be fulfilled.

When consumers make a deposit in an Federal Deposit Insurance Corporation (FDIC) insured account, including Certificates of Deposit (CDs), checking, savings, and money market deposit account, such deposits are automatically insured up to at least $250,000 per depositor, per FDIC-insured bank, per ownership category. In other words, the bank customers are protected in the event that the bank fails, as the FDIC insurance is backed by the full faith and credit of the US government.[1]

But this was not always the case. In fact, the FDIC was created as part of the Banking Act of 1933, or the Glass-Steagall Act, designed to "provide for the safer and more effective use of the assets of banks, to regulate interbank control, to prevent the undue diversion of funds into speculative operations, and for other purposes."[2] The bill was signed into law to restore public faith in the banking system following the stock market crash of 1929 and the subsequent Great Depression, where a large number of banks failed or suspended operations and many families lost their savings.

The one major difference with crypto products, however, is that they are not FDIC insured.[3] So when a crypto exchange files for bankruptcy, investors may not be able to withdraw their assets, as in the case of Voyager and Celsius, which are technically centralized finance (CeFi) (more on that later), and risk losing all the money, including crypto assets. In fact, this was clarified by the regulator in a warning to the crypto industry that FDIC protections are extended to banks but not to crypto companies that have bank accounts.[4]

Ensuring funds' availability is only one of the several consumer protection vehicles. The Fair Housing Act and the Equal Credit

Opportunity Act also contain provisions to protect consumers from predatory and discriminatory practices and deceptive marketing.

Of course, the system is far from perfect. Regulations governing every aspect of banking, lending, and trading are complex and processes are slow. Intermediaries from banks to lenders and exchanges set conditions and fees for access—to the extent allowed by regulation—and earn a percentage of every financial transaction.

There are other pain points with traditional banking infrastructure. They are often constrained by national borders. This constraint also applies to credit bureaus that the banking industry relies heavily on. Central banks control the monetary policy of their jurisdictions, and mobility across jurisdictions often means a reset of credit history for consumers.

In a war-torn world, where mobility for refugees must be as seamless as possible, traditional banking services just don't scale functionally. After a comfortable life with a credible financial status in a country such as Ukraine, if a family had to relocate to Europe and build their credit file from scratch, it could be a struggle. That should be the last thing the world imposed on consumers, particularly in difficult times.

To make matters worse, those who do not typically transact using products and services offered by conventional financial services often do not accrue credibility in their own jurisdiction. For instance, a farmer or an artist who regularly finds a consumer for their produce/creation, may not have an economic identity if they don't have a bank account or a credit card. Financial services must operate as a utility that cuts across industries without consumers realizing it.

Even in a fintech-powered world, embedded fintech is still in the early stages of development where those who use financial services in subtler ways are often excluded from having economic identities. Embedded fintech is often integrated with a lifestyle experience, but users are expected to still be part of traditional financial services infrastructure to be able to build an economic identity.

What if there were another way?

In our three-pronged approach to the metaverse, DeFi enables the economic layer. The economic layer in the metaverse is like the monetary engine of a country. It ensures there is enough capital in the ecosystem, transactions are seamless, access to capital for economic actors is provided, and most of all these are managed through robust risk management practices.

All parties using a DeFi application will have an identical copy of the public ledger, transactions will be verified and recorded in encrypted computer code, with no intermediary managing the system, nor any regulators driving policy making. The downside is also that there is no central body to act as guarantors of consumers' money. There are centralized crypto exchanges such as Celcius and stablecoin issuers like Circle that will be under the regulatory watch soon, but DeFi has somehow escaped regulations so far.

Before we get into the detailed DeFi use cases for consumers, it may be helpful to understand the layers that make up a robust DeFi application, as well as some basic terminologies in DeFi:

- infrastructure layer: Blockchain
- rules layer: Smart contracts
- assets layer: Tokens
- application layer: Dapps (decentralized applications)

As mentioned, DeFi runs on decentralized applications, also known as Dapps. Instead of residing in a database on a server controlled by the company that produces the app, the data for the decentralized application lives on a blockchain. Such a structure enables customized designs with different levels of decentralization, where some Dapps are controlled and managed by third parties.

The Blockchain Layer

The blockchain layer also allows a series of decentralized nodes to decide the order of transactions through different consensus mechanisms (such as proof of work), balancing access and control, scalability, as well as security.

WHAT IS A CONSENSUS MECHANISM?

A consensus mechanism is a method by which agreement, trust and governance are achieved in a decentralized network. Proof of work (PoW) and proof of stake (PoS) are the two widely known consensus mechanisms in web3. While proof of work has nodes using processing power to validate transactions, proof of stake depends on network validators using staked tokens.

For instance, a highly decentralized chain may struggle to perform fast transactions, but it is considered to be more secure as the level of decentralization increases. In contrast, more centralized chains with fewer nodes and validators tend to process transactions faster, but they are not considered to be as secure as the chains with a high degree of decentralization.

The Rules Layer

The rules layer is where the transaction rules are programmatically embedded. In a simple DeFi app, depositors get paid interest for contributing to the pool of capital and borrowers are expected to offer collateral. This layer ensures that these transactions are triggered by events that are tracked programmatically and the right commercial and contractual handshakes are performed through smart contracts.

For example, when a lending protocol does a smart contract-based handshake with the depositor to pay regular interest, and another handshake with the borrower on interest to be paid, the interest paid by the borrower is channeled to the depositor directly or through a pool of liquidity through smart contracts. These smart contracts are programmatically written, tested, and audited before they are mass deployed. The blockchains that these smart contracts are written on have the governance responsibility to ensure spurious smart contracts are spotted and exiled from the system to protect users.

In essence, the infrastructure layer acts as the *regulator* in DeFi and the smart contract layer executes the structure of the financial product.

The assets layer is where value is stored in the form of tokens. Transaction value locked is mentioned quite often in DeFi and is a critical element to assess the health and maturity of a DeFi ecosystem. Just as banks cannot exist without deposits, DeFi apps cannot exist without the assets that users bring to them.

WHAT IS TRANSACTION VALUE LOCKED?

Transaction value locked (TVL) represents the total value of assets (in $USD) deposited into the smart contracts of a DeFi application.

Finally, the application layer is where the user journey is defined. This is the layer that the user interacts with to perform a financial transaction. DeFi applications are often integrated into crypto wallets, and users can also visit a DeFi app on their browser, connect their wallets, and perform transactions.

WHAT IS A CRYPTO WALLET?

A crypto wallet is a digital location where users can store their digital assets. Most blockchains have applications that provide the wallet functionality that can support cryptos and NFTs that are built on the blockchain.

So, what's the catch?

At the peak of the last Bitcoin cycle in 2021, Ethereum-based DeFi apps had $160 billion in transaction value locked. Despite the recent growth in DeFi ecosystems, the industry is not without challenges.

Let's start with the infrastructure or the blockchain layer.

Decentralization—Utopia or Dystopia?

There are three key centralization vectors that layer 1 platforms exhibit.

WHAT IS LAYER 1?

Layer 1 is the base network, such as Bitcoin or Ethereum, and its underlying infrastructure. Layer 1 blockchains can validate and finalize transactions without the need for another network.

The First Vector

The first vector is where the network runs on a cloud infrastructure provided by one large provider, such as Amazon (AWS) or Microsoft (Azure). These cloud providers have distributed infrastructure across the globe, mitigating the risk of the server infrastructure being largely based out of one country. Yet, if 20 percent of the Ethereum network runs on AWS, it is reliant on the provider being in business and will therefore be exposed to it.

The Second Vector

The second vector that layer 1s exhibit is with token distribution. This is particularly true in chains that use the PoS consensus mechanism. As the web3 world moves on from energy-intensive consensus mechanisms like PoW to attract ESG investors, it is potentially moving on from a governance methodology that relies on relatively even distribution of energy across the world. For example, in a PoW world, if China chose to ban Bitcoin mining, the mining operation could quickly switch to Texas in the US and ensure the network was back on its feet within weeks. But in a PoS system, consensus relies on ownership of the token. A node that owns a large percentage of the token has a higher control on the chain. Imagine a scenario where Ethereum prices fell to $500 during a crisis, and effectively below $300 billion in market capitalization. In this scenario, the US or the Chinese government could buy a big slice of the pie to control the network.

At the time of writing, the Ethereum network is the largest blockchain network, with several million transactions. Yet, there is a scenario where PoS could be the beginning of a centralized Ethereum network.

The Third Vector

The third vector of centralization is driven by the transaction supply chain. In 2019, years after the Ethereum network was born, Phil Daian highlighted miner extractable value (MEV) in his paper Flash Boys 2.0.[5] More recently, with the move to PoS, MEV's new expansion has transitioned to "maximum extractable value," referring to "the maximum value that can be extracted from block production in excess of the standard block reward and gas fees by including, excluding, and changing the order of transactions in a block."[6]

From the point where a user triggers a transaction from their wallet to transaction completion, there are several economic actors involved in making the transaction commit on the blockchain. An Ethereum transaction involves the user, the miners or the validators (in PoS), and third-party searchers and bots. These economic actors are incentivized to perform their tasks on the transaction supply chain, and the incentives are charged back to the user who triggers the transaction.

On the Ethereum blockchain, "gas fee" is the term used to refer to the fee the user pays to the network for processing and committing the transaction. MEV becomes relevant when searchers run bots to identify high-incentive transactions and push these transactions to be included in a block. There are also instances where bot-generated transactions are used to artificially "sandwich" a user-generated transaction, resulting in the user paying higher gas fees.

What began as an incentive mechanism for miners is turning into an industry trying to manipulate the supply chain of transactions for third parties to accrue value for themselves. There are mitigation techniques to alleviate this issue. For example, miners may be limited to including but not ordering blocks; alternatively, layer 2 chains like Immutable X and Polyton can be used to batch up transactions to be committed to layer 1 chains like Ethereum. Such measures would reduce the number of MEV bad actors significantly.

While we will not dive further into the problem of MEV in Ethereum or other similar smart contract blockchains in the context of this book, it is beneficial to at least understand the scale and potentially serious consequences of it.

Beyond MEV, there are a few other challenges that DeFi faces.

User Experience

Web3 applications are notoriously clunky, and DeFi is no exception. Interfacing with a DeFi app will require the right wallet to be set up, and in some cases you will also need to know the right chain to connect to for the app from the wallet itself. For instance, if you are using the Uniswap Dapp you will need an Ethereum wallet such as MetaMask.

The DeFi ecosystem can be intimidating for newcomers, especially if they are not familiar with concepts such as staking, liquidity provision, swapping, impermanent loss, and many more. We will touch upon most of these in the use cases section, but it is suffice to say that DeFi and web3 could benefit from a facelift in user experience.

Dapps Centralization

Dapps centralization is a common theme and a challenge within DeFi. These apps can define the rules of engagement with their users quite loosely and exploit the ambiguity during times of crisis. This has most certainly created a backlash from the crypto community and hurt their progress. Consumers can also be affected by apps that misinform them of their rules, or mislead them with financial products.

This issue can be resolved as DeFi regulations tighten. Genuine decentralization of these Dapps can also help ensure community-driven decision frameworks are developed and used for governance.

Despite these challenges, DeFi is the most developed vertical within web3 that has helped the market capitalization of blockchains like Ethereum and Solana. Much like with mainstream banking, there are major areas of improvement needed with DeFi, and it has largely held itself together through the crypto bear market of 2022.

DeFi Hacks

DeFi hacks become more prominent as the total value locked in DeFi platforms continues to grow. Where money flows, scammers and hackers will follow; smart contract security remains one of the key challenges for decentralized smart contract platforms. Bad actors have exploited smart contract bugs, copy and paste errors, and faulty Dapp logic to their advantage. Phishing attacks targeting Discord servers are another pain point for web3 security, highlighting both the dependence of NFT projects on the social media platform for marketing to and engaging with their communities, but also the security risks that this can bring about.

Losses resulting from hacks, scams, and other malicious activities exceeded $10.2 billion in 2021, which was substantially higher than the $4.38 billion lost in 2020.[7] Over $2 billion was lost to hacks and exploits in Q1 and Q2 in 2022 alone, making 2022 an expensive year for web3 as well.[8] We will explore the security topic in a bit more detail later in the chapter.

Risk Management (Or the Lack Of It)

Risk management (or the lack of it) is another major challenge with DeFi. Most young Dapps in this space are led by technologists with very little understanding of risk management. It takes a banker to run and scale a bank. Many DeFi apps today are essentially providing banking services and therefore would need to draw inspiration from the traditional financial services industry.

Every DeFi app must have a clear stress testing framework, and perform scenario modeling and sensitivity analysis. Entrepreneurs leading these Dapps must have or hire risk specialists to understand the viability of their model in a crisis scenario. Dapps must also provide educational content to users. As this sector develops, DeFi platforms must go through similar rigor to what traditional banks must go through to stay in business.

A CONVERSATION WITH SOFIE BLAKSTAD, CEO OF HIVEONLINE

On the digital divide and opportunity gap:
Let's not forget that a vast portion of the world's population do not have a phone nor phone signal—whether due to the high cost of services or lack of infrastructure, because they live in conflict zones, or they are in rural areas. When we design new solutions, we must use clever and inclusive approaches to leverage and blend in existing social structures; otherwise, such innovation will benefit only the same people who can afford it. Instead of closing the digital divide, we might increase it.

On using technology for good:
Seventy percent of arable land in Africa is not farmed because farmers cannot afford the seeds. How can we best leverage technology to help these farmers manage cash flow, increase food production, and bring about transformational economic benefit?

Final thoughts:
We need to listen to the farmers and understand what they need. It is not always just about great tech.

A CONVERSATION WITH ADI BEN-ARI, FOUNDER AND CEO OF APPLIED BLOCKCHAIN

On blockchain and how it will impact banking:
When savings, borrowing, and lending can be done more efficiently and safely elsewhere, what will (eventually) happen to the banks? I think the models will change. But we'll still need banks for stablecoin issuance and custody services.

I don't think centralized exchanges will be going away because there is a need for people to use things in a way that is easy for them. The user experience is not an easy problem to solve. Obviously, from a technical perspective, self-custody is the ideal solution.

On the future:
I don't think I have seen any technology where so much real innovation is happening in such a short time. And what we have done so far is a lot of learning. We have barely scratched the surface of what can be done.

Use Cases of Distributed Finance

While still relatively new, different DeFi apps are being tested and implemented in a variety of use cases, many of which aim at replicating today's financial services functions.

Peer-to-Peer Lending and Borrowing

Due to its decentralized nature, anyone can become a lender in DeFi, making crypto lending and borrowing the largest single segment of DeFi in 2021, representing half of the value locked on the Ethereum blockchain at the time of writing.[9]

In modern-day finance, those who save earn interest from the banks through the money that they deposit with the institutions. Banks then provide loans to borrowers using the funds. Unlike traditional finance, where borrowers are vetted using credit score and other data points, DeFi platforms are reliant on collateral in order to align the incentives of the borrowers and lenders (depositors), due to the anonymous nature of the parties. While this could be a helpful alternate means for borrowers who lack creditworthiness to obtain capital (e.g., immigrants with credit thin files), the need for collateral, partly due to the volatile nature of crypto assets, can be a hindrance to true financial inclusion as those who do not have access to credit and formal financial services tend to have fewer assets to begin with. In the future, soulbound tokens could become a solution for under-collateralized on-chain lending, through provable reputation.[10] Suffice to say, there is still work to be done for us to attain the full potential benefits of decentralized lending.

Some DeFi applications such as Aave started as a peer-to-peer (P2P) lending protocol before pivoting to a pool-based strategy. In the P2P model, the borrower submits their lending request, and if it gets accepted the collateral is moved to an escrow and the loan is granted. In a pool-based strategy, the collateral is deposited in a smart contract. The valuation of the collateral happens using oracles.

Depending on the supply and demand equation of a specific pool of assets used as collateral, the interest rates would vary. Several DeFi lenders themselves have issued proprietary tokens. If lenders hold these tokens or choose to get paid interest on these tokens, their returns are higher.

As mentioned earlier, due to the anonymity that DeFi offers, it must take collateral to lend. The collateral is often digital assets in the form of Bitcoin, Ethereum, and more recently NFTs. This may not be a scalable model in an asset class that often sees 30–40 percent volatility in price within a week. It could create systemic risks and spiraling losses as the crypto markets get more interconnected and grow in size, as the Celcius episode revealed.

Collateralization is a good risk mitigation for anonymity, but DeFi users can stay anonymous and still have a credit file that is relevant in an ecosystem. This can be achieved through an innovation called soulbound tokens. Soulbound tokens are like credentials that users within a specific ecosystem can accumulate by adding value. For instance, a user can lend regularly within a DeFi platform and accumulate soulbound tokens within the platform. The platform will be able to see the contribution of the user to the platform from these tokens. As a result, they may get preferential rates if they choose to borrow from the platform.

Soulbound tokens are generally not meant to be transferable across users. They are tagged to a wallet, and cannot be sold in a marketplace like normal crypto or NFT tokens. This allows for them to be tagged to a user and gamification within DeFi ecosystems. As users collect more of these soulbound tokens, they are incentivized to interact in a way to benefit both themselves and the ecosystem.

Trading

Similar to foreign exchange markets, cryptocurrencies need a marketplace to facilitate buying, selling, and trading. While much of crypto trading today is still reliant on centralized exchanges, such as Binance, Coinbase, and Kraken, things may be slowly changing.

Decentralized exchanges (DEXs) are P2P marketplaces where transactions occur directly between crypto traders. They are not legally based in any jurisdiction, and anyone with an internet connection and access to a crypto wallet and funds can use them. Traders can conduct their transactions anonymously, which are settled directly on the blockchain, and no exchanges between fiat currency and cryptocurrency are allowed.

WHAT IS FIAT CURRENCY?

All forms of money that are made legal tender by a government decree are called fiat currency. In the web3 world, fiat is typically used to refer to USD, GBP, and other mainstream currencies.

To replace order-matching systems and custodial infrastructures, DEXs use autonomous protocols called automated market makers (AMM) that leverage smart contracts-based transactions to derive the price of digital assets and provide liquidity, eliminating the need for an intermediary to facilitate the trade. Whereas in traditional exchanges only high net worth individuals or companies can assume the role of a liquidity provider, for AMMs anyone can become a liquidity provider and deposit as little as a fraction of a token in the pool. In return, they are rewarded with a fraction of the fees paid by traders on the transactions executed. AMMs also issue governance tokens to liquidity providers and traders, providing them with the rights to vote on issues relating to the governance and development of their protocol. We will dive more into the governance aspects in later chapters.

There are currently more than 35 decentralized exchanges around the world, with Uniswap DEX being one of the largest ones. The Uniswap protocol is a P2P system designed for exchanging crypto-currencies (ERC-20 tokens) on the Ethereum blockchain. The proto-col is implemented as a set of persistent, non-upgradable smart contracts designed to prioritize censorship resistance, security, self-custody, and to function without any trusted intermediaries who may selectively restrict access.[11] Users can also participate in governing and maintaining the ecosystem via the Uniswap decentralized auton-omous organization. We will explore these in further detail in later chapters.

WHAT IS A DECENTRALIZED AUTONOMOUS ORGANIZATION?

A decentralized autonomous organization (DAO) is an organization governed by a community. The community typically includes the founding members of the firm, the users of the platform that the organization is working on, creators, developers, ecosystem members who contribute to the platform, and investors who have invested in the organization.

DAOs are formalized by the launch of a token through a token generation event (TGE), and the token holding is often proportional to the voting powers that community members have on DAO resolutions. This effectively makes decisions quite decentralized, unlike traditional capital market constructs.

While DEXs have been gaining traction in recent years, challenges remain. As mentioned earlier in the chapter, gas fees and user experience need to be improved before we will see mass adoption. Interoperability between different DeFi platforms in particular is crucial for a seamless ecosystem of decentralized P2P trading to occur.

Digital Identity

Identity is fundamental to a functional society. From birth certificate, social security card, passport, and driver's license, to student identity card, voter's registration card, credit card, and beyond, these are all various forms of documents issued by public and private entities to provide proof of one's identity and rights.

Unfortunately, these forms of identity are not available to everyone. According to the World Bank, an estimated one billion people in the world cannot prove who they are.[12] Not only do they struggle to access basic services such as finance and telecommunications, they can also face challenges with employment and property ownership, and lack the right to vote. Women and the poor, in particular, are at the greatest risk of being left behind due to lack of formal identification.

Digital identity has proven to be especially crucial as governments around the world looked for ways to respond to the economic and social consequences of the Covid-19 pandemic. Countries such as Thailand were able to leverage their digital identity systems to uniquely identify eligible recipients for government aid, enabling immediate cash transfer to the beneficiary's bank account.[13]

Even for those of us who have access to formal identity, the systems are often siloed and fragmented. Increasing instances of data breaches to critical systems often leave users with severe consequences from identity theft.

Could decentralized digital ID infrastructure be a solution—not only for the physical world but for what's to come in the virtual world?

Perhaps we can look towards AID:Tech, a decentralized digital identity startup, for clues. AID:Tech is a social enterprise that enables fast and instant disbursements over blockchain technology for disaster relief, by providing digital identity to end users with a mobile phone, which can be used to open bank accounts, get loans, and access social services.[14]

More interestingly, its decentralized reputation and reward-based system can be used to incentivize volunteers by providing opportunities for them to build on-chain reputation via their digital identity NFT and earn cryptocurrency for volunteering. These tokens can be traded as a currency and act as a utility in the network.[15]

Another interesting scenario can be found in gaming, with the combination of NFTs, soulbound tokens and zero-knowledge proof.

WHAT IS ZERO-KNOWLEDGE PROOF?

Zero-knowledge (ZK) proof helps to prove the truth of a statement without sharing the statement's contents or revealing how you discovered the truth. For instance, if a user wants to borrow money and the interest rates are decided by the asset he holds in his wallet, he can inform the lender that he has the necessary assets to borrow, without revealing the assets he holds in the wallet.

As mentioned in the previous chapter, "I am my ape, and my ape is me" is an emotional connection with a profile picture (PFP) NFT. Gaming platforms began modeling 3D rendering of these NFTs to leverage this emotional connection. These NFTs did not just create an emotional identity for the holders on social media platforms such as Twitter, they also created a community identity. Some ape holders are known by their digital friends based on their ape number, while their real-life name and identity remain anonymous, and in many cases are irrelevant to their communities.

While one may use their ape or Moonbird NFT to participate in a game or an economy and present themselves to other gamers as that ape, it is really when they win badges of honor (soulbound tokens) within the game that they are respected for the economic value and social status that they have earned in the system.

Now that emotional and economic identities are largely identified, ZK proofs can be used to create handshake mechanisms within the applications that these identities need to be used in.

ZK proofs are a cryptographic method that allows us to prove our identities without revealing private information. A simple example could be for a user to prove their financial credibility without having to reveal their bank balance. This can be used in a metaverse environment as follows. Imagine an ape NFT holder with a platinum badge (a highly respected soulbound token) within a gaming ecosystem. When they need to borrow money from inside a DeFi app in the game to buy in-game assets, ZK proofs can provide details about the user anonymously to the DeFi app and establish credibility with the DeFi app. Thanks to the user's identity in an ape, and the credentials in the platinum badge that reflect their participation within the gaming economy, they will stand a good chance of getting the loan approved.

Although cross-chain and cross-ecosystem identities feel like utopia from where we are, the web3 world often innovates with technology and business models at breakneck pace. It is safe to say that the criticality of interoperability to the maturity of web3 is not lost on the innovators. As we stand today, chain-based applications and ecosystems are focused on creating robust models that can scale within that context. Thanks to exchanges and cross-chain bridges, we are able to move value across chains and ecosystems manually where they are needed. In the future, we should be interacting seamlessly between DeFi apps sitting on different chains.

As users continue to spend time in the digital realm, whether through virtual events, an online learning platform, or a gaming ecosystem, they will continue to build up their digital footprint, which constitutes part of who they are and should stay with them, regardless of which virtual environment they are in.

In fact, this is what Sebastien Borget, co-founder and Chief Operating Officer of The Sandbox, has hypothesized: "Users will want to bring more than just the visual appearance of their avatar from one virtual world to another. They will also want to carry their online reputation, progression and achievements with them."[16]

As the metaverse continues to develop, users should be able to use all of their data as proof of who they are online, and such identity should not be confined within one walled garden platform.

Wallets

And this brings us to the topic of digital wallets, which play a crucial role in the metaverse and act as the home for all digital assets and transactions in web3. A wallet is where all the crypto tokens, NFTs, and soulbound tokens are held by a user. It can be visualized as a new age bank account. As the user journey within cryptos stands today, wallet is perhaps the single most important application that most participants will need to have.

As a user goes through a DeFi application, they connect their wallet to the Dapp through a smart contract handshake. This handshake allows the Dapp access to any information it needs from the wallet to enable a DeFi transaction. For instance, if a user wants to purchase Ethereum using USD Coin (USDC) on Uniswap, they must connect their MetaMask wallet to Uniswap. The Uniswap application offers an interface where users can enter the amount of USDC that they want to buy Ethereum for.

Uniswap receives information from the wallet about its USDC balance and creates a user journey to use the right amount of USDC. The user triggers the swap transaction between USDC and Ethereum with another smart contract approval from the wallet. Once the swap happens, the wallet will reflect an increase in Ethereum balance and a decrease in USDC balance.

An alternative to performing this transaction through a wallet is via a centralized crypto exchange such as Coinbase or Binance. However, that transaction would not be anonymous and will be performed in a more centralized infrastructure.

Wallet User Journey

Despite such a fundamental application that the wallet addresses, the implementation of digital wallets in web3 has been far from optimal.

It is often hard to know which wallets on a specific chain are credible. While Ethereum and the MetaMask wallet for Ethereum have been around for several years, wallets for other chains like Solana, Near, Polkadot, and Tezos are relatively new.

Wallets also require users to hold a private key and a 12-word recovery phrase. Private keys and secret recovery phrases have to be securely stored to ensure hackers do not get access to the wallet. "Not your keys, not your coins" is a mantra that the crypto world embraces, referring to the need to hold your own private keys associated with your funds. Thus handing over control of your assets (including NFTs) to a third party in a centralized exchange can be frowned upon by the community that believes in true decentralization.

However, such ethos may not always be scalable, and the web3 world can certainly seek inspiration from web2 innovation to create more frictionless and seamless user journeys. And we cannot emphasize this enough: If the ambition is to bring financial inclusion to different corners of the world, we need on-ramp solutions that will simplify user journeys, even if that means more controls to verify identity in order to onboard users.

Wallet Security

While user experience presents a challenge with wallets, a more serious issue is cyber security. As described earlier, wallets need to grant permission to Dapps through smart contracts to perform certain tasks. But an average user may not necessarily understand smart contracts nor what the permission really means to them and the assets in the wallets, thus creating opportunities for cyber criminals.

Apart from user mistakes through smart contract approvals, there are infrastructure issues as well. The ecosystem is just creating interoperability between chains. For instance, if a user holds USDC on an Ethereum wallet like MetaMask, and wants to buy Solana, they are effectively asking for a cross-chain transaction. This can happen through a crypto exchange such as Coinbase. But if they want it to be a DeFi transaction, this cross-chain handshake will need to happen through a "bridge."

These cross-chain bridges allow Ethereum wallets to connect to them, sending Ethereum-based assets to Solana wallets and buying-Solana based assets. But bridges have been a very successful hunting ground for hackers: the Solana Wormhole bridge hack cost the network $326 million.[17] Thankfully, the network had investors and backers that quickly mitigated the risk.

In essence, poor user experience and cyber security issues have reinforced the importance of better wallet infrastructure, which will be crucial in helping to scale web3 globally and drive user adoption.

Insurance

That leads us well into the insurance use case of DeFi. Of all the above use cases of DeFi we have discussed, insurance is perhaps the most nascent, with some startups developing insurance for losses due to smart contract malfunction. For instance, Etherisc is creating a protocol to offer DeFi insurance and Bridge Mutual is working on an aggregator for DeFi insurance.

But how will this work? Assume a user holding digital assets or performing DeFi transactions insures their assets with an insurance provider, with an annual premium of about 2.5 percent. If they lose their assets to faulty or spurious smart contracts (under a scenario that is covered with the insurance policy), then they can claim for their losses. The insurance provider can be a centralized organization that is prepared to underwrite the insurance for these products.

Alternatively, a DeFi insurance provider can be built on DeFi rails to offer services for the DeFi ecosystem. For example, a number of users can come together and choose to offer liquidity to insure assets on Uniswap. At the other end, we could have a number of users who want to buy insurance for their assets on Uniswap. If Uniswap gets hacked and the users lose their assets, the funds from the liquidity providers will be used to pay the users who have lost their money.

For now, this market is perhaps too nascent and too small for large insurance organizations to underwrite insurance products, and insurance products will largely be offered to other institutions who are looking to provide digital asset custody solutions. Retail-level insurance is very much in the future for institutional insurance firms.

Until then, there is nothing stopping the web3 community from building the rails of insurance products that will satisfy their needs, focusing primarily on cryptocurrencies and DeFi transactions around cryptos. But this could soon be extended to NFTs and transactions in the metaverse.

We have discussed a wide variety of DeFi use cases that are relevant in a metaverse context. There are other DeFi applications such as derivatives, analytics, and exchanges, but their synergies with the new paradigm are minimal at the time of writing this book. As mentioned earlier in this chapter, there are several challenges that still need to be addressed should DeFi scale and become an integral part of the metaverse experience.

A CONVERSATION WITH SEEMA KHINDA JOHNSON, CO-FOUNDER AND COO, NUGGETS

On digital identity in the metaverse:
The metaverse, a persistent virtual world where communications, finance, and personal profiles converge under one interoperable platform, requires a secure and trustworthy solution for digital identity. In many ways, digital ID is even more crucial in a virtual world than in real life. In the metaverse, people obfuscate their identity with avatars and personas, but sometimes you still need a way to prove elements of your identity such as age, available funds, or citizenship.

Likewise, the same security issues from web2, such as fraud, data breaches, social engineering, phishing, and theft, will become even more prominent in the metaverse—especially as we continue to share data more liberally. Self-sovereign decentralized identities (SSDID) will become essential in the metaverse to avoid becoming a target. This decentralized digital identity management system enables individuals to own and control personal data and online identities without requiring a central authority.

On privacy and security:
Combining the SSI approach with BBS+ verifiable credentials, cryptographic solutions such as zero-knowledge proof and PeerDIDs can guarantee privacy by allowing users to only share data they absolutely need—or no data at all. Moreover, tying payments, cryptocurrencies, bank accounts, and digital collectibles directly to digital identity enables users to securely transact in the digital economy, creating, buying, and selling goods without compromising or sharing their data.

The metaverse is poised to completely reshape the way we interact with digital services and each other. To succeed, however, this new digital frontier needs to be safer and more empowering than its web2 predecessor, and I believe decentralized SSIs will be an inextricable and integral part of this vision.

Roadblocks for DeFi

DeFi brings a more democratic approach to delivering banking and financial services to the modern customer. Even during the Luna/Terra crash episode in 2022, despite a systemic collapse across the crypto ecosystem, followed by a crypto contagion, DeFi has been relatively stable. On the contrary, the contagion from the Luna collapse hurt centralized crypto exchanges like Celcius and BlockFi more than the likes of Uniswap, Aave, and other DeFi apps.

While this stands as testimony to the robustness of the model, processes such as credit checks and know your customer (KYC) can bring more credibility to this market. They do not have to be centralized and opaque processes like we see in conventional financial systems, but they need to be there. Also, with a large portion of the DeFi market relying on Ethereum where there are questions on scalability, along with the next largest ecosystem on Solana, which has had security and stability challenges, much needs to be done.

Here are some areas of improvement for DeFi that are worth considering.

User Experience

We live in a digital era where we have come to expect seamless and friction-free user journeys. Yet, the same can't be said for web3 user experience. As described earlier in this chapter, in order for a user to hold Bitcoins or Ethereum in a wallet, the complexity involved in creating and setting up a wallet can be intimidating for most customers. While many of the web2 audience who are used to banking applications may not feel too worried about being hacked or completely losing access to their accounts, web3 users are largely on their own.

In the web3 world, in order to perform transactions through a wallet, or even between exchanges, we use addresses that are long hash codes; in contrast, in web2, we can initiate money transfers between bank accounts that bear the name of the account and account holders. While it may not be a big difference semantically, it is a new and different user experience.

The user journey associated with activities such as swapping, liquidity provision, or borrowing from a DeFi app can also be challenging at first. Most of these applications are browser-based, and users will need to integrate their wallet plugin into their browsers. The process of importing their crypto wallets from mobile to browser is another cumbersome touchpoint.

But, most of all, the process of signing off a transaction through a smart contract prompt to perform a swap can be a psychological headwind. What the smart contract does behind the scenes is often not clear to the user, and can often become a source of hacks.

Buying an NFT, becoming part of a new ecosystem such as an Ethereum Name Service (ENS), or playing a web3 game that is available on particular chains all serve to add more layers of touchpoints and complexity to the user journey. Later in the book, we will discuss how NFTs are critical to several aspects of the web3 economy, and yet the experience of getting on the NFT bandwagon is not simple.

Luckily, we are still at the very beginning of the evolution, with much still to be defined and improved. Onramper, Swapin, and MoonPay are some of the companies working to make the process of onboarding crypto users more seamless. We can also expect crypto exchanges and fintech challenger banks to join the effort.

Cyber Security

Cyber security has been a major issue in the cryptoverse. As mentioned earlier in the chapter, the financial losses from cybersecurity incidents have been mounting in the past few years. Some typical areas of vulnerabilities include:

- cross-chain bridge hacks
- smart contract hacks
- Discord hacks
- marketplace (opensea) hacks
- wallet hacks

The Poly Network hack and the cross-chain bridge hack involving Solana's Wormhole bridge and Axie Infinity's Ronin bridge are high-profile examples:[18]

- While the Poly Network hack remains the largest crypto hack at the time of writing, with the hacker making off with $611 million,[19] it has twists and turns that resulted in a happy ending: the protocol offered a bounty of half a million dollars, along with the opportunity for the hacker to become the network's chief security advisor.
- Another high-profile heist involved Solana's Wormhole bridge and Axie Infinity's Ronin bridge. While cross-chain bridges allow users to transfer cryptos from one chain to the other without the need to go to a centralized exchange, therefore facilitating interoperability between chains, they have brought about new and costly vulnerabilities. Combined, $878 million was lost.[20] Both platforms

were able to recover and replenish lost money due to their robust investor base. Yet, it revealed the need to address vulnerabilities with cross-chain infrastructure.

While cross-chain bridge attacks can be categorized as smart contract hacks, it is worth categorizing interoperability-based vulnerabilities separately. Smart contract attacks can be specific to an application or a protocol where certain vulnerabilities are exploited. In the case of Grim Finance, the protocol lost $30 million when a hacker exploited the absence of a reentrancy guard and fed a series of new fake deposits into a vault while the previous transactions had yet to be settled, allowing the hacker to trick the smart contract into releasing $30 million in Fantom tokens.[21]

In a different example, lending protocol Cream Finance lost $130 million in a flash loan attack in October 2021, after two separate incidents in the same year where $62.5 million was stolen.[22] Hackers were able to manipulate token pair prices to engineer a "flash loan attack" by repeatedly taking out flash loans across different Ethereum addresses. In fact, the ability to manipulate exchange (token pair) prices received through oracles has been a key vulnerability across DeFi applications.

While the above examples are more sophisticated hacks, there are other ones directed at the individual user level. These attacks are often systematically targeted at a user base with an expected behavioral pattern. For instance, Okay Bears is a collection of 10,000 PPP NFTs released on the Solana blockchain in April 2022. Its popularity and floor price skyrocketed, making it one of the most popular NFT collections on Solana. A few days after the NFT mint, several wallets that held the Okay Bears NFT were "airdropped" a malicious NFT by the hackers.

The malicious NFT had a text that indicated that it was a gift from the Solana team to the Okay Bears community. Several holders fell victim to the scam and clicked on the links confirming the transactions, allowing the hackers to wipe out any Solana balance left in the wallets.

We have seen such clever social engineering techniques on Discord, the social media platform that is popular amongst NFT projects.

Tactics include phishing attacks linked to NFT minting scams deployed through compromised Discord server administrator accounts. In some instances, once the hackers gained control of the accounts, they would send out links to promotional giveaways and exclusive NFT mints by creating a false sense of urgency that would trick unsuspecting users to connect their wallets to malicious websites. In other instances, users are tricked into providing private details of their accounts to actors pretending to be customer support, thereby gaining access to their wallets.

These social engineering techniques get cleverer every day and sometimes even the most experienced web3 users can fall prey to them. While smart contract and cross-chain bridge issues are not dependent on user behaviors, they can be generally addressed by high-quality audits. Many organizations like ConsenSys and even PwC are building capabilities to provide such audits to web3 organizations.

The user-based hacks can be addressed by education and users creating safeguards to protect themselves. A tiered wallet system involving hot, warm, and cold wallets is one possible solution. Web3 users can keep one wallet connected to all applications as the hot wallet, one wallet that stays connected to the internet but not connected to the apps as the warm wallet, and a cold wallet like Ledger that very rarely connects to the internet.

This will ensure there are very few assets stored in the warm wallets, and increasingly more assets held in the colder wallets, reducing the possibilities of a hack and the size of losses when hacks happen.

Model Risks

The web3 ecosystem has come on in leaps and bounds in innovation and maturity. Each time a well-established firm such as Blackrock or J P Morgan gets involved in the ecosystem, it gives us a little more comfort that the system is slowly maturing. Yet, there is no denying that this is still a trillion-dollar *experiment* that can potentially fail. Both the Luna Terra crash and the lack of basic risk management within Celcius are good examples. These are modeling failures where the founders failed to perform stress testing, scenario analysis, and sensitivity analysis on their business models to understand where the vulnerabilities lie. If the web3 ecosystem knew about these methods, or were forced to implement them, billions of dollars of hard-earned money from retail customers could have been saved.

As controversial as it might sound, this can only be resolved by suitable *governance*.

While web3 governance is often the role of the decentralized network, most ecosystems are not matured enough to spot vulnerabilities, run continuous assessments, and implement timely fixes. At least until that point, it would make sense to rely on risk management practices from traditional financial markets along with regulatory oversight, to bring guidance and discipline to a still maturing industry.

We will study these risks and the potential regulatory implications in greater detail in later chapters in the book.

GameFi— Experiential Pillar of the Metaverse

05

Technology is best when it brings people together.

MATT HULLENWEG

In Chapter 4 we saw how micro transactions, lending, payments, and other aspects of DeFi contributed to the economic aspects of the metaverse. As the most mature pillar within web3, DeFi will remain a key cog in the metaverse wheel. However, experiential elements are as important as the economic elements of the metaverse. This is where GameFi plays a critical role.

GameFi is the growth hack that metaverse needs to become mainstream: it is to metaverse what social media was to the internet. Even when the internet was seen as vastly useful in the 1990s, it was really messaging, microblogging, and socializing applications that really brought the world into the internet and kept them there.

As the web3 narrative blossomed, largely since 2016, most of the focus for newcomers has been either acting as retail investors looking for speculative returns, or building the infrastructure layer to build the nuts and bolts of the internet of value. Only in the last couple of years have applications with meaningful use cases started to emerge. DeFi was the most significant application layer that saw major growth in 2021. GameFi and SocialFi are the next wave of application layers, with GameFi emerging in 2021.

We believe the heydays for GameFi and SocialFi are ahead of us as they mature in size and stability. There are several aspects of GameFi that make it the heart and soul of the metaverse narrative. To start with, it is the most alluring of the three application layers due to the experiential elements that come with games.

As a building block of the metaverse revolution, GameFi offers the experience as well as value accruals for those who embrace web3 gaming. If web3 gets these two right, there is huge scale to be achieved in attracting the 2.5 billion gamers into web3. Later in the chapter, we will discuss how web3 models within GameFi can solve some of the economic downsides that online gamers have today.

But first, let us look at how online gaming came about and the key business models within the gaming industry. We will also look at the pain points of the current online gaming world from a gamer's perspective and deep dive into how web3 gaming can help address them.

The Rise of Online Gaming: A Look Back

It all started with "the Brown Box,"[1] originally called TV Game Unit #7. It was a prototype with basic features that most video games consoles still possess today: two controls and a multigame program system. By flipping the switches along the front of the unit, it could be programmed to play different games, including ping pong, checkers, four sports games, target shooting, and a golf putting game. Developed by Ralph Baer and his colleagues at Sanders Associates in 1967, the Brown Box represented the first multiplayer, multiprogram video game system.

The system was licensed to Magnavox, which released it as the Magnavox Odyssey in 1972, though it was discontinued shortly after. The Atari was introduced in June of the same year by Nolan Bushnell and Ted Dabney, the pioneers of gaming. Propelled by the likes of Space Invaders, Pac-Man, and Donkey Kong, the first large-scale gaming *community* was born. But while the concept of arcade machines became popular in shopping malls and bars, multiplayer gaming was still limited to players competing on the same screen.

The gaming industry began to evolve with the introduction of personal computers and the creation of games such as Gun Fight, which marked the first example of a multiplayer human-to-human combat shooter, along with a new style of gameplay with two joysticks per player: one to move the cowboy and the other to change the shooting direction. The release of Windows OS and more affordable Ethernet cards helped to push the social aspect of gaming to a whole new level and multiplayer gaming platforms became more popular.

The Internet Revolution: A Tech Race

As the cost of internet access decreased and computer processing technology became more powerful, the new age of gaming was born. Online multiplayer gaming experience took centerstage, and new online storefronts changed the way people bought games and interacted with each other. And as mobile access became more prevalent with new smartphones and app stores, gaming evolved along with it, changing not only the way people played, but also widening the demographics of those who played. Beyond the likes of Microsoft Xbox and Nintendo Wii, big technology players such as Apple and Google slowly became key players in the gaming ecosystem due to the dominance of the app stores. In fact, it was Apple's iPhone that marked the turning point for the mobile gaming market.

Playing rival to the dizzying pace of mobile development was the console war. The Super Nintendo was released in 1990 with much fanfare, boasting upgraded 16-bit graphics over the original Nintendo Entertainment System, with more than 49 million units sold worldwide, focusing on high-quality games including hits such as Super Mario Kart. This was followed by Sega in 1993 and Sony PlayStation in 1995, with the latter being the first console in history to sell more than 100 million units.[2]

The Anytime, Anywhere, Connected Era

With increased connectivity came opportunities. Video games in the 2000s were dominated by the likes of Microsoft, Nintendo, and Sony. Sony PlayStation 2 was released in 2000 and became one of the bestselling video game consoles. Microsoft launched Xbox Live in 2001 with a monthly subscription fee, which included value-added services such as multiplayer matchmaking and voice chat, just as Saga pulled out of the console war. Mid-decade, Nintendo released the Wii, which revolutionized the industry with more interactive gameplay. Its new wireless controller could function both as a motion sensor for gesture recognition or a pointing device towards the TV screen, or as traditional controls. The Wii was Nintendo's first home console to directly support internet connectivity, and quickly became the best-selling console.

Meanwhile, graphic innovation continued to drive sales and development of the gaming industry, transitioning gameplay from two-dimensional video games to fully immersive three-dimensional high-definition ones. The lower cost of technology, servers, and the internet led to popularization of games such as World of Warcraft in 2004, a massive multiplayer online role-playing game (MMORPG) with a peak of more than 14 million monthly paying subscribers.[3] Along with multiplayer online battle arena games (MOBA) that gained popularity as a form of electronic sports, the battle royale game format also became widely popular with the release of PlayerUnknown's Battlegrounds (2017), Fortnite Battle Royale (2017), Apex Legends (2019), and Call of Duty: Warzone (2020).

Starting from March 2020 citizens around the world were placed in various waves of lockdown due to the Covid-19 pandemic, leading to dramatic increases in the adoption of remote work as well as increased consumption of digital content, from entertainment to exercises and social commerce.

According to PwC, video games revenue, which rose 32 percent between 2019 and 2021, will rise at an 8.4 percent compound annual growth rate (CAGR) through 2026, creating a $321 billion industry.[4] Investments in e-commerce in gaming environments and the metaverse are also expected to increase, with brands vying for opportunities at the convergence of virtual and physical environments.

With mobility comes opportunity. In 2022, mobile games are projected to account for more than half of global gaming market revenues, per figures from Statista.[5] Console gaming remains the second-strongest segment, with a 27 percent market share. It's worth noting that mobile gamers have spent $41.2 billion in the first half of 2022 alone and downloaded games 30 billion times. While this is slightly less than the $44.5 billion spent for the first half of 2021, it represents an increase over the $36 billion in the first half of 2020.[6]

With increased interests in metaverse and advanced technology such as virtual and augmented reality, the gaming industry is poised for another evolution.

Before we proceed to expanding on the GameFi ecosystem and its economic actors, it's worth reviewing some of the notable players in the industry including Epic Games, Roblox, Axie Infinity, and PUBG

Epic Games

Potomac Computer Systems was founded by Tim Sweeney in 1991 in his parents' house in Potomac, Maryland. In 1992, the name changed to Epic MegaGames, Inc. Sweeney relocated the company to Cary, North Carolina, in 1999, and thus became Epic Games as many of us know it today.

Some of the most popular games include Fortnite and the Unreal, Gears of War, and Infinity Blade series. The Unreal Engine was named "most successful video game engine" in 2014 by Guinness World Records.[7] Through the years, the company has gone through multiple evolutions, from producing personal computer games, to developing on-console systems, to delivering games as a service (GaaS). The latter model allows companies to monetize video games through subscriptions and microtransactions, which encourages players to continue paying to support the game by providing a long tail of monetized new content over time.

Fortnite, released in 2017, was one of the most successful online video games developed by Epic Games. Fortnite Battle Royale, for example, drew more than 125 million players in less than a year, earning hundreds of millions of dollars per month. The game is monetized through the use of in-game currency (V-Bucks) that can be either purchased with fiat money, or earned through completing missions. In 2021 alone, Fortnite generated $5.8 billion in revenue; it has about 400 million registered players, 83 million of whom play at least once a month, with over 60 percent of the players aged 18 to 24.[8]

eSport events, a form of competition using video games, can be found around Fortnite as well.

Roblox

Roblox is an online game platform and game creation system developed by Roblox Corporation in 2004 and grew in popularity during the Covid-19 pandemic. It is free to play, and the game is monetized through in-game purchases with its virtual currency, Robux. Since 2013, creators have been able to exchange Robux for real-world currencies through its developer program, where developers can create their own game modes and worlds. And through the same program, Roblox makes money by taking a cut of the revenue earned by the developers. In January 2023, Roblox rolled out the Creator Hub for developers, giving them central access to a suite of tools and documentation, a marketplace to share and sell assets, and a talent hub to recruit from the Roblox creative community.

Roblox generated $2.2 billion in revenue in 2022, representing a 16 percent increase year-over-year. It had about 65 million daily active users in January 2023, with around 5 billion total hours engaged, up 19 percent year-over-year.[9] More interestingly, Roblox paid $624 million to its global community of game developers in 2022, compared to $538 million in 2021, highlighting the growing importance of user-generated content and the creator economy.

Axie Infinity

This is an NFT-based online video game developed by Sky Mavis, where players battle, collect, and raise digital pets known as Axies. The game is built on the Ronin Network, an Ethereum-linked sidechain developed by Sky Mavis. There is also an in-game economy where players can buy, sell, and trade resources they earn in the game. Similar to other games with a "play-to-earn" model, players can earn an Ethereum-based in-game cryptocurrency by playing. In addition to owning Axies, players can also own plots of land that they can customize and monetize.

According to ActivePlayer.io, the Philippines account for 40 percent of Axie Infinity's user base.[10] The monthly number of users averaged around 700,000 in October 2022, a far cry from its peak of 2.78 million users in January 2022.[11]

PUBG

Tencent's PlayerUnknown's Battlegrounds (PUBG) was released in December 2017, and at the time of writing maintains over 275 million players every month.[12] PUBG Mobile, which is free to play, had about 127 million downloads in 2021 and about 30 million daily active players, despite losing half of its user base when it was banned in India. An additional 50 million users play the Chinese version, Game for Peace, which is responsible for half of PUBG Mobile's revenue generation. PUBG Mobile was the highest-grossing game of 2021 and 2022, with $2.492 billion and $2.012 billion respectively.[13] And it scored the highest number of active users in 2021, followed by Roblox and Candy Crush Saga.[14]

The GameFi Ecosystem

The rise of GameFi coincided with the previous Bitcoin bull market. There were several gaming projects such as Axie Infinity that rose to fame during this time and that led to the introduction of new key participants in the ecosystems, including:

- game studios
- creators
- game economies
- NFT holders, renters, and gamers
- gaming guilds
- scholars
- game marketplaces

Game Studios

These are the organizations that typically build the game and own the entire ecosystem. Many GameFi projects have drawn a line in the sand between the firm that identifies the game creation organization, and the firm that manages the game economics. This distinction has helped game studios be better capitalized for the long development process to develop games and build online worlds, enabling them to tap into the private market for venture funding on their game studio organization, as well as public funding through token launches for the game tokens.

Creators

While game studios are the initial creators on a GameFi project, there are ecosystems that actively develop their creator communities. These creators contribute to the game creation process or enrich the experience for the gamers through in-game assets, developing weapons, game environments, wearables, etc., that gamers can purchase or earn through gameplay. In a web3 construct, creators get a large portion of the sales proceeds, often as a paid royalty for secondary sales of their creatives.

Game Economies

While game economy is more of an abstract element that refers to the collective strategizing, modeling, and execution effort behind creating the economic model, there are also players that provide this as a solution. As game economic models go through a similar evolution, once they are built, solution providers will be able to replicate them for other GameFi platforms. Instead of offering to build the entire game economy, solution providers may also be able to offer a small subset of the game economics as a technology solution.

For instance, web3 games have a smart contract layer where the rules of the platform are executed, and game economies rely on these rules being automatically executed right up to the microtransactions. This layer alone can be built as a product and offered to game studios, which will allow game studios to focus more on the gaming environment, experience, and strategies rather than worry about the smart contract layer.

NFT Holders, Renters, and Gamers

These players can generally be grouped as "users" of the platform. GameFi projects build their communities around their NFT holders, who later turn into game players. While some NFT holders are able to participate by playing games, many may just choose to simply be NFT holders and rent their NFTs for other gamers to use and enjoy. Users who typically rent NFTs are those who cannot afford the full cost of the NFTs but still want the game play experience.

It is critical that a game economic design process addresses the needs of all these actors and ensures that the right behaviors are incentivized.

Gaming Guilds

Gaming guilds are participants who came into the limelight through 2021 when Axie Infinity began to expand across Southeast Asia. Guilds invested in games and bought NFTs. They would train gamers using the NFTs they owned and let them play the game for a fixed rent. They would also take a commission in the earnings that the gamers made from playing the game.

As the "play-to-earn" model proved to be unsustainable, many guilds have pivoted their models to become either technology providers or marketplaces for games. In parallel, many web3 games have now moved on from NFT-based entries and offer free entry for their users, making the guild model largely obsolete.

Scholars

These are glorified gamers that the guilds have groomed to ensure they have high returns on investment (ROIs) for the NFTs that they have lent to the gamers. These gamers are selected based on their skill levels to ensure they earn well and can provide a payback for their investment as soon as possible. However, as the guild models have pivoted, scholars are struggling to find their feet in the GameFi ecosystem.

Marketplaces

Marketplaces are also called aggregators for game enthusiasts. They bring together the best of the games for listing on their platforms. In some cases, guilds that already had a substantial pool of gamers would sign up, pivoting their unsustainable guild models to become marketplaces, providing the distribution capability that games would need through their platforms.

Now that we have discussed the GameFi ecosystem, let us look at the qualitative elements that differentiate the web2 and web3 games.

Web2 vs Web3 Gaming Economies

The gaming industry is one of the fastest-growing ecosystems in the last decade. In 2020 alone, the in-game asset market grew by 20 percent to $180 billion.[15] The rise of gaming has been fueled by faster connectivity, as well as more affordable and better home computing and hardware infrastructure. Gaming infrastructure continues to be critical both for performance and for the play experience. Yet, the gaming industry in its current form has a skewed incentive model, with several pain points that could be addressed by web3 structures.

Asset Ownership

The online gaming industry has a big asset base that gamers spend and are dependent on. These assets include weapons, clothing, shoes, vehicles, or any other props that serve to improve the gaming experience. As gamers onboard the game, they immerse themselves in the experience and start collecting experience points (XP), building credentials and progressing along the way through purchase of in-game assets.

For instance, players in a shooting game like Call of Duty can upgrade their weapons through XP cards. However, gamers can also upgrade their game assets by paying for them. These game assets are a major source of revenue for game studios who launch these games. For the gamers, these in-game assets make them feel vested in the game. As they upgrade and accumulate more assets, they feel more connected to the game, or they feel more compelled to stay with it, for fear of losing the fruits of their hard work. It's a conscious economic model that the game studios adopt to reduce gamer churn.

Yet, when a gamer purchases an in-game asset like a weapon, and upgrades it through XPs, they must own the asset. Unfortunately, this asset may not mean anything if the game studio chooses to launch an upgraded version. This happened recently, when Call of Duty launched Warzone 2.0 and the assets accumulated by their gamers became worthless in the new gaming experience. All gamers' progressions were also lost, resulting in the gamers having to start from scratch, losing both time and money.

It may not be standard behavior for all web2 games to just move on from one gaming experience to another, effectively rendering the in-game assets useless. Yet, the ability for gaming studios to make gamers' assets worthless, particularly as this market has grown to hundreds of billions of dollars, is unacceptable. Value retention of gaming assets is a major differentiation between web2 and web3.

Since the advent of web3 games, they have relied on NFTs to ensure gamers own their assets within the ecosystem. Many game platforms first launched their proprietary NFT collections and built a strong community around the NFTs. Since these were mostly PFP NFTs, as community members got more engaged, these assets became a form of identity, as we described in an earlier chapter. This has allowed web3 firms to launch games for these NFT communities, and holders of these NFTs are able to experience the game through the digital avatars that they own. In addition, gaming assets, such as weapons, vehicles, and other game props were also launched as NFTs, which gamers were able to earn or purchase from gaming studios and effectively own from that point.

> I happily played World of Warcraft during 2007–2010, but one day Blizzard removed the damage component from my beloved warlock's Siphon Life spell. I cried myself to sleep, and on that day I realized what horrors centralized services can bring. I soon decided to quit.

> Vitalik Buterin, Co-founder of the Ethereum blockchain.[16]

Value Permanence

Looking at another dimensionality of game assets, the money used by gamers to buy them is considered as revenue opportunities for the game studios. Therefore, there is no incentive for the game studios to allow value retention of these assets. Another source of revenue for games like Fortnite is battle passes. Battle passes capture the progression of a gamer through the game environment.

As a gamer wins higher levels of the game, they are rewarded with game assets and are also able to move to a higher tier of battle passes. Moving to a higher tier might require gamers to win a difficult level in the game, accumulate XPs, or sometimes pay as well. The higher the tier of the battle pass, the better are the rewards that the gamer would receive.

Despite all these revenue models that the gaming studios use to accrue value to themselves and their shareholders from the engagement of their gamers, there is very little tangible value that gamers can accrue. Ensuring value permanence is the first critical step in changing the status quo—and a building block for web3 games, through which users can own, retain, and monetize assets, using game NFTs.

As long as the gaming ecosystem is thriving, the NFTs should retain their value for their holders; having asset interoperability across chains and gaming ecosystems is critical in attracting and retaining web3 gamers.

For instance, if a gamer buys a weapon within a gaming ecosystem, they should be able to connect their wallets with another game and use the same weapon, as long as the two games have established interoperability, providing utility across games in different chains. Similarly, supporting interoperability across battle passes will allow top-tier battle pass holders to start their journey on a new gaming platform at the same level attained elsewhere. Such future state capability will help to extend the horizons of value permanence with web3 games.

Asset Transferability

Asset transferability is a feature that assumes game asset ownership and value permanence as a given. Therefore, this feature is largely possible only in the web3 gaming world. A gamer who has collected a number of in-game assets would want to liquidate and profit from them. Most web3 gaming platforms offer a marketplace feature, where gamers can list their assets for sale.

This feature is generally not available or even possible in a web2 gaming construct, as gamers don't typically own their assets, thus missing out on the opportunity to monetize their efforts in accumulating the pool of assets.

As interoperability between gaming platforms and the blockchains that they are built on improves, gamers should be able to move these assets to other games or blockchains. Where a gamer owns NFT assets earned through their gaming efforts, they should be able to use NFTFi (NFT+DeFi) tools that allow them to borrow stablecoins if they collateralize their NFT assets.

These models blur the boundaries between web3 GameFi and DeFi ecosystems. Touching upon the concepts of economic identities discussed in previous chapters, as gamers build their credibility within the gaming ecosystem, their asset holdings, XP points, and battle pass tiers should determine their ability to borrow, regardless of their geographic location or other demographics attributes.

We anticipate a future where identities will be ecosystem specific: Ecosystem identities, rather than real-world identities in the traditional sense, will be more critical for DeFi transactions that happen within a GameFi context, especially for participants with large asset holdings and a track record. This is similar to Amazon being able to offer business financing solutions to small and medium-sized businesses without the typical lengthy paperwork and long wait. The availability of transaction history and other data of the businesses on the Amazon platform enables Amazon to assess risks and make quick lending decisions.

On a similar note, DeFi within these ecosystems will rely on lenders offering products through predefined contracts. As ecosystem users and super-users achieve certain ranks, smart contract-based lending can be offered more seamlessly without any need for manual underwriting intervention. This should be possible even when the user's identity in the real world is unknown.

Creator Incentives

Value accrual in an ecosystem must be focused on those who genuinely add value to it. Web2 games have models that look very similar to their social media peers, focusing on accruing value to the business entities and to their shareholders, with minimal incentives to credit creators who are adding value.

Let us take Roblox, a popular web2 game, as an example. As mentioned earlier in the chapter, Roblox have created a platform that brings gamers, creators, and developers together. In doing so, they are able to create rich gaming experiences for their users across 180 countries in the world, with over $2.2 billion in revenues in 2022, and more than 65 million daily active users.[17] In 2022, Roblox distributed about $624 million to its creators community, accounting for around 28 percent of its total revenues. While it is common for gamers to have to pay for the experience and for creators to generate revenues with their content, it is worth asking if the gaming platform is treating the creators fairly, and if this is appealing and lucrative enough for the creators.

Web3 could flip this incentive structure, offering more to the creators and less to the platform, thus attracting more creators to the ecosystem as it matures and scales. As inclusive incentives driven by tokenomics and asset ownership and transferability through NFTs mature, creators will have the incentive to switch to web3. With better gaming experiences and larger adoption from the gaming community, creators should see better value within web3 than in web2 over time.

User Experience

We have seen several economic model features that are inherently better with web3 than web2. However, if there is one key area that web3 has so far struggled with it is the user experience and user journey. If there is one takeaway for application developers from the Steve Jobs and smartphone era, it is that the user experience must be seamless and frictionless in order to attract a wider audience.

Web3 games have a major challenge in onboarding new customers, particularly those who are not native web3 users. There are several steps in onboarding a new user to a game, particularly where it is an NFT-gated gaming platform.

Let us go through the user journey step by step, as we did for the process of buying an NFT in Chapter 2:

1 Before the user begins, they must understand that an NFT is needed to play the game.

2 Next, the user finds out how to buy the NFT via the game's website.

3 Next, the user downloads a digital wallet that supports the chain where the NFT resides.

4 Next, the user purchases ETH, SOL, or any digital token that is needed to purchase the NFT, either from an exchange or from the digital wallet itself, and sends the cryptos to the wallet.

5 Next, the user visits the marketplace where the NFT is sold and buys the NFT.

6 Next, the user goes back to the game's website and connects the wallet to the platform.

7 And, finally, the user gains access to the game and starts playing.

In a web2 context, the user wouldn't have to know about the NFT nor the chain they need to use to purchase the NFT. They would typically register as a user, enter a form of payment, buy the NFT through one seamless transition of screens, and connect to the game from there and start playing.

The web3 onboarding experience can become even more complicated if NFTs have metadata that is critical to gameplay abilities or the ability to accrue value within the gaming platform. The user must then go through the metadata features, understand the type of NFT they need, settle at a price they would be willing to pay, and wait for it or buy it right away.

Needless to say, these steps can be quite daunting for anyone to navigate, particularly those who are new to the environment.

Cybersecurity

With web3 we are not just building data networks, we are also building value networks. Therefore, when a network is hacked, it is real money that gets stolen. Unfortunately, as many infrastructure-level experiments happen, such as creating cross-chain bridges to create interoperability across blockchains, the users become easy prey to hackers. These infrastructure layers must be built with high levels of cyber security controls.

However, the decentralized nature of development within web3 means controls are often ignored. This leads to gaming ecosystems built on vulnerable infrastructure. As these games grow in size, they expose their gamers and their assets to hackers. One such high-profile incident was the hack in March 2021, where Axie Infinity suffered a $552 million hack of its Ronin bridge. The firm had to raise a further $150 million from Animoca Brands and Andreessen Horowitz to return lost funds to its gaming community. This may not be possible with other gaming ecosystems as they may not have the deep pockets that Axie Infinity commanded at that time.

While cybersecurity must be built into any digital economies and not as an afterthought, the nature of web3 makes this an even more pressing priority.

Economic Models

Throughout this book we have discussed how blockchain is not just a technology, but also a foundational layer for economic models that can drive a more inclusive form of capitalism. But there is data that warrants skepticism. Several GameFi projects that rose to fame in 2021 and 2022 have struggled to scale their economic models.

Axie Infinity

Sky Mavis was founded in 2018 to make Axie Infinity, the first project to achieve a relatively significant user base amongst web3 GameFi projects, using an innovative model for its gamers. Among the investors for the Vietnamese blockchain game company were Mark Cuban,

Alexis Ohanian, co-founder of Reddit, and John Robinson, President and COO of 100 Thieves, one of the world's most valuable esports companies.[18]

In Axie Infinity, gamers buy digital pets called Axies, which are NFTs that can be bred and prepared for battle. As the Axies battled and won, the owners of these NFTs were rewarded with tokens of the game called Smooth Love Potions (SLP). This GameFi model was termed play-to-earn (P2E).

Sky Mavis launched their game Axie Infinity in early 2020, and by December 2020 there were more than 600,000 monthly active users on the platform. The usage peaked a year later in January 2022, with over 2.8 million users. By March 2022, Axie Infinity had sold over $4 billion worth of NFTs in the form of Axies and the virtual land that the gamers typically owned within the gaming environment.[19]

The gaming user base for Axie largely came from Southeast Asian countries. At the time of writing, 40 percent of Axies users are from the Philippines.[20] Thailand and Vietnam also make up a significant portion of Axie's user base. The demand for Axies drove their prices up, and the cheapest Axies seldom won battles for the gamers. Therefore, serious Axie players had to buy rarer Axie NFTs just to earn from the game in SLP tokens.

SLP token price was a good indicator of in-game economics and its health. Until the crypto bear market set in, SLPs had a good run; the price had gone up to 36 cents in January 2021 but slowly fell to almost 1 cent in April 2022. At the peak, an average Axie gamer could earn 4,500 SLPs per month, which was worth roughly $800, or $25 per day per gamer. As the number of users increased, SLP tokens were endlessly increasing in supply via wins within games. With over 2.5 million players and a large portion of them from emerging markets eager to earn their daily wages by playing games, that is more than $60 million of sell pressure for the SLP tokens per day, $22 billion worth of sell pressure per year.

Needless to say, Axie's game play couldn't match the supply with SLP burning mechanisms to keep the price steady, and the model proved to be not sustainable. From the get-go, the game relied heavily on users buying their NFTs. However, those micro-revenue opportunities were nowhere close to the amount required to mitigate the sell pressure created by Axie's P2E gamers.

This led to the inevitable. SLP tokens tumbled in value from 36 cents in 2021 to almost a third of a cent at the time of writing. Axie Infinity in the meantime have tried to introduce several game mechanics that allowed for some burning mechanisms of SLPs, thereby reducing the supply. However, those measures have so far proven insufficient.

There are several principles that are relevant while developing game economics and we will highlight them later in this chapter. However, it is critical to remember that game experience is ultimately what drives users to the game. If users come to play the game just to earn, and do not enjoy the gameplay experience, the model is not sustainable.

This philosophical pivot that gaming platforms realized through late 2021 led to the transition from P2E to play-and-earn. In a play-and-earn gaming platform, there is more focus on making the gaming experience more enjoyable for gamers, rather than simply playing to earn.

StepN

Another interesting GameFi project is StepN, who kicked off the move-to-earn (M2E) phenomenon. The project's inception was in August 2021. Their team came up with an innovative concept of compensating users for their daily walks and runs, via a mobile application, where users had to buy their NFTs to start using the app. After a period of beta testing, StepN did their token launch in March 2022.

When the Solana blockchain suffered the Wormhole hack and lost several hundreds of millions worth of Ethereum in early 2022, the rise of StepN helped the Solana ecosystem recover from that event. By June 2022, StepN recorded their peak with just over 700,000 monthly active users.[21] At the time of writing, users of StepN had recorded over 67 million miles.[22] However, their game economics came crashing down as their user base skyrocketed.

StepN offered Green Satoshi Tokens (GST) to their users who walked. Depending on the number of NFTs and their levels, users were able to earn from walking. GST reached a price of about $7.8 in May 2022, which largely coincided with the rise in the user base as well. However, what started as an earning opportunity of $5–50 per user per day proved to be unsustainable in the long run with the large number of active users. While StepN had several supply mitigating mechanisms where users would end up burning the GSTs they earned from their walks, it was never nearly enough to reduce the sell pressure of GSTs.

At the time of writing, the price of a GST is 2.5 cents, and the days of $7 per GST seem like a fairytale. StepN suffered from the same issues that Axie Infinity did: they didn't have enough economic actors and activities to add value to their model. As millions of value extractors were able to earn GSTs and cash out, there were simply no mitigation mechanisms to hold the price of GSTs high enough. StepN was a poster child for the Solana ecosystem for many months until the GST prices started collapsing without a floor in sight.

The StepN and Axie episodes left the GameFi world looking for solutions. There were several players with strong teams, great games and experiences. However, the search for a robust economic model, one that can withstand a difficult market downturn, continues.

Here are some key takeaways:

- Tokenomics alone cannot create a sustainable business model. It has worked effectively so far with layer 1 blockchain networks such as Ethereum and Solana. However, those systems have different structural dynamics and ecosystem network effects that drive demand for the token. They have several built-in burn mechanisms for the tokens to reduce supply as well. These levers are easier to use in an infrastructure platform like Ethereum, rather than an application layer like Axie Infinity.

- When web3 businesses design their tokenomics as the bedrock of their economic models, they must model both value extraction and value addition activities. If value extractors dominate the economy, the price of the token will fall; on the contrary, if there are more users who add value to the economy, the price of the token will go up.

- These activities must also be modeled with the correlation the token displays with the mainstream crypto market. If the token price will fall alongside Bitcoin and Ethereum in a bear market, that scenario must be factored into the economic model.

- Sensitivity analysis of economic model elements is important. It would help to understand the sensitivity of the token price to each of these economic activities. Web3 economic models must take some inspiration from risk management practices in banks, where sensitivity analysis, scenario modeling, and stress testing are standard practices to understand how a portfolio would react to a market crisis. When sensitivities of a token are modeled, and the token prices are stress tested for market downturns, the team should be equipped with a risk framework.

- Every economic model hypothesis must be A/B tested with the market and the economic activities that make the model must be slowly released for market feedback.

- While web3 allows us to explore and experiment with token models, the principles of building a sustainable business do not change between web2 and web3. Tokenomics is not a silver bullet that can be a replacement for a mediocre business model.

The sustainability of economic models is one of the biggest challenges that GameFi projects need to address. However, in order for web3 to attract the 2.5 billion people from web2 gaming, the user experience must improve. Unlike web2 games, web3 games store assets that have real-world value for the users, and therefore for the hackers. Cybersecurity is an increasingly big concern for not just GameFi but for the entire web3 industry; security measures must be built in, and not an afterthought.

Last but not least, with a substantial percentage of Roblox users being under 13, it is essential that there are ample controls on how they interact with their peer gamers. Children must be protected from antisocial elements that can come in different forms.

On a similar note, being more inclusive with game strategies is critical as well. Based on a study conducted by Newzoo,[23] 49 percent of gamers are women. Yet, a vast majority of games are created for male gamers. There is also a large underrepresentation of women within the gaming industry. As the ecosystem gets more inclusive, content will become more inclusive too. That is a critical step to the growth and maturity of the industry.

Despite all these challenges, the fundamental building block of web3 economies can be applied to games too. As games find their footing with this new economic paradigm, they will soon be able to attract billions of global audiences and lay the foundations for the metaverse experience.

In fact, the inaugural gaming fund from Andreessen Horowitz (a16z), Games Fund One, might provide just the boost of confidence that the games industry needs. Launched in May 2022, the $600 million fund, dedicated to game studios, gaming-related consumer apps, and infrastructure, is founded on the belief that games will play a pivotal role in defining how we socialize, play, and work over the next century.[24] The famed venture firm believes that gaming infrastructure and technologies will be important building blocks of the metaverse, an opportunity it says could be much bigger than the current $300 billion game industry itself.

A CONVERSATION WITH MARCO VAN DEN HEUVEL, CO-FOUNDER AND CEO OF MERIT CIRCLE

Merit Circle is a decentralized autonomous organization (DAO) focused on gaming.

Lessons learned:
On sustainability: With the Axie Infinity model, you need a continuous influx of new people and new capital. The model becomes unsustainable when the majority of your community is value extracting rather than value adding, and there are more people looking to make a quick buck rather than looking to actually play the game for fun. The play-to-earn model is hard to scale.

On gaming experience: You need more experienced web2 developers joining the web3 ecosystem to build proper games to attract the right audience to create value. Start with free-to-play games to build value—so they don't have to buy themselves into the game. And it is still going to be a few more years before game companies actually start supporting each other as entities and you see wider usage of NFTs between games.

Key takeaways:

Pay attention to what matters most. Focus on making the game fun to attract and retain gamers. Take your time to build a proper game and engage with your community—don't leave them in the dark. Complete decentralization is likely utopia as most games don't care as much about decentralization as they care about the gaming experience.

How you build value matters. What is your cost per user acquisition and how much time do they spend playing the game? How much value is the gamer adding to the ecosystem?

Improve the UI/UX: Many successful web3 games will be using a custodian wallet—gamers don't want to have to deal with private keys. Bring the UI/UX and onboarding experience from the web2 world to make it easier to play web3 games.

Fun fact according to Marco:

"There are more Filipinos with Ronin wallets than there are Filipinos with credit cards."

The Metaverse 06

When unreal feels real, we have made the choice to close our eyes to see more. Perception indeed then is the reality.

SRINIVASAN MUTHUSRINIVASAN

Ever heard the advice from seasoned commentators: "Treat everything as a scam, until they prove otherwise"? While this might be sound financial advice when it comes to investment opportunities within the metaverse, being overly cautious might sometimes cause us to miss out on new opportunities and overlook new ways to do things. There is a fine line between being too risk-averse and being reckless. Taking action is about taking calculated risks, not completely avoiding risks; having an open mind is essential to understanding innovative trends within this emerging ecosystem.

Get a Horse

"Get a horse!" That was the response the world had to the invention of the automobile. People were opposed to cars conquering their roads even well into the 20th century. Times have changed; we have become so reliant on four-wheeled machines over the years that we are now demanding they be fully autonomous. But let's take a step back and think about how we got there.

Babies are born to be curious. They learn by observing, exploring, and trying new things. They get into everything and become mesmerized by things that we think are mundane' such as gravity. As they get older, they tend to ask fewer questions, and slowly begin to lose the sense of curiosity. Perhaps it's comfort in conformity—in not standing out by asking why too many times. Perhaps it's comfort in familiarity and keeping the status quo—in staying within boundaries. And as adults, we tend to perceive new paradigms as riskier ones.

"If I had asked people what they wanted, they would have said faster horses" is an old adage on innovation that was often attributed to Henry Ford in reference to the Ford Model T in 1908—though without proof. But the lesson remains true, regardless of the origin of the saying. Often the most groundbreaking inventions are hard to comprehend at the start. The further they veer from the status quo, the more alien they feel to the average user. That is manifested in the rate of innovation adoption; new ideas and technology must progress beyond niche appeal and reach critical mass in order to self-sustain.

In the past few decades, however, technological progress has been increasing at an exponential rate and the relative timespan for new technology adoption has been decreasing as well. From cellular phones and tablets to social media and smartphone usage, modern technologies have demonstrated fast-rising adoption rates compared to older household appliances and products.[1]

Yet, the instinctive skepticism surrounding potential leapfrog innovation remains rampant in some pockets of the population. This was true when people were against automobiles, and remained true when Amazon was initially met with skepticism as a Ponzi scheme rather than a Wal-Mart of the Web.[2] This distrust is perhaps even more pronounced when it comes to web3. Web3 entrepreneurs have taken a very technology-heavy and insular approach to describing their innovative ideas, thus alienating a substantial ecosystem of potential stakeholders. Web3 has also been plagued by several frauds, hacks, and not well-thought-out approaches to scaling potentially promising ideas. Celsius, Three Arrows Capital, and the Luna Terra episodes are all examples of how innovators have pushed the "scam" tag onto web3.

As we progress through the next few chapters, we will dive deeper into how the innovative models of the last few years within web3 have allowed for the metaverse to be envisioned as the new internet. It would have been preposterous in the 1990s when a business was asked for its website to prove its credibility. In a similar vein, a presence in the metaverse would feel rather superfluous or too intangible to us today. Yet, we are witnessing an amazing era of innovation unfold in front of us; spending some time in that rabbit hole can help us better understand the possibilities and shape a future that we can all aspire to.

Here we lay out the "metaverses" we have today, and the series of innovations, namely NFTs, DeFi, GameFi and SocialFi, that have established the foundation for internet 2.0.

What is the Metaverse?

The term "metaverse" is not new. First coined by Neal Stephenson in his 1992 book *Snow Crash*, he referred to the metaverse as a place where digital replaced the physical. According to the Merriam-Webster Dictionary, the metaverse is now viewed as "a persistent virtual environment that allows access to and interoperability of multiple individual virtual realities."

The definition really starts with the experiential differentiation that the metaverse would bring. It is a place where one could go to with a wearable and perhaps enjoy an evening with friends, watch a concert, play games, or learn. Such *experience* is the first "E" we have discussed right through this book. That is something most existing players such as Meta and Fortnite are targeting through hardware technologies like augmented reality, virtual reality, and mixed reality headsets, as well as other mobile and desktop devices. Many of them are also looking to tap into software tools like Unity and Unreal Engine to develop metaverse environments. Others are focusing on the engineering challenges that lie underneath, such as that of managing thousands of states of users on the metaverse simultaneously.

All this innovation contributes to the experiential aspects of the metaverse. Yet, there are the economic and empowerment elements of the metaverse as well. The hypothesis that we are working on with this book is that *both* the economic and empowerment aspects must be delivered by the metaverse, which would effectively become the Internet 2.0 for the new ages.

For this chapter, let us focus on the experiential elements of the metaverse, existing metaverse firms and their approach, the technologies that contribute to this innovation paradigm, and the use cases we see as low-hanging fruits before the more utopian ones are achieved.

Is it "a Metaverse" or "the Metaverse"?

It's worth discussing the fine nuances when we interchangeably use "a metaverse" with "the metaverse." Through this book, we have used the term metaverse to generally refer to the immersive virtual space that could become the future of the internet. However, there are several companies we will be discussing in this chapter, where we will refer to each of their limited versions of the gated metaverse as "a metaverse." So how and when would we transition from multiple such "metaverses" to "the metaverse"?

To understand this, maybe it would help to go back to the early days of the internet. The internet saw its inception in the 1960s through the efforts of the Advanced Research Projects Agency (ARPA), the US military's research arm. ARPANET, as it was called, was a network for safe communication between military research efforts and universities across the US.

However, it was not until the mid-1970s that networks like NORSAR, a US–Norwegian system to track earthquake activity, connected with the ARPANET. This slowly led to other regions and their networks connecting to the ARPANET and laid the infrastructure foundation for the seamless exchange of information, helped by the standards that had been created back then.

However, the user experience in accessing rich content was still missing. Enter the World Wide Web (www), with Tim Berners-Lee, a CERN researcher, who developed the key technologies that are the bedrock of the Web and published the first website on August 9, 1991.[3]

Since then we have seen the world innovate at breakneck speed. Could the metaverse narrative follow the same path in a much shorter period of time than it took the original internet to evolve and be adopted at a mass scale?

Crucial to this development are tech companies that are creating their instances of the metaverse that are analogous to the ARPANET, as well as standards that these metaverses must conform to, led by organizations such as The Metaverse Standards Forum. As these standards drive interoperability, the much-needed bridges will need to be built across metaverses for us to achieve the utopian state of "the metaverse."

It is important to note that the metaverse is not just a web3 paradigm. Companies such as Roblox, Fortnite, and Minecraft have successfully created immersive experiences for their respective communities. These ecosystems are thriving with different revenue streams, creator economies that are tried and tested, along with highly engaging concerts and events that have attracted and retained a very engaged user base.

In contrast, web3 metaverses are still in their infancy. The experiences that Decentraland and Sandbox offer are nowhere close to their web2 counterparts. Since the crypto market crashed through late 2021 and through the first half of 2023, the number of active users in these metaverse platforms has also dropped significantly.

Let us look at some of the more popular metaverse initiatives and understand how their product and growth strategies compare to each other.

Roblox

In the previous chapter on GameFi, we discussed some of the players that have played a crucial role in the gaming industry. One of which is Roblox.

Unless you lived off the grid in the last decade, you would have heard of the rise of this popular web2 game, which was founded by David Baszucki and Erik Cassel in 2006. In the simplest terms, Roblox is a virtual universe of games and events where users can create, own, earn, and enjoy the immersive experience. Roblox allows users to create their own spaces and convene with friends, buy and sell assets within the world, and earn in the process.

The Roblox platform uses a token called Robux that is used as the currency within the ecosystem. Gamers can earn Robux through their in-game experience and use that to buy assets. Creators can build their own spaces, but also can scale their creativity to build games using Roblox Studio.

As mentioned in the last chapter, Roblox has over 65 million users as of February 2023.[4] As these users create experiences that attract players, it results in more revenue opportunities for these creators and the platform in the form of in-game purchases. Based on Roblox's 2022 financial results, with revenue at $2.2 billion and developer fees at $624 million, Roblox shared 28 percent of revenue[5] with around 3.5 million game creators in 2022.[6] According to the company's filing, 17- to 24-year-olds demonstrated the highest growth in the fourth quarter of 2022 at 31 percent, accounting for 22 percent of all daily active users.[7] Overall, the number of daily active users over the age of 13 has surpassed that of under 13s.[8]

There are instances where these users have managed to generate substantial amounts of income from their creations on Roblox. For example, Alex Balfanz, the co-creator of Jailbreak, one of the top games on Roblox, made enough money to pay for all four years of his college tuition from Roblox earnings. In a little over two years, the game made Balfanz and his partner millionaires.[9]

To encourage more creators to experiment with the platform and develop games for the community, Roblox introduced a $35 million Game Fund for special up-and-coming games with "compelling cross-platform gameplay, engaging social mechanics, dynamic in-game avatars, and creative economic models."[10] Each approved project will receive a minimum of $500,000.[11]

But Roblox is more than a creator economy and a collection of immersive games. It is also a massive social network where friendships are forged daily on the platform as users connect with each other in their virtual world.

As the platform becomes more popular with younger children, it is becoming increasingly common for parents to offer monthly allowances in the form of virtual currencies. Games including Roblox are catching on to the trend and began to sell virtual currency as monthly subscriptions, similar to an allowance.[12] It will be interesting to see how fintech and incumbent financial services institutions can learn from these demographics and evolve their services, in order to better serve a generation that is accustomed to money movement in a virtual world.

Brands have been experimenting with the platform as well with content strategy to appeal to this relatively younger demographic. Here are a few examples:

- Gucci Town features a central garden that connects mini games and a virtual store for players to purchase virtual Gucci outfits for their Roblox avatars. It is one of the luxury fashion brands that have made a foray into the metaverse.[13]

- Through collaboration with Roblox, Nike added an immersive AR experience to its Fifth Avenue flagship store in New York City, to create a virtual-first playground for kids.[14] According to Roblox, Nikeland, the virtual world created on Roblox, saw 7 million visitors over the first two months.[15]

- Lavazza Arena is a new Roblox game launched by Italian coffee brand Lavazza, designed to raise awareness of the impact of deforestation.[16]

- Walmart Land and Walmart's Universe of Play are two new spaces created by Walmart, with the former being a virtual store of merchandise for avatars, whereas the Universe of Play consists of different toy worlds for players to explore and earn rewards.[17]

Beyond gaming and fashion, Roblox also introduced a $10 million Roblox Community Fund in November 2021 to provide grants to educational organizations, to develop immersive educational experiences on Roblox. Through the Roblox Community Fund, the Museum of Science in Boston launched "Mission: Mars" to engage with students online.[18]

Fortnite

Fortnite is a virtual gaming experience that is doubling down on its metaverse strategy as well. As mentioned in the previous chapter, in 2021 alone Fortnite generated $5.8 billion in revenue; it has about 400 million registered players, 83 million of whom play at least once a month, with over 60 percent of the players aged 18 to 24—which is slightly older than those in Roblox.[19] As one of the most successful online video games developed by Epic Games, Fortnite stole the limelight through its Battle Royale game, where the goal is simply to be the last person standing in a battlefield of 100 players. Much like the Roblox model, Fortnite's revenue streams also rely on in-game purchases by the users.

There are two main differences in the user base between Roblox and Fortnite. In addition to the age difference, where Fortnite players tend to skew a bit older than those from Roblox, an overwhelming percentage of its player base are men.[20] One of the possible reasons can be attributed to the use of Unreal Engine by Fortnite, which has allowed them to build more intricate and detail-oriented areas. One of these is the Fortnite Battle Royal Island, which in turn brings more hardcore gamers onto the platform. Figuring out how to promote gender diversity is a challenge that will affect every stakeholder in the ecosystem, present and future.

Through the years, Fortnite has introduced different live concerts and events to bring players together and to grow its user base, including an Ariana Grande concert, a Star Wars event, and Travis Scott concert, with the latter (in April 2020) attracting over 27.7 million unique players in-game participating live 45.8 million times across the five events.[21]

Fortnite also uses an in-game currency called V-Bucks. However, Apple banned Fortnite on its App Store as the in-game purchases were not honoring the 30 percent commission rule that Apple had set for all its applications. The antitrust lawsuits are in progress, yet this sets the tone for future web3 applications, as such a steep commission can seriously impact creators' revenues.

Fortnite has solved several problems that metaverse platforms have. They have brought growth through immersive gaming experience and events; they have also converted their users from visitors to returning players who make in-game transactions, resulting in healthy revenue numbers.

Yet, scalability from an engineering perspective still remains a challenge. Battle Royale games are limited at 100 users per experience because metaverses are expected to manage states of the metaverse for each of those users. It has proven to be an exponentially harder problem to solve as the number of users increases.

Here is an example describing the problem in greater detail, and it is essential to understand why it is critical for the mass adoption of metaverses. Imagine a game where two players (A and B) are trying to survive in a forest. They are discovering weapons in the forest, and the one with the most powerful weapon would win the game comfortably. If player A reaches the weapon first, the state of the game should change so that the weapon is not available for player B to own.

Now bring it one notch higher, where 100 players are trying to acquire an inventory of weapons to survive in a Battle Royale experience. Each of their acquisitions would change the state of the experience for others. This engineering problem is difficult to scale, but it is essential to solve to ensure the metaverse experience is what it promises to be.

With infusion of funding into Hadean—a firm that specializes in metaverse infrastructure—from Fortnite creator Epic Games and others, we expect this will help to lay the foundation for a richer and scalable multi-user experience.

Sandbox

Sandbox is a platform for entertainment experiences in a virtual world developed by the game studio Pixowl in 2012, and which grew to about 40 million downloads over the years.[22] They gained public attention after being acquired by Animoca Brands in January 2018 and pivoted to develop a creator-driven blockchain-based 3D open world game.

Part of the Sandbox ecosystem is SAND, an ERC-20 utility token built on the Ethereum blockchain and used as the basis for transactions and interactions throughout Sandbox. Players can buy LAND, a digital piece of real estate in the Sandbox metaverse, in one of the LAND sales, and they can then rent them or populate them with games and assets to increase the LAND's value. Players can also create and sell assets on the marketplace as NFTs.

Sandbox's new incarnation is still in alpha mode. The Sandbox Alpha Season 3, which went live on August 24, 2022, was their largest so far with 17 million visits, a threefold increase over Season 2, according to Sandbox's own report.[23] This new season also attracted 4.1 million total wallets, twice the number compared to the Alpha Season 2 in March 2022.[24]

Sandbox's direction seems to be a mix of both Roblox and Fortnite. While their virtual world experience is pixelated and of lower quality compared to Roblox, they have a strong focus on creators building their own games and virtual assets.

Similar to Roblox, Sandbox also offers a Game Maker Fund, to support game designers and help them produce and publish games in The Sandbox's metaverse. The Game Maker Fund is funded by the Sandbox Foundation, which supports the ecosystem by offering grants to incentivize content and game production in The Sandbox, including NFTs, play-to-earn tournaments, and Community Rewards and Ambassadors program. As players contribute to the Sandbox ecosystem, from playing and creating games, to creating and selling assets, they also earn SAND tokens.

Sandbox is also doubling down on their focus on social activities, art exhibitions, fashion events, charity auctions, and even a virtual space for large corporations. This is reflected in their partnership strategy as they have forged relationships with HSBC, UNICEF, Snoop Dogg, Smurfs, and many more.

While Sandbox is closer to being a centralized metaverse much like Fortnite and Roblox, it differs in one key aspect. Since SAND is a governance token, holders of the SAND token can participate in the governance of the Sandbox ecosystem via a DAO structure, and exercise their voting rights on elements such as the Foundation grant attributions to content and game creators and feature prioritization on the platform roadmap.[25]

As creators chip in with more games and experiences, the network effects will help the platform scale to a similar level of success that Fortnite and Roblox have enjoyed. With the required level of ecosystem scale and maturity comes decentralized governance to ensure creators can define and refine policies that become the rule of the virtual land. But, as mentioned earlier in the chapter, putting a heavier focus on making their experiences fun and engaging, with the experiential elements that attract the older audience demographic that Fortnite boasts, will be one of the keys to success.

Decentraland

Decentraland is a decentralized 3D traversable virtual world built on the Ethereum blockchain. It was founded by Ariel Meilich and Esteban Ordano in 2015 and launched on February 20, 2020, with the establishment of the Decentraland DAO.[26]

Decentraland is made up of parcels of LAND tokenized as an NFT called LAND tokens. Owners of the LAND or virtual plots can monetize by creating assets on top of the land they own. They can be virtual houses, billboards, games, or event venues that will increase the value of their land. Separately, Decentraland LAND owners can also rent out their virtual plots to tenants to be used to host events and deploy experiences. MANA is the in-game currency of Decentraland. It is an ERC-20 token that players can use to buy LAND and trade avatar wearables and other virtual goods within the game.

While large areas of land on the platform can be empty, there is healthy foot traffic around areas with the art galleries, games, and events such as Art Week, Metaverse Fashion Week, and Pride Week.

Major brands, especially fashion and luxury brand names, have also been experimenting with virtual spaces in Decentraland:

- Samsung opened a virtual version of their 837 flagship store in New York, called 837X, which serves as a creative hub that transcends the physical and digital, and to connect with their customers via events such as the Metaverse Music Festival and Climate Week.[27]

- The Metaverse Fashion week saw participation from big fashion houses including Dolce & Gabbana, Tommy Hilfiger, and Estée Lauder, amongst others.[28]

If a user holds a piece of land in the neighborhood of such high-profile events, the land is expected to be valued higher than others, mimicking real-world characteristics. Decentraland has also addressed the engineering challenges around implementing a metaverse, where multiple concurrent states have to be managed.

Yet, there are a few challenges with the model that Decentraland has adopted. The game experience is subpar due to pixelated avatars used to represent the player in the virtual world. The second key element rests with both acquisition and retention of players. Apart from large spaces of lands, with events conducted from time to time, Decentraland has very few features today to actively bring users onto their platform on a regular basis to keep them engaged. This is in stark contrast to Roblox and Fortnite that have millions of daily active users.

It was therefore not hugely surprising when the daily active user count dropped from several tens of thousands in December 2021 to a few hundred in October 2022. Without a basic gamification and habit-creation mechanism, coupled with poor user experience, active user engagement becomes difficult.

As the ecosystem matures and with more developers actively participating, more enriching in-game experiences can be created to attract and engage with users on a regular basis, bringing forth a more promising future for the web3 metaverse platform.

ZEPETO

Riding the metaverse wave in the East is ZEPETO; a K-pop and fashion-focused avatar-centric social platform, it is the largest in Asia.[29] It was created by Naver Z Corporation, a subsidiary of Naver Corporation, a South Korean internet conglomerate that operates Naver, the search engine. With over 300 million users, who are predominantly female and aged between 13 and 21, along with 2.3 million ZEPETO studio creators, it has a similar business model to Roblox, though smaller in scale. It operates mostly via the smartphone app, which allows the users to create and customize their own 3D avatars, design and trade virtual fashion items, play games, go on quests to win coins and zems (the in-game currency for ZEPETO), and interact with other avatars in the virtual worlds.

Its extensive partnerships span household names from luxury fashion to appliances and consumer retail, including Adidas, Gucci, Ralph Lauren, Hyundai, Samsung, Disney, Pixar, BT21, and Peanuts. The well-known four-member Korean girl group Blackpink also made their entrance in ZEPETO as avatars first in mid-2020, before winning the first-ever MTV Music Awards Best Metaverse Performance, a new category introduced by MTV in 2022 as a nod to the increasing popularity of virtual concert. The virtual fan signing event held by Blackpink and Selena Gomez, for example, drew more than 46 million fans worldwide.[30]

As part of the larger trend in South Korea, which is eyeing to become an incubator for metaverse projects, ZEPETO announced the plan to pivot to web3 with ZEPETO X (ZTX), a new crypto-enabled version of the metaverse built on the Solana blockchain. According to the company's white paper, ZTX, a joint blockchain initiative of Jump Crypto and ZEPETO, will be built on ZEPETO's existing software component architecture while leveraging the existing pipeline of partnerships with global companies and brands. Unlike other popular web3 games, ZTX users will receive a free plot of land upon which they can further develop through asset crafting and building.[31]

A CONVERSATION WITH RENÉ SCHULTE, DIRECTOR OF GLOBAL INNOVATION AT VALOREM REPLY

What is a metaverse, in the simplest sense?
Think of it as "metaverse embedding the real world into computing." It has a physical reality and is not purely virtual.

It is device-independent and it needs to be accessible to anyone with any devices, including mobile and desktop.

It is always on. Persistence is a key attribute because users need to be able to save the state. From a technology standpoint, this requires a lot of computational power.

It is the new immersive internet, but you can go into it with virtual reality, or it can come to you as augmented reality.

Do you think we have all of the basic building blocks that we need for that to go mainstream?
I think most of the building blocks are there. A company that doesn't have a metaverse presence in the future will probably be like being a company that doesn't have a website today. And although nobody has gotten the experience right so far, we have to realize that we're just really at infancy.

But companies also need to be clear about what they are trying to achieve in the metaverse. It is important to have the right brands providing an experience to the users that makes sense and adds value, not because they are afraid of missing out. It is not about "We have something there, but I don't know what to do with it."

What gets you excited about the metaverse?
Our human brain works spatially. I can remember how things work and I can connect to things in the real world much better if I see them in a room spatially. A fully immersive experience will be quite a benefit, especially when you have globally distributed teams and you can do things in a more engaging way.

I can own my assets, and I can connect my avatar as an NFT to my decentralized identity. In other words, "Your wallet is your identity."

What are some of the major hurdles that we still need to overcome to increase more user adoption and make it more mainstream?
The devices we have today are too bulky and expensive. Will users want to wear these headsets for an extended period of time? What if we have displays in the room instead so they don't need to put on special glasses, and the effect will look somewhat like holograms?

Having some form of regulation is crucial to foster responsible usage. We need to provide a safe place for everyone to enjoy. Interoperability between different platforms is also important. Sustainability is another area that will need a bit of work as well.

Metaverse Use Cases

Broadly speaking, we are still in the very beginning of a rapidly changing world. While we can never be certain what the future might hold, we also cannot afford to simply sit back. Beyond gaming and entertainment, it is worthwhile to review how jurisdictions around the world are planting seeds and experimenting with the concept of metaverse.

Metaverse Seoul, for example, is an effort by the municipal administration of Seoul, South Korea, that seeks to create an immersive ecosystem for all areas of its municipal administration, such as economic, cultural, tourism, educational, and civic service.[32] Imagine having a digital square where citizens can explore cultural events, learn, and get access to public services at their leisure, without the constraint of time and space associated with a physical environment. Or businesses can get support from a virtual Seoul Fintech Lab and collaborate with others in virtual coworking spaces as if working in a real office. Or where avatars can advise foreign companies interested in collaborating with the Korean startup ecosystem, and host networking events in virtual receptions. From a global perspective, South Korea's investment of $177.1 million in this new ecosystem is definitely among one of the first such investments to be made by a national government.[33]

Use cases are not limited to public services, either. MAVE:[34] a K-pop group by Kakao Entertainment, for example, is a band created entirely in the metaverse and debuted in 2023.

Elsewhere in Asia, a couple, or rather their avatars, tied the knot in The Sandbox's first metaverse wedding set in Singapore's historic Alkaff Mansion.[35] Though we are not sure if many people are ready to say "I do" in the metaverse, it does open up possibilities for friends, family and loved ones from afar to join in the celebrations wherever they are.[36] In the age of hybrid everything, why not a wedding?

Weddings are not the only events that might go phygital. The Hong Kong Philharmonic launch The Metaverse Symphony live and in the Sandbox in May 2023 in a re-creation of Hong Kong's Statue Square, marking the world's first symphonic work to be performed in both a concert hall and the metaverse.

Dubai and other emirates in the UAE have also taken steps to integrate the metaverse into their larger economy and society. The Dubai Metaverse Strategy, announced in 2022, aims to create 40,000 virtual jobs and add $4 billion to the Emirate's economy over five years.[37] These initiatives will build the skills of Emiratis and create a large metaverse community in Dubai to include metaverse companies, startups, investors, and users. Dubai's Virtual Assets Regulatory Authority (VARA), an independent authority to regulate the sector through the Emirates, also became the world's first authority to enter the metaverse with its MetaHQ.[38]

Would visiting an embassy or a tax office in the metaverse be in your future? Barbados seems to think so, as it embarks on a partnership with Decentraland to become the first sovereign nation with a diplomatic embassy in the metaverse.[39] Separately, Norway is also planning its entry into Decentraland with the establishment of a virtual tax office, as part of a broader initiative to educate a younger audience about taxes related to DeFi and NFTs, and to explore additional web3 services, including DAO, digital wallets, and smart contracts.[40]

As countries are increasingly confronted with the devastating impacts of climate change, some turn to the metaverse as a way to preserve a nation's culture and heritage. Tuvalu, an independent island nation within the British Commonwealth in the South Pacific, plans to become the first digitized nation in the metaverse. According to Tuvalu's foreign affairs minister, Simon Kofe, at high tide, up to 40 percent of the country's capital, Funafuti, is underwater. Back in 1989, the UN designated Tuvalu as one of numerous island groups most likely to be submerged in the 21st century due to global warming. Experts predict the island nation, home to 12,000 people, could be uninhabitable within the next 50 to 100 years. While creating a digital twin will not directly reverse the climate trend, it will hopefully help to raise awareness on the urgency of the climate crisis, while in parallel preparing the country for the worst-case scenario.[41]

Beyond these experimental efforts led by the different jurisdictions worldwide, there are also some real applications that an immersive metaverse experience can fulfill. For example, a Columbian court held their first judicial hearing in the metaverse, using Horizon Worlds to simulate the virtual space, and avatars to represent the participants in the procedures.[42] This is likely just the beginning of more to come.

To bring these use cases to life, we will look at some applications of augmented reality (AR) and virtual reality (VR) that can be leveraged in two practical use cases: education and work.

Education

Most of us had a schooling experience where a number of students watched a teacher walk through a syllabus with chalk, a blackboard, and a projector. Or at best a PowerPoint presentation on a screen. What if we can reinvent the experience to make it more engaging?

Imagine a world where students could switch on their headsets, see their classmates next to them, and listen to the teachers as they walk them through their geography lessons, while being immersed under the Northern Lights, on top of Mount Everest, or in the ocean with a blue whale. AR in the education market is expected to reach $41.8 billion by 2027, growing at a CAGR of 77.2 percent over the period 2020–27.[43] Startups such as zSpace, TutAR, and PlayShifu are working on education applications using VR and AR. Through the use of such technology, these edtech startups are able to virtually transport students back to 250 million years ago, show them what earth looked like back then and allow them to see dinosaurs walk around them; or bring the virtual Solar System into the classroom and provide them with an immersive experience with orbiters, landers, and rovers.

Other use cases include providing students with a realistic experience of looking into human anatomy. Teachers can zoom into parts of the human body, rotate them, provide different views, and resize them to help students take a closer look at human body parts. Imagine seeing the heart pumping blood right in front of your eyes, and the teacher explaining the mechanics of it all.

VR solutions within education can offer not only better learning experiences, but also more global experiences. Traditionally, a student completing an undergraduate degree at the University of Oxford must do so in person. What if students from villages in Asia and Africa can take these courses in the virtual classroom, with a similar level of personal interaction experience with cohorts and teachers? That would be a truly inclusive use case that breaks global barriers and offers a cost-effective way for those who otherwise do not have access to high-quality education. In fact, with MetaHKUST, the Hong Kong University of Science and Technology plans to overcome geographical constraints by opening the world's first physical–digital twin campuses in the metaverse, enabling students across borders to attend classes together.[44]

Similar technologies can also be deployed for workplace training, which can help to reduce cost and time, and improve job mobility for workers by providing more upskilling and reskilling opportunities. According to a report from CB Insights, Bank of America provided VR training to 50,000 employees across a variety of scenarios from fraud detection to customer management. And the effort resulted in four times the speed of learning compared to traditional environments.[45]

We are just scratching the surface with the potential of education technology. With more mainstream and cost-effective hardware, coupled with reliable and affordable internet around the world, crossing physical borders to educate oneself could be a thing of the past.

The Future of Work

The second practical, scalable, and viable use case of AR/VR technologies is around the future of work. While the world was going through turbulent times with Covid-19, most organizations switched to remote work almost overnight. Thanks to the highly connected world we live in, the transition from a daily commute to a video conference call life happened relatively smoothly.

As a result, critical businesses continued operations online, resulting in a lower cost base as commercial real estate was hardly needed. International conferences, business meetings, and travel were drastically reduced. The lockdowns through April 2020 saw a 17 percent drop for the month, and a 7 percent drop in 2020 annual carbon emission. While this was harder to sustain as economies reopened, by creating better ways to work together digitally, we could consciously reduce international travel and physical commutes to work.

Working together through VR technologies in the metaverse could prove to be more sustainable in the long run, without sacrificing the personal interactions in physical settings. While nothing can truly replace a face-to-face conversation and the trust that it helps build amongst colleagues, a vast majority of work conversations could happen in a highly immersive virtual environment, leaving in-person meet-ups for special occasions and a small subset of team-building events. Work is no longer a physical place that we go to—conversations are now taking place anywhere and anytime, transcending digital and physical boundaries.

When Mark Zuckerberg delivered his vision of transition to Meta, he called AR/VR "work teleportation" devices that would shrink distances between employees and allow for more seamless communication within the organization. As part of the journey towards that vision, they delivered a VR headset, Meta Quest Pro. In October 2022, Microsoft announced partnership with Meta to enable people to interact with content from Microsoft 365 apps within VR on their Meta Quest devices, and connect and collaborate with each other as though they are physically together in person.[46]

As hardware and software capabilities converge, the future of work will become more immersive and engaging. Much like the education use case, physical borders, distance, and even a lack of personal interaction will no longer be a barrier for a global team to collaborate and innovate seamlessly.

The experiential element of the metaverse powered by AR/VR technologies can become more impactful, particularly when delivered for day-to-day activities. Yet, there are still technological limitations that need to be addressed to achieve a seamlessly scalable and immersive experience. Let us look at the technology journeys we have been through in the past few years that have converged to make metaverses possible.

A CONVERSATION WITH DIANA WU DAVID, AUTHOR OF FUTURE PROOF

The Future of Learning and Development

The metaverse can be used to heighten the experience in order for learning to be more embodied and to create shared experiences. Onboarding, once done in person at a corporate campus, becomes a branded experience for new joiners or digital offsites as employees around the world visit the digital twin of headquarters or share simulated virtual team experiences like yoga, meditation, or skydiving.

In diversity, equity, inclusion, and belonging training or empathy training, VR allows people to enter an immersive world as a minority and see in real time in a group how they might be treated differently. Customer service reps can role-play real-time interaction with angry customers.

Virtual training might be used when the cost of training or getting to training is high or safety is an issue. Pilots can do early simulation training in their home countries anywhere in the world and then come in for more advanced training. Offshore oil rig repairers can be trained for dangerous situations with minimal risk.

Finally, new immersive environments lend themselves to more gamification of learning and even work. This will yield in the next phase a wealth of data we can use to further improve opportunities to work and learn via the metaverse.

A CONVERSATION WITH CHRISTOPHER LAI, DIRECTOR, KOREA AT HONG KONG TRADE DEVELOPMENT COUNCIL

While the metaverse is still a nascent space, Asia has the biggest potential due to demographics (overall growing population and rising middle class), as well as the fast pace of technological development and adoption across the region.

South Korea, in particular, could see major growth and progress. It had the world's third largest number of metaverse-related patent applications from 2011 to 2020,[47] while the Korean Government's aggressive Digital New Deal includes an outlay of over 220 billion won to developing metaverse technologies and platforms. In fact, the domestic metaverse market is expected to reach 400 trillion won by 2025.[48]

Hong Kong, as an international business platform with a robust capital market as well as core strengths in finance, professional services and logistics, is also well placed to be a strategic hub for the global metaverse ecosystem.

Potential Use Cases in Hong Kong and Korea

There are multiple interesting use cases for the metaverse that are worth mentioning. Let's start with those in Hong Kong:

- Education:
  - Hong Kong University of Science and Technology (HKUST) will become the world's first physical–digital twin campus in the metaverse with MetaHKUST, an extended reality campus for both HKUST and their Guangzhou counterpart. It is envisioned that the members of the two universities will be able to generate their own avatars, NFTs, tokens, or virtual art works for the virtual world, along with blockchain-secured diplomas or transcripts, and online–offline events.

- o Separately, metaverse learning platforms such as Soqqle, can encourage knowledge transfer and idea generation in more immersive ways that were not possible before.
- Household name brands and gaming platforms:
  - o B.Duck was designed by Eddie Hui in 2005, originally as a gift for his children. Over the years, it became the largest domestic character IP in China in terms of licensing revenue in 2021.[49] To extend from apparel and gifts into new markets such as gaming and the metaverse, the brand partners with gaming platforms and grants them licenses to use B.Duck IPs in the scenario and character designs of games. B.Duck recently launched its first NFT collection via a collaboration with MADworld, a well-known Animoca-backed NFT Origination Platform. This first batch of 4,000 B.Duck NFTs was sold out within five hours of public sales. In the future, B.Duck NFT owners can travel through various B.Duck-themed applications in the *Duckverse* for more immersive gaming experiences and earn awards.
  - o And, of course, we cannot talk about the metaverse without talking about The Sandbox, an open metaverse and a subsidiary of Hong Kong-based Animoca Brands, which allows users to own land as well as their own created content in the form of NFTs in play-to-earn games. They can also host functions, produce new games, experience different brands, and enjoy concerts. The Sandbox counts big brands such as Adidas, Snoop Dogg, The Walking Dead, South China Morning Post, The Smurfs, Care Bears, Atari, CryptoKitties, and Shaun the Sheep as partners.[50] Its land holders also come from diverse sectors, including fashion brands, banks, telecoms operators, and the hospitality industry.
  - o We can also create new immersive experiences by bringing the physical and digital worlds together. Hong Kong fashion designer Vivienne Tam, for example, brought the streets of Hong Kong virtually to her 2023 New York Fashion Week runway show, with the help of NFTs/PFPs.[51]

The ecosystem is also very vibrant elsewhere in South Korea:

- Telecommunications:
  - o After the initial launch in Korea in July 2021, Korean operator SK Telecom has now rolled out its "ifland" metaverse platform in

49 countries from Asia and the Americas, to Europe, the Middle East, and Africa, supporting multiple languages including English, Chinese, Japanese, and Korean. The telco carrier is also planning to collaborate with local partners such as Japan's DoCoMo to tailor content for local markets.[52]

- Education:
  - A metaverse version of the King Sejong Institute will be launched in 2023 to help foreigners learn Korean anytime and anywhere. The institute, a government-funded Korean language education brand, had 244 centers in 84 countries as of the end of 2022. Having the virtual platform will enable more people to study and experience life and culture in Korea.[53]

- Government:
  - The Seoul Metropolitan Government launched the world's first virtual public administration platform in early 2023[54] with the first phase of Metaverse Seoul, an online platform where people can use public services offered by the city government, including administrative services, economic matters, tax, and education.
  - The second phase of the five-year plan is expected to include additional content on public safety, real estate, a support center for foreigners, as well as a digital replica of Dongdaemun Design Plaza.

- Banking:
  - The Shinamon metaverse platform includes a finance zone, a health zone, an art zone, a sports zone, and a store, providing financial and non-financial services to customers.

- Healthcare:
  - The metaverse can also be a valuable educational tool for healthcare. In 2022, Medical IP, a digital twin-based medical AI solution provider, signed a memorandum of understanding with the Korean Association of Anatomists to start joint research for the development of a digital anatomy education project—the Metaverse Education Research Association—and the creation of a medical IT ecosystem.[55]

- Entertainment and gaming:
  - Owned by Korean tech group Naver, ZEPETO is Asia's largest K-pop and fashion-focused avatar platform.[56] Its users are

predominantly young females, and partnerships include well-known fashion and household brands such as Gucci and Samsung.

Challenges and Opportunities

Some challenges are to be expected in the next three to five years, especially around regulation and security, mental health, inclusion, and sustainability. Regulations need to be in place to protect the well-being of citizens and consumers, preserve data and identity security, and to prevent illicit activities including money laundering.

We would likely see a new digital divide, for those who are unable to, do not wish to, or cannot afford to, access and use the metaverse. On the flip side, new mental health challenges may arise with those who become addicted to the metaverse and withdraw from the real world.

While this ecosystem is still being proven, we might see some business campaigns and activities that could be ill-advised or under-developed, leading to unsatisfactory results and poor customer experience. From a sustainability perspective, we would need to address the environmental concerns that arise, as the exponential increase in computing power required will likely lead to an unavoidable and sustained increase in energy usage.

But with challenges come opportunities.

Specifically within financial services and fintech, we expect more immersive digital banking experiences, new developments in payments and lending, and digital assets trading. We can also leverage the technology platform to conduct virtual training for professionals and next-generation talents.

Deployed thoughtfully, the metaverse can help to improve access to services and experiences, from public services to education and healthcare. The new economic dynamics and technology paradigm can also enable new business and employment opportunities, and create new ways of working and real-time collaboration across geographies. Businesses can leverage the metaverse to expand their digital footprints and build new communities where fans can interact and connect with each other. New business models will emerge as a result. For instance, breweries can mint NFTs for collectors and investors when offering limited releases, which can be traded directly in the secondary market without the need for additional third-party authentication, due to the nature of blockchain-based NFTs that allow investors to ascertain product origin and authenticity.

Technology Advances

The metaverse needs several technological elements to be in place to go mainstream. Each of these technologies adds a specific attribute to the way metaverses can be implemented. The attributes and the respective technologies are as follows:

- Immersive experience delivered by AR/VR.
- Rich environments in the virtual world designed in Unreal Engine/ Unity (and other such software platforms).
- Graphics processing units (GPUs) to process these digital experiences.
- Blockchain to offer the economic model and store the data (optional).

While it must be clear by now that blockchain technology would be one of the building blocks of the metaverse, there are metaverse experiences that we discussed in this chapter that do not use this technology, and these platforms have done quite well in scaling to millions of users.

In the next chapter we will explore in greater detail the reasons why the blockchain can help with the metaverse. Later in the book we will also delve into what limitations the technology must overcome to achieve scalability. Before we do that, let's take a closer look at some of the limitations presented by the hardware and software tools of today, and their impact on the experiential experience of the metaverse.

VR and AR

The concept of virtual reality was seeded in 1838 when Sir Charles Wheatstone identified that the human vision came about when the brain combines images from both the eyes to create a 3D version. The concept was termed "stereopsis" and has been leveraged in stereoscopes in VR systems to create the illusion of depth.

The technology has developed in leaps and bounds in the past two centuries. Yet, it has struggled to gain mass adoption. For the metaverse narrative to scale, it is crucial for AR/VR technologies to mature and become part of our daily experience.

Usability

The biggest challenge with AR/VR has been the usability of the headsets. Even with the most recent launch of the Meta Quest Pro announced in Q4 2022, the experience is not close to what we are used to with 2D laptop screens. While image quality, haptic feedback, spatial audio quality, and eye tracking have improved the experience, usability issues remain:

- Headset weight can cause discomfort with extended use.
- Peripheral vision is absent with a VR headset.
- Mixed reality that brings experiences into your living room is still nascent.
- Traversing between applications can still be slow and delayed.
- Headsets and the handheld controls still make the experience less compact.
- Poor battery life makes it inconvenient to use.

While usability aspects are certainly improving, we will not be able to get to mass user adoption unless we can create a variety of hardware and application ecosystem lineups that can cater to different uses, not only for gamers and entertainers, but, more importantly, for professionals and everyday consumers.

Application Ecosystem

The rise of Apple and Google mobile operating systems was led by the application ecosystems that came with it. As the depth, breadth, interoperability, and data sharing across applications grew over the years, it created the much-needed network effect for mass adoption. These applications now need to find their equivalents within the virtual worlds.

We highlighted the importance of the partnership between Meta and Microsoft in creating a home workspace. Imagine sitting in your living room wearing your VR glasses and being able to see three large

80-inch screens and work across them. While that future is not too far away, to deliver the desired experience, we will need rich professional applications to be developed. This is where combining mixed reality with virtual reality can be critical—to enable visual view of the real keyboard and seamless transitions across applications.

Cost of Manufacturing

VR headsets are quite expensive to manufacture and the consumers typically bear the brunt of it, with costs ranging from $250 to several thousand dollars. This, combined with limited daily use and a shallow application ecosystem, hurts adoption. However, this is a natural cycle most technologies have faced in their early days. It was not that long ago when mobile phones were too bulky and expensive for everyday consumers.

We are almost at a similar stage for VR technologies today. But that could quickly change if the competition heats up, especially when Apple enters the market and taps into their extensive application ecosystem.

In essence, addressing the friction points within AR and VR will catalyze the growth of the metaverse.

Software Tools

So far, we have discussed the experiential elements and the hardware components that help catalyze the growth of metaverse. However, advances in software tools are equally important. Thanks to advances in gaming experiences over the years, there are many options available, including but not limited to:

- Unity
- Amazon Sumerian
- Unreal Engine
- Google VR for Everyone

The quality of graphics offered by these software platforms is critical to the gaming experience. Unity, for instance, has better interoperability across devices, while Unreal Engine excels on graphic quality.

Understanding the target use case and audience is therefore crucial. For instance, for companies building an entertainment portal or a game for hardcore gamers, who have the hardware capabilities and expect high-quality graphics, Unreal Engine may be a better fit. However, for casual gamers in their early teens who want a Roblox-like experience on the go, Unity may be a more suitable candidate.

The ability to deliver good-quality graphics is also reliant on having good computer hardware capabilities, especially when it comes to processing power. GPUs are purpose-built processors for rendering images. Over time, they have evolved from graphics accelerators to much more. Their parallel processing abilities have now paved the way for better visual effects, realistic graphics, shadowing techniques, data mining, big data applications, artificial intelligence, and deep learning.

While central processing units (CPUs) are typically used by conventional laptops, the emergence of GPUs changed the way creators could develop content. Over time, as technology continues to evolve, GPUs might replace CPU rendering systems completely, delivering delightful experiences and optimized performances with the speed and low cost that consumers demand.

A CONVERSATION WITH DR MELISSA SASSI, CEO AND CO-FOUNDER OF SKILLS HUSTLE

I used to think web3 was pointless and centered around trading digital art. For me, the metaverse was yet another slippery pathway of allowing technology to engulf our lives more than it does already. While I like gamified and interactive experiences, I wouldn't consider myself a gamer. These two use cases didn't fire me up and were irrelevant to me.

As I began to better understand the history of money, inflation, fiat currency, and economic and monetary policy, I became enthralled with the concept of decentralization. Similarly, I became more aware of the lack of control all of us currently have over our data. These two factors make me realize I misunderstood the true value proposition of web3.

The same epiphany happened when I stumbled upon an incredibly powerful use case for the metaverse. We all know justice systems across the globe are broken, and the legal industry is a late bloomer when it comes to digital transformation. Legal systems are often biased, paper-based, slow, not accessible for all, and filing a legal claim can often be more trouble than it's worth. MetaCOURT is the first legal metaverse, and an early-stage startup democratizing access to the legal system for minor disputes requiring mediation and arbitration. Who needs to talk to an attorney or go to a physical court to fight a minor contractual dispute? Why not gain access to lawyers in the metaverse? Having escrow-based smart contracts for freelancing could stipulate that contractual disputes could be mediated through the metaverse with solutions such as those offered by MetaCOURT.

While I may not be trading digital art or collecting random cryptocurrencies as I game all day, web3 has significant power to create new business models, entrepreneurs, and opportunities for disruption and innovation. Here's to decentralization, blockchain-based solutions, more control over our data, and rethinking the role tech can play to digitally transform the world around us!

The Journey Continues

In this chapter we have deliberately focused on the experiential elements of the metaverse. With the convergence of hardware and software advancements and as the world becomes more creator-centric, we are not too far away from these experiences being integrated into our daily lives.

However, there are other questions to be answered in the journey. What role does blockchain play in the metaverse of the future, and what are the economic and empowerment aspects for creators in the process?

With the experiential elements for the user addressed, and an economic framework to empower the creator developed, we can sit back and watch the network effect of our lifetime unleash itself in front of us.

The Metaverse Economic Models   07

It is not always wise to move fast and break things. But you also cannot make progress by living the status quo.

A technology paradigm goes mainstream not because of the buzz it receives, the number of users it has, nor its valuation. A technology goes mainstream when there are several viable business models that are built on it and it is adopted beyond a niche market segment. This was true with the internet era as several startups saw rising usage and valuations, but over time managed to also get to viable business models.

Metaverse as a technology paradigm is very nascent and the definition of the metaverse is still not crystallized. Different ecosystems define "metaverse" based on their view of what the paradigm is. It can be a gaming ecosystem, an art ecosystem, a private workplace for bankers, or an esports ecosystem. However, every avatar this paradigm takes will need to find a firm footing through commercial viability.

We have discussed experiential elements through virtual reality and foundational building blocks like NFTs, DeFi, and GameFi that can help metaverse become Internet 2.0. NFTs can bridge the web2 audience into web3, virtual reality experiences can draw the crowd in, and DeFi can help set up the underlying financial transactions and models. However, the experiential elements can only act as the dopamine carrot that pulls in users. Metaverses need to improve across several user adoption yardsticks to get closer to a viable technology to become part of our shared future.

So, what are the benchmarks that a metaverse should measure its progress against? How and when can a metaverse, a multiverse, or the metaverse of the future claim to have sound fundamentals? Let us draw some inspiration from the pirate metrics that venture capitalists use to gauge consumer adoption for a product. A metaverse's unit economics can be judged using this framework more broadly as a paradigm, but also focused on specific platforms.

Pirate metrics have been historically used as a framework to judge the progress that a consumer platform is making. The framework looks at five stages of consumer adoption:

1 Acquisition: Where a user is targeted through SEOs and marketing channels and directed to the platform.

2 Activation: Where a user who is on the platform registers as a user.

3 Retention: Where a registered user feels compelled to come back to the platform on a regular basis.

4 Revenue: Where a loyal customer makes a purchase, bringing revenue for the platform.

5 Referral: Where a user becomes an advocate and spreads the word, which in turn brings more users to the platform.

While we will largely use the above framework, there is one other key dimension with web3 platforms that will need to come ahead of the acquisition stage. That is "attention." With web3, user acquisition and community adoption of a platform often rely on how well the founders of the platform are able to draw attention, particularly on social media platforms such as Twitter. While the platform of choice to get the word out might change in the future, user adoption is typically highly reliant on how well the platform gains user attention and keeps them excited for long periods of time.

Attention

The way a metaverse platform draws attention to its brand, its platform, its token, and ecosystem is critical to its user adoption. In the previous Bitcoin bull run of 2021, we saw several web3 brands leverage Twitter and Telegram effectively to grab attention. Some of them were technology platforms looking to launch a token, while others were NFT collections looking to launch their genesis NFT collection. Some of these strategies include:

- Community competitions and rewards for winners.
- Airdrops for those who engage with the social media content of a web3 platform.
- "Ask me anything" (AMA) sessions featuring celebrities endorsing the platform.
- Content distribution by paid influencers on social media platforms such as TikTok and Twitter.
- Loyalty points and rewards for the most loyal community members through Discord activities.
- Witty content posted by founders and community members, also known as sh*tposting.

WHAT IS AN AIRDROP?

An airdrop is a mechanism where web3 projects give away their tokens to their loyal community members for free. Community members are identified through on-chain interactions with the project, and wallets that have had interactions get rewarded with airdrops.

While there is no shortage of ideas to gain attention, the general yardstick for attention-grabbing communities is when their social media posts appear on the social feeds and echo chambers of completely unrelated participants on the social media platform. This is often a planned strategy where crypto and NFT teams leverage web3 influencers and whales to distribute content.

WHO IS A CRYPTO/NFT WHALE?

A crypto or NFT whale is someone who holds a large quantity of a particular crypto token or an NFT collection. The entry of a whale into an

NFT community is often seen as a bullish sign for the price of the NFT. We also see the reverse, when a whale leaves an NFT collection and the price drops. Therefore, whales can often make (or break) the future of an NFT collection/crypto token both by bringing a lot of attention, but also helping the price of the asset.

As whales and influencers take notice, they'd typically claim publicly on Twitter that a particular community has managed to flood their social media feeds. They'd study the project and engage with the founders, and often take a huge position either in crypto tokens or in the NFT collection of the project. For crypto/NFT enthusiasts, this is considered a big win and brings a lot more attention to the project.

As projects constantly strategize to win customer attention, the community often rallies behind the founding team. Channels on Discord are set up to allow community managers to share social posts with team members, whales, and influencers, who interact with the content systematically through responses and memes to attract further attention. Rallying the community to attract attention to the project has been a key strategy used by projects in web3 through the last cycle.

How well a project in web3 is positioned to gain attention is also a key criterion for investors who back the project. Social media following, as well as the quality of the top and bottom of the social media funnel, are all considered by investors as key metrics that add value to community capabilities of the firm.

Any metaverse project that is looking to scale will need to be at the top of their game in attracting attention from their community and potential community. Unlike hardcore web3 use cases, metaverse projects have the additional burden of onboarding web2 metaverse enthusiasts as well. Therefore, on top of attracting the native web3 audience, they have to go further and get the attention of web2 consumers who could potentially be part of their community.

Acquisition

As metaverses get better at getting the attention of their customer, they need an acquisition strategy to onboard them to their platform.

While content and social media strategy are handy in getting their attention, it is typically a rewards mechanism built on a growth hacking exercise that helps acquire customers.

The reward can be monetary or experiential, depending on the metaverse's strategy. Through the last Bitcoin cycle, several top projects such as Uniswap, ENS, and Aptos used airdrop strategies to acquire and hold on to their customers. Some DeFi projects offered airdrops to Uniswap customers to create a cascaded growth hack effect through the Ethereum DeFi boom in 2021.

Monetary Rewards

Airdrops have not only helped bring attention to projects, but they are also used to acquire and retain customers by top web3 projects. So what are users expected to do to earn an airdrop and what are the new strategies that are being explored?

Some projects have explicit ranking and gamification mechanisms to get their community members to rally behind them on social media or to get them to beta test their platform. Users are ranked on a loyalty leaderboard depending on how close they have been to the community and whether they have helped with either product testing or social media messaging. Every user activity is tracked, with users submitting evidence of activities that are likely to get them rewarded or moved up the loyalty leaderboard.

As these activities and leaderboards get automated, there are now providers who build these leaderboard platforms as-a-service and offer it to web3 platforms looking to acquire and retain users through their community activities. Sui, a decentralized, PoS blockchain and Blur, an NFT marketplace, are two platforms that are actively using community leaderboards for users to register their activity results. Often these results are picked up from on-chain data, while in some instances users submit them to win points in the ecosystems.

Blur, in particular, uses airdrop strategies not only to acquire but also to retain customers and create regular active usage. For example, Blur leverages a leaderboard for its three-drop strategy, and users can view the points they have acquired by listing, bidding, or buying NFTs on the platform. A snapshot of user activity is taken in multiple phases, and a dedicated airdrop is performed per phase. The size of the airdrop increases through successive phases as users rally behind the project to show their loyalty and gain as big an airdrop as possible.

"Plain vanilla airdrops" have seen mixed results when compared to traditional web2 models, based on the cost of acquisition of customers (CAC). And some of the more recent strategies that phase out airdrops and try to change user behavior through activities have seen better results with lower CACs.

Airdrops could be an effective tool for metaverse platforms as they can leverage it for a phased approach, and at the same time also have their ecosystem do airdrops to their users. Metaverses could easily have a number of infrastructure and application-tier projects that piggyback off their growth. As a result, metaverses could collaborate with these ecosystem projects to reward their user base for their loyalty. As users use more of the metaverse features, there could be more rewards in play for them.

Experiential Rewards

Earlier in this book we discussed StepN and Axie Infinity in relation to the failure of play-to-earn (P2E) models that focus purely on giving tokens to acquire and retain users. While monetary rewards are often considered an expensive hack to growing a user base, experiential rewards can lead to more sustained growth. The failure of the P2E model that we described is a great example of how buying users with tokens cannot be a sustained long-term solution.

Within the GameFi space, we have seen an increased focus on games that offer immersive experience to users as a way to acquire and retain them. This experiential reward is also why GameFi would be a key growth hack for metaverses. Metaverse platforms that look to scale their user base, particularly from traditional web2 ecosystems, will have to rely largely on gamify experiences to onboard users.

While the rails are in place to onboard users at scale, clunky on-ramp solutions can often dampen the experience right at the start. Therefore, metaverses must build on-ramp solutions themselves to onboard users seamlessly, without them having to create a wallet with private keys, buy NFTs, and go through all the other friction points typically associated with a traditional web3 application, as explained earlier in the book.

Simplifying the onboarding process is a key step to ensure users can enjoy experiential rewards. And it is not just about games and immersive experiences either. How seamlessly a web3 user can navigate the ecosystem across DeFi, NFTs, and other verticals without feeling overwhelmed by the experience is also crucial. One ecosystem that is spot on with their user journey is Solana. While their onboarding process still relies on wallets with private keys, their NFT platforms, DeFi platforms, and, most important of all, their frictionless, low-cost transactions, make the entire experience very pleasant.

Most other layer 1 ecosystems have had high CACs, and only time will tell if they manage to extract good lifetime value from these customers. Comparatively speaking, Solana has set the benchmark high with their user experience, which has helped create a very tight community around the chain.

> You need centralized exchanges for fiat on and off ramps for people to enter and exit the crypto economy. You can't live your life within the crypto economy; centralized exchanges need to exist.
>
> Mike Dudas, founder and General Partner of 6MV

Activation and Retention

One of the key challenges that metaverse projects have is around activating users and holding on to them at scale. Most metaverse projects that are live in web3 today lack the user experience and the product strategy attractive enough to bring users back to the platform on a regular basis. For instance, while Decentraland is a well-known brand, and they are leaders when it comes to the engineering behind metaverse, they lack the ability to entice users to come back.

Metaverses not only need to have ways to attract new users, they must also be able to retain them, and entice them to keep coming back on a regular basis. They might have to be a household narrative before such high levels of retention can happen, and they need use cases beyond gaming and events, such as retail. In the short term, gaming promises to be the user retention carrot for metaverse platforms. In the medium term, however, VR/AR infrastructure needs to improve and become household systems that we use on a daily basis. This implies the digital divide must be closed, with access becoming available and affordable. Use cases for the metaverses must scale to include education and future of work, and for more people. Users must have seamless access to open and closed metaverses depending on the context of usage. The convergence, which we will address in more detail in the next chapter, will bring about behavioral changes as we become more accustomed to interacting with each other in the metaverse on a regular basis, thus improving the lifetime value of customers on metaverse platforms.

While the fundamentals to attract and acquire users into a metaverse are relatively well understood today, retention requires several other technologies and corresponding use cases to mature. Till then, this will remain a boat with a hole. While these platforms will continue to spend investors or token holders' capital to acquire users, without a clear retention use case and a strategy they will struggle to make any of their revenue models work. User retention is often seen as the most critical metric by venture capital investors in the traditional web2 world. That is not without merit. High user retention demonstrates the platform's ability to try new business models with these users and a pathway towards profitability.

Revenue

Acquisition, activation, and retention are meaningless for long-term viability if a metaverse platform cannot identify sustainable revenue sources. Fortunately for the metaverse narrative, there are multiple revenue streams that have been identified. Some of them are inspired by traditional web2 metaverses and technology platforms, while others are native web3 revenue lines.

Digital Assets

The valuation of cryptocurrencies has been a difficult task for even the most experienced financial mind. But NFTs and digital real estate have taken this challenge to a completely different level. Metaverses are built on digital real estate, and these real estate plots are often sold to users to raise capital in order to build the platform and the business. Some metaverses have used token gating as a way to provide exclusive access to perks, content, and events, available only to token holders, a common method used by NFT project teams to create value for their community members. Sometimes these NFT holders also receive subsidized pricing for other digital assets, as well as faster progression, if the metaverse is based on gamification. Holders of Gary Vaynerchuck's special VeeFriends NFT, for example, receive exclusive access to the annual VeeCon event in Minneapolis for three years after the NFT's purchase.[1]

The year 2021 saw the rise of several NFT communities and successful sale of digital real estate, including, for instance, the sale of Sandbox's LAND NFT. Most of these NFTs and land sales not only result in revenues from primary issuance of these assets, but also bring royalty revenues on secondary transactions. Therefore, as these platforms demonstrate that NFT and land holders accrue value in the ecosystem over time and market these offerings suitably, demand for these digital assets sky-rockets.

Apart from the PFP NFTs and land sale, metaverses also have different ecosystems where creators design and develop other forms of digital assets. For instance, a gaming metaverse can offer game-based digital assets including weapons, ammunitions, armor, and vehicles. These are designed by expert creators and are sold on marketplaces for gamers and users of the metaverse. While the creators typically receive the large portion of the proceeds from the sale, the metaverse platform provider or the DAO that leads the platform development often receives a commission from the sale as well.

Digital assets will continue to be a key source of revenue for metaverse projects. Not only do they help bring much-needed income, they can also rally the community together through PFP NFTs that the community members can identify themselves with.

Transaction Commissions

We touched on transaction commissions when we described digital assets in the previous section. Transaction commission is a broad revenue line that can apply to most transaction types on metaverse projects. While the secondary sale of digital assets can bring commissions as revenues, a metaverse can also have commissions on several other types of transactions:

- Land owners can construct event venues and lease or rent them out. Metaverse platforms will receive a commission from the sale and leasing.

- Shopping malls can be rented out to firms who want to sell their merchandise in the metaverse. If the malls are designed by the metaverse firm, not only are they able to earn revenue from the sales, they can also earn commission (or tax) when the owner of the mall rents out the space.

- Metaverse e-commerce is a source of transaction commissions where the metaverse business gains a small percentage of the commission from sales transactions.

- Events can be hosted on the metaverse, and the sale of tickets and merchandise from the event can all generate revenue for the metaverse. If the metaverse team hosts the event, they can also receive a large portion of the proceeds. Where a third party hosts the event, the metaverse may receive only a commission.

- Land and landmark owners can use their strategic positions in the metaverse to host ad banners. When the firms pay the land owners to advertise in the metaverse, they often pay a commission to the metaverse business as well.

- Metaverse projects can also become launchpads for other micro-economies on their platform. For instance, an art metaverse can encourage a group of artists to launch their own micro-economy and tokens if viable. This can in turn contribute to the broader metaverse ecosystem through various commission and token exchange models.

Many of the above sources of revenues have already been tested by the metaverse projects that have seen some success.

While all of the above revenue models are largely focused on the metaverse application layer, there can be other business models also, including metaverse protocols and metaverse-as-a-service.

Metaverse Protocols

Most of the layer 1 and layer 2 blockchain protocols that metaverse projects have used, including Ethereum, Solana, Polygon, and Immutable, have broad ecosystems and application categories. However, as blockchain technologies have evolved, we have already begun to see modular blockchains that are built for specialized use cases, such as the Fuel blockchain network, which focuses on high throughput with high levels of security.

As modular blockchains mature, we could see metaverse-specific blockchain protocols that address specific architectural requirements of the metaverse. Lamina1 is an open protocol implementation that focuses on metaverses. Neal Stephenson, who coined the term metaverse in his bestselling book *Snow Crash*, is also a key stakeholder in the Lamina1 project. As projects focus more on the protocol layer rather than the application level, their revenue model will become more reliant on the applications that are built on top of the protocol. As applications on the protocols see more user adoption, network effects would result in better unit economics and a more robust revenue model for the projects.

However, these are early days for modular blockchains and it will be a few more years before they get mainstream adoption and attention. But they are a model that metaverse projects should consider.

Metaverse-as-a-Service

One significant business model that is being explored is metaverse-as-a-service (MaaS). This model can assume different approaches depending on whether the target client is looking to set up an open or a private metaverse. Let us briefly look at the key differences between an open and a private metaverse and how MaaS offerings can help both these approaches.

Open Metaverse

An open metaverse is analogous to the internet where content creators, ecosystem developers, artists, consumers, gamers, and e-commerce providers are all free to operate. There would be some broad rules that they may have to follow for cyber security and compliance reasons, but the metaverse must be an open forum for all stakeholders to participate, create value, and benefit from the experience.

In both these instances, there are revenue opportunities for MaaS providers. The process of building an open metaverse has several stages and components. For instance, building a gaming metaverse will require the project team to develop the metaverse experience, the games, the gamification engine, the economic model, and the back-end infrastructure. While the metaverse look and feel, the game strategies, and themes will be different across projects, the gamification engine, backend infrastructure, and the economic model engine can be replicated across projects.

As a result, projects like Moonstream.to have built the infrastructure to support gaming metaverses and gamify projects. They bring the GameFi engine, blockchain infrastructure, and the plumbing needed by gaming projects. Projects like Moonstream.to offer gaming studios and metaverse creators the space to focus on their core proposition and help progress faster. As this space matures, there would be more MaaS offerings like Moonstream.to that would target specific capabilities that metaverse initiatives need.

As Neeraj Kashyap, Founder of Moonstream.to, told us: "It's important to build tools that make blockchain easy to interact with, for both developers and players. This lowers the entry barrier for players and makes games more sustainable."

Closed Metaverse

A closed metaverse is like the intranets that large organizations typically create within their firewalls. This allows them to form a forum for their member stakeholders for specific activities, in a closed and secure fashion. A metaverse for banks with trading floors could be a good example of a closed metaverse. As we see this space mature, we should see closed metaverses set up by universities for their students, and by corporations for their employees.

The partnership announcement between Meta and Microsoft was perhaps one of the biggest developments for closed metaverses. A partnership between the tech giant that is considered as the leader of the metaverse narrative, and the largest enterprise software provider in the world, allows us a glimpse into the future. Add to this Microsoft's acquisition offer to Activision Blizzard for $68.7 billion.[2]

This acquisition would provide Microsoft with a stronghold in the GameFi space that could serve them well to be leaders in closed (enterprise) metaverse offerings. We will examine that more in the next chapter.

Closed metaverses, where organizations have the ability to offer an immersive work experience to their employees, with the entire Microsoft stack integrated into it, are a future that is not too far away. While this may sound like a space that Microsoft could dominate, this is similar to the cloud infrastructure migration that many organizations embarked on over the last decade. As closed metaverses mature, software providers will need to make their tools compatible with the metaverse experience, leading to the development of new apps to enable compatibility across VR/AR/XR devices.

Based on these developments in MaaS, there will be no shortage of value creation and revenue opportunities for creators and game studios in this next version of the internet.

Metaverse Support Infrastructure

As innovation has ramped up around the metaverse since 2021, so have risks. Unlike the internet of the past, where users shared data in an open environment, with the metaverse users will have digital assets in an open environment. For instance, a post on Twitter by a user is just a piece of data openly shared by the user. But when a metaverse creator publishes their digital asset, it has tangible value. Often these assets and transactions are on-chain and a smart hacker can assess the net worth of a creator or an artist in a metaverse based on the sales they see in the ecosystem.

This opens up the doors for bad actors, hackers, and money launderers to exploit naive creators in the metaverse. According to Chainalysis, scammers collected over $3.5 billion from victims in 2022.[3] Another estimate from Privacy Affairs indicates that the loss could be as high as $4.3 billion worth of cryptocurrency.[4] And this is just the beginning. As the market capitalization of the industry goes up, the size of assets lost to illicit activities will likely go up as well.

How is this a revenue opportunity, though? Cyber experts, anti-money laundering analytics firms, and parental control experts have been building solutions to protect crypto and NFT users from these actors. Wallet providers have built controls that show the details of a smart contract before a wallet holder signs a transaction.

Previously, smart contracts were quite opaque, and often users would have little to no idea of what a transaction usually entails. But now, with new wallet plugins like Fire,[5] users can finally see clearly what assets would leave their wallet and what would come in when they sign a smart contract.

This is of course a simple example of how tools and applications will need to be built in order to protect users in a metaverse context. There will also be other fintech products, such as cyber insurance, that are data and smart contract driven to protect digital assets in the metaverse. These fintech products can be integrated into the commission fees that metaverse projects charge their creators, reducing the financial burden on creators while providing them with additional protection.

We also need to consider mental health solutions that need to be in place before users are subjected to dopamine addiction through immersive metaverse experiences. Meditation and mindfulness solutions and centers will likely see a lot of demand in a metaverse and will most likely be tracked through on-chain activities. As with what we have experienced in today's virtual worlds, how do we best ensure the mental well-being of users? Who should be held accountable, if anyone? And what are the ethical guidelines for engagement?

While it is extremely important to create a robust support system around metaverse users to ensure they are protected and supported at all levels, there are more questions that will need to be addressed. Apart from the projected market capitalization for the metaverse as a paradigm, these support infrastructure elements would also be a big space that would see growth and value creation.

Referral

We have been through several criteria from the pirate metrics framework to see what metaverses should do to get to good unit economics and become viable long term. Referral is a key metric that shows how pleased the user base is with the product. After all, a happy customer that is willing to vouch for your business is the best customer; having a high referral rate typically indicates a satisfied user base.

However, a higher referral rate may depend on several random user experience factors, too. For instance, in the initial days of LinkedIn, they had a button that allowed users to invite their email contacts to the platform. The LinkedIn product team noticed that the rate at which users clicked on this button increased as soon as this button turned red, and the "redder" the button, the more likely users would click on it. While this was a serendipitous solution that LinkedIn stumbled upon, metaverse projects may have to consider and conduct planned referral experiments. They have gamified experiences and token economics as two key tools to bring more users onboard. Token economics may be a purely financial upside for referrals, while gamification may be more than that.

Using gamification for referrals could also mean that soulbound tokens could find utility. Users who contribute to the ecosystem with referrals could win soulbound tokens, stamps, and badges that would give them financial and non-financial benefits within the ecosystem. Many of these techniques were tried and tested through 2021 and 2022. While some of them were successful, new projects are improving on referral models and the incentivization structures around referrals.

Summary

There is no shortage of ideas that have been implemented and tested when it comes to web3 metaverse business models. The web3 ecosystem has seen varying degrees of success with these models, which can be largely attributed to high levels of reliance on tokenomics.

Often, the financial upside for the consumer to get them to use a product may prove unsustainable in the long run and across different business cycles. However, due to the Bitcoin cycle, many of these unsustainable practices and models have been exposed through the bear market. Metaverse projects that emerge through this downturn and survive through a couple more web3 cycles will be more likely to thrive and become templates for other new projects to draw inspiration from.

The Metaverse Convergence 08

I was taught that the way of progress was neither swift nor easy.

MARIE CURIE

The CEO of Animoca Brands, Robbie Yung, explained to a crowded room at the Web Summit 2022 that "there is no metaverse without web3, because you need to have that transaction layer so that you have interoperability between content and you can bring it from place to place."[1] He added that virtual reality could be a distraction to the metaverse narrative.

The thesis behind this book is very much the view that true metaverse experience can only be achieved through the next generation of the internet, along with web3 fundamentals. However, we also believe augmented reality and VR are very much part of the journey and definitely not a distraction.

Quite early on in this book we identified three key qualitative elements that a metaverse should ideally build on: experiential, economic, and empowerment. The experiential aspects were covered in Chapter 6 where we discussed the evolution of AR and VR over the years. We also touched upon the challenges of using these technologies and the issues that need to be addressed before VR can go mainstream.

While there are still headwinds and hurdles in getting the right experience of the metaverse, there are other fundamental challenges that we need to address as well, including maturity of the economic models and empowerment. What more needs to be done to create a metaverse which offers not merely immersive experiences, but also provides inclusive incentives and keeps creators at the heart of its economic model? What would be the role of blockchain in this next version of the internet?

A Summary of Friction Points

Before we get into our take on how "the metaverse" will be constructed, let us quickly revisit the fundamental friction points we have with today's internet. In highlighting them, we will also address how they are and/or could be addressed in the new future as we see it.

Centralization

Most internet applications we have today are centralized entities, and they are centralized across two key dimensions that matter. The first is governance, where the rules of the platform are decided; and the second is incentivization, where the value created on the platform is distributed across its stakeholders. Both of these aspects are a challenge with the current internet. Imagine building up a sizable presence on a social media platform such as Twitter, only for the rules of the platform to be changed such that your posts are no longer visible. And now imagine if the algorithm functions like a black box and users have no chance to appeal.

Misaligned incentive is another common risk in many internet applications. Amongst all the stakeholders in your ecosystem, whose interests are you serving? Advertising models on platforms like Meta have long been a key friction point that has raised scrutiny. For platforms such as Meta and Twitter that rely primarily on advertising revenues to sustain operations, it brings forth not only questions around long-term viability, but also incentive structure. Social media is no longer just a tool for entertainment and communication; it is a crucial part of our daily lives and an enabler for how communities are built and sustained. While such tools, employed by millions of people worldwide, are *free* to use, the data generated by the users often becomes the source of monetization for the platform. Remember the old adage, "If you are not paying for the product, then you are the product"? What if we can provide visibility on where data resides, and protect not only the privacy of one's data but the ownership of it? Would this help to shift the power from the platform back to the users and creators, and create a healthier version of social media?

Making the transition will surely be a heavy lift, and one that will take time. But it is heartening to see different efforts being made, including from the likes of Mozilla.[2]

Ownership

We touched upon ownership of data when we discussed centralization earlier in the book. But ownership goes beyond user data. There are other forms of creator content that are being generated on the internet and social media, where this content primarily serves as a revenue engine for centralized entities under most of the current models.

While platforms act as service providers and a conduit to these creators, ownership of the content should ultimately reside with the content creators. Platforms, in this case, can charge a fee to facilitate the delivery of the content. But the ownership of data, the assets, and other forms of content must lie with the creators themselves.

As discussed in previous chapters, creators owning their creatives must become a new business design principle. That will not just serve the digital business models but also real-world use cases like agriculture.

Creator Centricity

The last few years in web3 have demonstrated clearly that creators would create and accrue value, often faster than even business people do. If more businesses base their models around creators owning their content, that could certainly be true. Yet, there are very few instances in today's internet focused around creators with incentives fairly shared with them.

In 2021, Twitter rolled out a product called Super Follows, a subscription-based product that allows fans to see exclusive content from creators whom they pay to support. However, it is unclear how the product has fared and how much creators have been able to benefit from it. Apart from ownership and economic models around creators, value retention is critical as well. For instance, if Roblox decides to upgrade their game version and creators have to redo all their work in the new version, the assets in the old version of Roblox could become worthless, with creators having little to no say over the outcome.

Beyond economics, the new internet would also need to bring a strong empowerment vector. As creators accrue value in an ecosystem, their credentials improve, giving them a power user status. That should be linked directly to economic benefits. We will expand on the empowerment angle later in this chapter through SocialFi principles.

Ecosystem and Community Focus

All three qualitative elements of the metaverse, namely, experiential, economic, and empowerment, rely on a deep community and ecosystem focus. Web3 metaverses can quite easily develop the experiential qualities for their users in a community environment. Bringing together musical concerts, gaming clubs, art events, or just simple chatting with friends within the metaverse, can foster a strong social bond in the virtual space. However, metaverses will also need to enable good economic and empowerment constructs within the ecosystem.

For instance, an art metaverse should provide better economic support to creators of art. Top artists with a huge following would feel more empowered within an art metaverse, as would top gamers within a gaming metaverse. This ecosystem and the community-driven incentives for creators transcends national boundaries as well as real-world social and financial status. Status is no longer limited to being wealthy or well known in the real world. Simply put, if you are a big hitter in a virtual community, you should also have economic and social swag.

As discussed earlier in the book, the principle of empowerment should percolate from digital ecosystems to real-world ecosystems. A farmer who has been serving their community for years shouldn't need to have a bank account and transactions in it to prove their status for a loan. They need to show their credibility within the farming ecosystem where their product has been cultivated and sold at a healthy rate. The banking system must embed itself into this agricultural ecosystem to serve the credible farmer.

Before we proceed further, it is important to summarize the three key qualitative elements of the metaverse that we have discussed in the book so far:

- Experiential: Experience brought about by the convergence of hardware (AR/VR headsets) and software advancements (tools such as Unity and Unreal Engine).
- Economic: Decentralization and inclusive incentives achieved through tokenization and DeFi; identity addressed by NFTs, soulbound tokens, and cryptographic techniques like zero-knowledge proof; and asset ownership and value retention achieved through NFTs.
- Empowerment: Creator empowerment through soulbound tokens and SocialFi models.

While we have discussed most of the above in detail, and given examples in previous chapters, SocialFi is a relatively new trend. This adds interesting elements to creator empowerment.

SocialFi Models

The challenges with web2 social media models have been well documented and discussed, especially in recent years with the rise of misinformation and the lack of transparency around content moderation, the misalignment of incentives, and digital ownership (or lack thereof). User profiles, connections, and the digital content are all locked into the network that the user belongs to—in other words, a walled garden.

Could SocialFi offer a different path forward?

As the name suggests, SocialFi blends together the principles of social media and decentralization. At the heart of the SocialFi movement are platforms with a vision of bringing a decentralized approach to creating and managing content, where the creators and users can have more control of their data and are able to find ways to monetize their engagement.

SocialFi Platforms

There are several organizations that are creating new SocialFi platforms using different design frameworks that keep creators and users at the heart of the entire narrative. A few examples are included below. With the exception of Lens protocol, all the others are backed by a16z crypto, the venture fund from Andreessen Horowitz investing in cryptocurrency companies and protocols:

- Farcaster is a decentralized social network built on top of Ethereum. Its open protocol can support different client applications, and users can move their social identity between each.[3]

- Lens protocol is a composable and decentralized social graph built on the Polygon proof-of-stake blockchain, designed to empower creators to own the links between themselves and their community.[4]

- DeSo, short for decentralized social blockchain, is a layer 1 blockchain built to power storage-heavy applications and decentralize social media.[5]

- Golden is a web3 data startup building a decentralized protocol for knowledge. It is in the testing phase at the time of writing. The startup plans to use public data NFTs and fractional ownership to build value and revenue-sharing rights.[6]

WHAT IS COMPOSABILITY?

Composability is the ability that a platform offers for seamlessly combining existing applications, or their code to create new products. Features like smart contracts, APIs, and software development kit (SDK) allow web3 platforms to be composable.

While all of the above companies are pioneering different approaches to achieving a decentralized social media and content framework, architecturally they all share a common aspect. They are all protocols and not just applications like the previous generation of social media. As protocols, they can support multiple applications and provide a multi-app experience to users. For example, the Lens protocol has grown in leaps and bounds in the first six months since launch, supporting nearly 300 applications and hackathon projects.[7] Some interesting examples include:

- Alps Finance, for social DeFi investing
- ClubSpace, for a live listening party
- Freelansers, for freelancing
- Lensta, for curated feed of images
- Lenster, for micro-blogging
- Lenstube, for video-sharing
- Orb, for professional social media
- Superfun, for meme artists

Perhaps it is by design, but it is hard to miss the functional similarities between some of the popular social sites like Twitter, Instagram, LinkedIn, and their decentralized equivalents. While the user experience could be similar, the infrastructure and the economic layers are designed ground up.

For instance, the DeSo protocol has its own layer 1 blockchain for storing data needed for social media interactions. Whether this blockchain would be able to efficiently handle large files like videos at scale is yet to be seen. However, the optimization that DeSo protocol offers at the layer 1 level should be able to support efficient social media interactions.

Some examples supported by the DeSo protocol include:

- DaoDao, a web3 fundraising platform
- DeSo Messenger, an encrypted messaging platform
- Diamond, a web3 Twitter
- Entre, a web3 professional network
- Mousai, a home for musicians and artists looking to earn in web3
- Pearl, a place for creators to engage and earn with their fans

- ViberHut, a video conferencing platform
- Zirkels, a blogging platform

While Farcaster also supports a suite of applications using the Farcaster protocol, including one that works like Twitter, called the Farcaster, the other applications built on the Farcaster protocol appear to be more focused on making the Farcaster application experience better rather than enriching the application tier.

Design Principles

There are a few design patterns emerging from the rise of SocialFi that are relevant for the metaverse narrative:

- Focus on being a protocol, and not just an application: Creating a social media superapp-like experience by focusing on being a protocol and not just an application can provide users with a lot more flexibility. A move from Twitter to LinkedIn in the new paradigm would no longer require a user to rebuild their connections from scratch, as long as they are within the same ecosystem.
- Cross-chain interoperability: It is clearly too early to think about carrying over network credentials and following from one protocol to another at this stage. But much like cross-chain bridges enabling DeFi transactions across chains, we will likely see cross-chain bridges for SocialFi develop over the next few years.

WHAT IS A CROSS-CHAIN BRIDGE?

A cross-chain bridge helps transfer cryptos from one blockchain to another.

In recent times, we have had several new blockchain ecosystems emerge. Some of them have followed Ethereum and built layer 1 protocols, while others have built layer 2 protocols that would help enhance the functionalities of layer 1 chains.

As a result, developer ecosystems have emerged across each of these blockchains, and as decentralized applications are launched on these blockchains, users start accumulating cryptos. If a user has accumulated Ethereum, but wants to transfer those tokens onto the Solana blockchain, they would need a cross-chain bridge like Wormhole bridge.

Without a cross-chain bridge, crypto currencies would have to be moved to a centralized exchange, where Ethereum could be exchanged for Solana (or any crypto within the Solana network), and the Solana bought could be moved into the Solana wallets.

- Creator centricity: The ability to move social media following from one application to another within a protocol gives users control of their following. In addition, data analytics applications that query protocols enable users to see precisely the type of content that resonates with their network. Unlike Twitter and LinkedIn, users are not at the mercy of the applications to tell them what they can see about their data and what they cannot.

- Finite state to infinite state blockchains: While mainstream blockchains struggle to handle large volumes of data, for web3 to scale beyond DeFi apps, which have a much lower number of transactions, we need a blockchain that can handle infinite-state applications such as decentralized SocialFi, with much larger amounts of data that needs to be stored, indexed, and queried. The cost of storing on-chain for the DeSo protocol is much cheaper compared to Ethereum and Solana.

- Soulbound tokens: As mentioned earlier in the book, soulbound tokens (SBTs) are NFTs that are sent to the wallets of users to mark the credentials of a user and affiliation to a community. Unlike mainstream NFTs, they cannot be transferred from one wallet to another. For instance, as web3 apps providing a LinkedIn-style professional network go mainstream, organizations can drop an SBT into their employees' wallets on the network, allowing the network to verify if the wallet owner is really who they claim to be. A soulbound credit score system is another use case for SBTs, to expand opportunities for DeFi users and enable them to build credit and get loans. For example, Masa Finance not only enables users to build web3 identity, it can also provide a credit score computed from the user's web3 activities on the Ethereum blockchain and the real world.[8]

- Social tokens: Last but not least, social tokens are a concept that is particularly being pioneered by the DeSo protocol. These tokens are associated with the profiles of creators and social media influencers, and the price is often indicative of their social influence within that ecosystem. Followers who want to interact with the content of an influencer must own the social token of the influencer. As the creator grows in stature within an ecosystem, the value of their social tokens increases as there will be more followers buying their token to interact with their content.

Social tokens represent the third tier of tokenomics that has emerged from web3, with governance tokens being the first tier and utility tokens the second. It is important to note that social tokens are still early in their lifecycle and the precise mechanism of valuations and exchanges is still unclear. However, as this space matures, the protocol and application ecosystem should develop with more clarity.

All of these elements above that are being built within the SocialFi ecosystem are focused more on the creators and less on the platforms and protocols. As creators become more empowered socially and financially through these systems, that lays the foundations for the internet of the future—the metaverse.

The Metaverse Convergence

This is the moment we have been building up to—the real metaverse experience and what it would feel like. To summarize, here are the fundamental building blocks of the metaverse:

- experience (AR/VR)
- engagement (GameFi models)
- economics (DeFi applications)
- empowerment (SocialFi applications)

All of the above will largely be built on blockchain rails, using fungible and non-fungible tokens to achieve the economics, identity, and credentialing aspects of the ecosystem.

Let's run through the scenarios of what a user may encounter in the gaming metaverse:

1 Onboarding:

   a The user must be able to sign up to a metaverse experience just as they would to any web2 application, using their email, Google, or apple login.

   b A web3 wallet tied to their email address could be created on sign-up without the user having to know or think about their private keys.

   c The user enters the experience with a VR/AR headset on. As the onboarding process continues, the user could be asked to choose from and customize a few avatars.

   d More experienced users must be able to connect their wallets and choose the NFT they want to use as their avatar in the metaverse.

   e The metaverse creates a 3D version of the avatar in real time, and the user starts exploring the environment.

2 The immersive experience:

   a The metaverse has various elements, including hardcore gaming portals, casual gaming experiences, a bulletin board for the events, multiple event venues, an asset marketplace, a metaverse advice center, and a creator hub.

   b The user can choose to play hardcore games by entering one of the portals in their NFT avatars.

   c This experience will further expand by offering the user a view of their status in the game, their game assets, the value of the in-game assets, and their battle pass details.

   d The user can choose to play the game or enter a leaderboard competition within the game to win game tokens.

   e The wins could also deliver soulbound tokens to the user, pushing them within the top 5 percentile of the game players.

f The user goes to the asset marketplace and buys a new weapon that they have been saving up for weeks. The user also chooses to sell some of their existing weapons and armor that they feel are no longer needed.

3 Other casual experiences:

a The user exits the portal and plays some casual games while ordering food within the virtual environment.

b While waiting for the food to arrive, the user wants to better understand how their recent win has helped their status in the ecosystem.

4 Convergence of DeFi and SocialFi:

a The user goes to the metaverse advice center where they check that they have earned a new role in the ecosystem through the game victory. The win now gives them an NFT that offers them access to two special gated clubs.

b The user collects the NFT and heads towards the first club.

c Using the NFT, the user gains access to the first club, where an advisor is waiting for him. The advisor provides the user insights into the games in the ecosystem that offer them the advantages in building their profile. The advisor also looks at all the DeFi services within the metaverse that would offer the best returns for the user's in-game assets. They also advise the user on the risks associated with each of those DeFi options.

d The second private club that the user gains access to gives them free access to all airport lounges in the world. The user is delighted, and collects the lounge access pass that instantly gets added to their wallet.

e The user chooses the DeFi application suggested by the advisor and obtains a good rate of return to deposit their assets there.

f The food gets delivered at the gamer's real-world address. After a good few hours spent within the metaverse, the user takes a well-deserved break.

There are also a few other scenarios not depicted above. For example:

1 The user can move their assets across ecosystems or even metaverses.

2 If the user has a big following, they can launch their social token.

3 The marketing team can approach the user and invite them to be a gaming ambassador by virtue of their credentials in the metaverse.

4 The user can leverage the creator hub in the metaverse to build their own experiences that others can use through low-code technologies.

The above is a set of experiences in the metaverse, the building blocks of which are all already in progress. It is also worth noting that all these experiences are possible while keeping the real-world identity of the gamer completely anonymous.

Similar experiences can be drawn out for metaverses focused on art, education, and more. However, the more formal a metaverse context becomes, the more the link will be between their real-world and virtual identities. In essence, top contributors, content creators, and developers participate in the ecosystem, add value, earn ecosystem credentials, and convert those credentials into virtual and real-world assets. Something to note is that perks that users gain within the metaverse can also have real-world relevance. But only by integrating virtual and real-world experiences can the metaverse narrative scale.

What About the Big Techs?

This brings us to the topic of the big technology companies, the titans of web2, if you will. What role will they play in this future version of the internet?

The biggest advantage that such players have is the sheer scale that they enjoy. Take Google, for example. The company has come a long way, and it has shaped our digital world in ways that we never thought would be possible. From the humble beginnings of a search engine with an original server housed in LEGO bricks,[9] Google now has a vast array of services available to and used by billions of people worldwide personally and professionally.[10]

So What Would Google's Entry into the Metaverse Look Like?

For one, Google is not new to the concept of the convergence of digital and physical reality. Google Glass (or simply, Glass) was launched in 2014 with much fanfare. Unfortunately, the product did not live up to its hype and Google pivoted the wearable to a different version focused for enterprise customers. While there were multiple challenges with the initial prototype, ultimately it came down to privacy and security concerns of the wearable itself and its lack of utility. Imagine wearing a built-in camera that could be recording or taking a photo at any time. What problem was the product actually solving and what benefits did it offer to consumers with an instant feed from the internet right in front of your eyes (literally), at a $1,500 price point?

While Google was not able to find success with the earlier consumer version of Google Glass, the subsequent Google Glass Enterprise Edition 2 fared far better. The lighter-weight design is packed with high processing power, enabling developers to incorporate computer vision and machine learning into the glasses. In addition to speech recognition, users can also control the wearables via built-in touch sensors. The wearable can also translate language in real time. But, perhaps most importantly, those wearing the glasses can share what they see with others via live stream, making it easy to collaborate with coworkers on complex tasks, solving a real workplace challenge where it is becoming increasingly common for teams to work in decentralized locations.

Remember how we mentioned in Chapter 6 on real use cases as being one of the critical factors for success for new technology innovations? If Google can continue to build on the momentum for the Google Glass business needs and evolve real-world applications, it might have found a pathway into the future of mixed reality.

Google is, of course, far from being the only tech giant pursuing the potential of the next iteration of the internet. Facebook went to lengths to rebrand itself as Meta, in a bid to become a prominent voice in trying to shape the future of the metaverse.

Will Meta Revolutionize the Metaverse?

In late 2021 Facebook, the social media giant, decided to change its name to Meta, as a signal of its commitment to the metaverse, a composite universe melding online, virtual, and augmented worlds that people can seamlessly traverse.[11] Interestingly, according to Oxford University Press's research, usage of the term metaverse "increased almost fourfold from the previous year in the Oxford Corpus," driven in part by Facebook's rebranding to Meta.[12]

With powerful smartphones being ubiquitous, powering the transition from desktop to mobile internet, what will be the future version of devices that can help us further transition to the metaverse?

Perhaps it should not be too surprising that much of Meta's investment since the branding change has been focused on virtual reality headsets: Meta Quest 2 and its pricier Meta Quest Pro (for the enterprise market). In late December 2022, Meta announced the acquisition of Luxexcel, a smart eyewear company headquartered in the Netherlands that specializes in 3D-printing prescription lenses for smart glasses.[13]

While Horizon Worlds, Meta's social VR platform, was opened to the public at the end of 2021, it has so far failed to gain significant traction. While Meta's social media products, including Facebook, Instagram, and WhatsApp, attract more than 3.5 billion average monthly users combined, Horizon Worlds has reportedly gained fewer than 200,000 monthly active users.[14] Steep price point for the hardware can certainly be one contributing factor; lack of an economic model for creators is likely another. Without incentives in place for creators to help build out the metaverse with engaging content to attract and retain users, it will be hard to envision the next billion-user virtual world.

Can Apple Lead the Revolution?

We can't talk about the role of big tech in the future world without talking about Apple, which has played an outsized role in how we use technology in our day-to-day lives. The iPhone, which was first released in 2007, has spawned new industry verticals and countless new businesses. It has quickly become an integral part of how we live and work, acting like a Swiss Army knife for every facet of our lives. We no longer have to carry a camera, a Walkman or mp3 player, a planner, or a watch separately. We read our news, check our emails, connect with our friends and colleagues, navigate the city, order a ride-share, shop for a present, pay bills, and transfer money, all via the portable device which packs more computing power than many laptops. It is no wonder that adults in the US check their phones 352 times a day on average.[15]

Playing to the brand's strength, we would imagine an Apple product with hyper focus on user experience, with an array of capabilities to complement the vast iOS ecosystem. Irrespective of whether it would be a mixed reality eyewear or an AR/VR headset, it will be interesting to see if Apple can help nudge more users into the metaverse.

Microsoft's Entry into the Metaverse

So far, we have been focused primarily on the consumer market. What if the workplace is the next holy grail? How does Microsoft, the productivity powerhouse, plan to shape the future of work? Microsoft's entry into the metaverse appears to be twofold. Eyeing the massive opportunity in the gaming market, Microsoft has been making waves by acquiring companies and content to help develop the gaming ecosystem for Xbox.

Beyond gaming, the tech giant is also seeking to extend the capability of Microsoft Teams and its suite of Microsoft 365 applications with the partnership announcement with Meta Quest devices. Through this collaboration, Microsoft seeks to deliver immersive experiences for the future of work and play, and to enable people to connect and collaborate as though they are together in person. One of the low-hanging use cases is new employee onboarding. With its extensive existing ecosystem of corporate partners, it is not hard to imagine Microsoft playing a key role in this future version of the work internet.

A CONVERSATION WITH DARAGH MORRISSEY, DIRECTOR DATA AND AI, WORLDWIDE FINANCIAL SERVICES, MICROSOFT

Lens into the future:

On getting started: Given the changes in the past few years, more employees have been able to realize the benefits of working from home. So more companies are trying to figure out how to create a hybrid workplace that can provide flexibility, drive more engagement, and allow choices for their employees. Things such as hosting company events, onboarding new employees, or conducting classroom-based training are great use cases for banks to explore.

On avatars: We have learned that appearing on video on back-to-back calls can generate fatigue, and avatars can help reduce the mental overhead of seeing yourself on video. The key is to make it optional for participants, so they can choose to use them if they want to. Some companies also like the use of avatars during video interviews to reduce unconscious bias and make the hiring process more inclusive.

On devices: At Microsoft, our vision for the metaverse is to make it an inclusive space and accessible to everyone. To get to a full virtual reality experience for mass adoption, it will need to be done on devices that are lighter, cheaper, and more affordable to everyone. We are enabling access to the metaverse across all device form factors. How are you going to bring everyone along? We also need to address the issue of trust: Can consumers trust the environment they will be in?

Banking in the metaverse:

On the evolution of branches: Let's think about how banking has evolved. A long time ago, we started with just branches. Then we added ATMs to the branches. After that, we added websites for internet banking, followed by mobile banking apps. So you might ask, do you still need a physical branch in the real world? Maybe not for day-to-day retail banking. But for small businesses and certain scenarios, you still need to have a branch.

On the future of banking: In the metaverse, it's not about whether or not there is a bank branch for customers to go to. It will be more about what scenario you want to address. Would the metaverse act as a contact center on steroids? Could technology offer a more immersive way for human advisors and relationship managers to engage with their clients, and a chance for organizations to scale to new market segments with more personalized and empathetic connections?

Key takeaways:

- Why should we care about kids and Roblox? Ask yourself a simple question: What is your brand, and where are you going to be in this conversation? I bank with a main street bank, but my kid doesn't know what that is. So, as a bank, you have to be ready to be able to win them over and engage with them as they get older.

- How do you bring the technology to everyone, regardless of what device they are on?

- The move to the metaverse will be more of an evolution than a revolution, and many of the elements are in place today.

The Best is Yet to Come

The future of the internet is certainly interesting, to say the least, with innovation happening at all corners of the ecosystem. Key challenges such as scalability still need to be overcome, especially with SocialFi, which is still in its infancy. However, there is undoubtedly great potential for the future of decentralized platforms and creator centricity.

In the next chapter, we will go into more detail on the next dimension of the metaverse: creating sustainable economic models.

Community   09

Community is the new commodity; attention is the new currency.

A community is commonly defined as a unified body of individuals with a common characteristic or shared interest living together within a larger society. The word was first used in the 14th century. While the concept of community existed way back in ancient times, the Neolithic Revolution, also referred to as the Agricultural Revolution, marked a major turning point in human history where the previously nomadic hunter-gatherers began to domesticate animals and cultivate plants, enabling them to establish permanent settlements instead of roaming and foraging for food.[1] When communities began to grow, civilizations flourished, bringing about religion and culture. Such human evolution also signified economic revolution, as different social and economic classes emerged, enabled by a complex web of labor and the emergence of different professions from farmers, fishers, traders, and builders, to religious leaders, artists, scholars, and political leaders.

Throughout history, interconnectedness has been a hallmark of community. But think about how communities have evolved and how far we have come along—from enclaves and tribes that are geographically driven, to digital nomads that transcend physical boundaries. And we are more connected than ever, not by bridges made of steel, concrete, stone, and asphalt, but by bits and bytes via data pipes buried deep under the sea and across continents.

Regardless of how communities are formed, one thing remains constant: technology is the means to an end. From analog to digital and beyond, we are closer together than ever before.

Community is the New Commodity

At the heart of it, web2 and web3 are built for one thing in common: community. While the way the economic models are constructed might be different, ultimately, it is about bringing communities together. From gaming and social networking to enterprise collaboration and productivity tools, community is the heart of what makes it work and ultimately drives adoption and success.

Consider the big social networks such as Facebook (now Meta), Instagram, LinkedIn, Twitter, YouTube, and TikTok. What attracts users and what brings them back on a regular basis? Similarly for gaming platforms such as Roblox and Fortnight, and countless others before them. People won't flock to an empty digital townsquare regardless of bells and whistles; they spend a significant amount of time there because they want to interact with other like-minded people, and consume content created by those who share common interests.

A great example is YouTube, which was launched in 2005 and acquired by Google for $1.65 billion in late 2006. Over 2.5 billion people access the video streaming app once a month, generating $28.8 billion in 2021, a 46 percent increase on 2020 figures.[2]

Similarly for Discord, a social platform that allows you to communicate with others via text, voice and video chat, as well as join different Discord servers with special interest communities. While the early days of Discord were dominated by gamers, it has grown beyond those roots, with 78 percent of its 150 million monthly active users indicating that they use Discord for non-gaming activities.[3]

But beyond spending money purchasing different items and digital assets, people also spend their time on these platforms engaging in online activities, commenting, and helping to spread the word and grow the communities. Such network effect is helpful not only for social networking sites, it's also instrumental for the growth of digital content streaming sites such as Netflix, which logged 223 million paid subscribers worldwide as of the third quarter of 2022.[4]

Taking the concept of community to the next level is Mastodon, a decentralized social network built on open web protocols, made up of independent servers organized around different themes, geographic locations, topics, or interests. Each server has its own administrator and governance, and users interact with other instances in an interconnected community called the Fediverse, regardless of which instance they reside in. While Mastodon was founded in 2016, it has gained immense attention since October 2022 after Elon Musk bought Twitter.

Since inception, the microblogging network has relied on user donation to keep up with server maintenance. Interestingly, Pawoo, operated from Japan since 2017 and one of the largest Mastodon instances, was acquired by a web3 firm, Mask Network.[5] With about 800,000 users, Pawoo has drawn users from all over the world including illustrators, anime fans, novelists, and music enthusiasts. It remains to be seen how this might change the dynamics and economic model of the federated network.

Most of the firms and products described above have been focused on building a community around their products. They roll out their product, have a clear community management strategy, and go on executing the strategy to achieve the much admired "network effect." However, with the advent of web3 brands, often community comes first. Projects declare their vision and the narrative around their brand. In doing so, they attract a following from users with whom the vision and the brand language resonate. Product often comes after this.

As described in Chapter 7, founders spend a substantial amount of time building their communities through platforms like Discord, Twitter, and Telegram. They run "ask me anything" sessions and Twitter spaces to engage continuously with their community even before the product, product strategy, and business models are developed and published. Entrepreneurs like Ryan Carson and Frank Degods (founder of DeGods NFT collection) have successfully built communities that rally behind them even before their product.

In a web3 context, this also becomes a necessary tweak to the way founders approach the community build out. Many projects these days start with announcing what their vision is, followed by a community-building effort through growth hacks and engagement exercises. This is shortly followed by an NFT launch, where the community rallies behind. The better the founder and the community are in grabbing attention, the faster it grows. Once the NFT is rolled out, most project insights are gated exclusively for the holders. The rest of the followers of the project would typically hear any project or business announcements much later than the NFT holders.

Projects like Proof Collective and DeGods have exclusive giveaways through collaborations for their NFT holders. New NFT mints that only NFT holders can participate in are a common model to offer the much-needed "alpha" that communities demand these days. With all these community-building exercises, drawing attention and building a brand following often takes center stage. Product often comes only after this stage.

Some communities like Okay Bears have been able to keep their community together for almost a year, without any product strategy. These firms have built a cult following to their brand language, and plan to tap into that brand equity for revenue opportunities. This is often done through partnerships with physical products like merchandise, wearables, and even food products. The expectation is that these firms can expand their brand presence beyond the virtual world, and become household names. Therefore, if product was a means to achieve a community during the previous wave of innovation from the dot-com era, the community is the means to achieve brand and product in the new wave of innovation led by web3 founders across the world.

While community is the new commodity, attention is the new currency. Regardless of the business, one fundamental question remains: What motivates communities to stick around? As brands scale, what's in it for the communities, the founders, the creators, and the brands, you may ask? This is where the web3 ethos comes into play.

Unlocking New Opportunities For Impact

For technology to gain wide adoption, it needs to be more than just technology for technology's sake. Leveraging technology for good for new use cases and solving new problems is just as important. Beyond gaming, nothing portrays passion and community more than the impact space. And we can look toward some recent developments from the United Nations Development Program, as well as the global community of developers, for inspiration when it comes to the potential of web3.

The 2030 Agenda for Sustainable Development, adopted by all United Nations Member States in 2015, provides a shared blueprint for peace and prosperity for people and the planet, now and into the future. At its heart are the 17 Sustainable Development Goals (SDGs), which act as a call for action by all countries—developed and developing—in a global partnership.[6] Could the new technology paradigm provide us with a more effective means of cross-border aid disbursement and collaboration, enabling a wider range of people to benefit from the new asset class?

GoodDollar

GoodDollar is a community-driven, distributed framework designed to generate, fund, and distribute universal basic income as a public good via the GoodDollar token (G$), an ERC-20 digital asset built on the Ethereum blockchain.[7] The idea of the bottom-up approach (as opposed to trickle-down economics) is fairly straightforward. Every day, a quantity of G$ is minted and distributed as basic income to verified users. G$ token is an automated-market maker, backed by a monetary reserve of additional cryptocurrency(ies). The value in the reserve backing G$ is generated by supporters (known as stakers) who deposit capital to decentralized third-party protocols and direct their earnings to support the GoodDollar ecosystem. As new value is added to the reserve, G$ coins are minted, which are used to pay out liquidity mining rewards to supporters and G$ to those making daily basic income claims.[8]

In addition to receiving social rewards in the form of Social Annual Percentage Return, these stakers are also included in regular distributions of GOOD governance tokens, which gives them membership in the GoodDAO, and thus a voice in the future direction of the GoodDollar economy.

Apart from the stakers and those who claim UBI in G$, merchants who accept G$ in exchange for goods and services are also a vital part of the GoodDollar economy, in order to help stimulate retail demand.

According to stats from GoodDollar, they have distributed $360,000 for over 485,000 claimers since launch in September 2020.[9]

Gitcoin

Gitcoin is a global community of builders and creators who start, fund, and scale different open source projects. According to Gitcoin, since its launch in November 2017 the community has facilitated almost 3.5 million transactions to over 11,000 unique earners, bringing about over $72.8 million funding for open source software, in the form of bounties, tips, grants, and more.[10] Developers can place a bounty and delegate work to developer and designer Gitcoiners in the community; they can also submit their own web3 project ideas and crowdsource funding (grants) from contributing donors on the platform.

While developers often contribute to open source projects with little to no compensation, Gitcoin was created to change the status quo by compensating developers who want to contribute to public goods projects through community-funded grants and bounties for the web3 ecosystem. With more programs like this and at scale, such a paradigm shift can change the way we drive innovations by harnessing the power of network effects.

ReSeed

In Chapter 2, we wrote about how web3 changes the future of trade and the dynamics between the creator (e.g., farmers and artists) and consumer of value. Another interesting opportunity using web3 as an enabler for farmers centers around climate action and regenerative economies. ReSeed, based in Wyoming, USA, is a community-based suite of tools that verifies and provides ongoing direct revenue based on measurable current carbon stocks managed by small-scale farmers around the world. The network works with over 8,000 small farm partners who manage over two million metric tons of carbon stock worldwide, by helping them inventory and map the carbon stock they currently hold and manage, and turning them into carbon protection and removal credits to be sold.[11] The tokenized carbon can be linked with live satellite imagery of the farms and verified by AI, bringing traceability and insights to the market. In addition, smaller bundles of carbon can be sold to individual investors and family offices instead of just large institutions and professional investors, thereby expanding the opportunities to everyday investors.

The end goal for ReSeed is to increase revenue for small regenerative farmers and incentivize them to draw down legacy carbon from the atmosphere. The marketplace also provides an opportunity for buyers to bring capital to the ecosystem and to reduce their carbon footprint. According to ReSeed, these farmers have been able to double their family income through the partnership.[12]

Regen Network

Another interesting player in the climate financing and carbon market is Regen Network, which aims to build a foundational fintech infrastructure for ecological claims and data. With its marketplace, institutions and government entities can buy, sell, and retire tokenized carbon on the blockchain for carbon offsetting purposes.

Regen ecocredits are designed and managed by a decentralized community. These tokens are issued according to the criteria set within each Credit Class on Regen Ledger and listed for sale in the marketplace. They can be purchased by anyone interested in offsetting their carbon footprint and having a positive climate impact.[13] In 2020, for example, Regen sold and retired over 120,000 CarbonPlus Grasslands credits to Microsoft on the Regen Network blockchain.[14]

Separately, the network also launched the Regen Ecosystem Fund, which focuses on strategic early-stage investments to stimulate the adoption of Regen Ledger and $REGEN token.[15]

Stellar

The UN Refugee Agency, along with Stellar Development Foundation, launched a pilot first-of-its-kind blockchain payment solution for "digital cash distribution to internally displaced persons (IDPs) and other war-affected people in Ukraine."[16] The project, done in coordination with the United Nations International Computing Centre (UNICC), seeks to disperse aid (US Dollar Coin) into the hands of those who need it quickly and transparently, and without the need for bank accounts or credit or debit cards. The recipients can then convert the coins to US dollars, euros, or other local currencies, and withdraw them at MoneyGram locations.

If successful, the pilot can pave the way for humanitarian aid to be dispersed for other countries.

Since the space is still evolving, many of these use cases and economic models will likely continue to evolve. As the new technology paradigm continues to unfold, we will be able to create new innovation ecosystems and unlock new ways of creating a positive impact on our society.

A CONVERSATION WITH DR MARTHA BOECKENFELD, DEAN AND PARTNER, METAVERSE ACADEMY

Lens into the future:

What is the metaverse? Trying to define the metaverse is akin to trying to define the internet when the internet wasn't there. At this stage, the metaverse is still a vision. While the technology components such as artificial intelligence and blockchain are not new, convergence of these technologies is novel and still evolving.

What are the opportunities? In this future vision of the internet, the immersive virtual world and the real world will be interconnected and the ecosystems interoperable. Imagine being able to leverage such technologies for education, giving others a chance to gain expertise that they otherwise couldn't attain.

What are the challenges? While the technology is developing exponentially, regulators are not keeping up. The ecosystem is also fragmented, with each jurisdiction doing something different, bringing in different experience and expertise.

Predicting the unpredictable future:
With the proper hardware, experience, and use case, the metaverse can connect and empower a multi-generational global community. Platforms such as Roblox are no longer just a gaming platform, but a social platform. This will be the key to success in the future: Brands cannot just have presence in the metaverse but without interactions and meaningful engagements. What is the ultimate experience you want to create for your customers, and why do they want to stay?

Drivers and Enablers

While we have touched on the importance of communities, and the central role they play in the viability and long-term success of a business, it is important to understand the drivers of these communities.

When we think of brand communities in technology, Apple is likely one of the ones that has the most loyal customers. According to Marketing Charts, it is the most valuable brand in 2022, beating out the likes of Amazon, Domino's, Disney+, and TikTok.[17] Not only do Apple customers buy from the big tech firm, but they are also actively engaged and emotionally invested. Their customers are some of the most fierce advocates for the brand. Apple's relatively high net promoter score (NPS) compared to its peers (such as Amazon and Google) also puts it in the top-performing brands when it comes to customer loyalty.[18] Developed in 2003, the NPS is a metric used to gauge brand loyalty and is often considered a crucial measure for customer experience. Apple's focus on brand community also helps to set it apart from its competitors. Apple users, for example, have their own customer communities where users can turn to each other for help. These forums also act as social spaces where members, experts, and brand evangelists around the globe connect with each other. Apple also has an Apple Community+ program, where it collaborates with a small group of contributors.

When it comes to community and user engagement, another great brand with a loyal following is LEGO. Founded in Billund, Denmark in 1932 by Ole Kirk Kristiansen, the global enterprise has come a long way over the past 90 years, growing from a small carpenter's workshop to one of the world's largest manufacturers of toys.[19] It has evolved with time and grown with its audience, from extending gameplay with robotics and AR/VR immersive experiences, to building out exclusive sets for different demographics beyond children. In fact, "enthusiasm to all ages" is one of LEGO's ten characteristics that are core to its development throughout the years.[20]

LEGO tugs at the heart of what powers a brand and what energizes its communities. LEGO Ideas, for example, encourages fans to share their creations, enter challenges, and showcase their proposals for new LEGO Ideas sets, with a chance for their creation to become a real LEGO set. LEGO fans around the world have set up their own communities to share ideas and commentary on new LEGO announcements and sets. BrickFair, for example, is a well-attended multi-day LEGO fan convention and expo in North America, and it is run by fans for fans.

So it should not come as a surprise that, in 2022, LEGO announced a partnership with Epic Games "to build an immersive, creatively inspiring and engaging digital experience for kids of all ages to enjoy together."[21] Such strategy is in line with what has guided the LEGO brand through the years. In the previous chapter, we talked about the building blocks needed to facilitate the convergence of physical and digital worlds. At the time of writing, not much is known about the extent of this partnership and what products and services would be rolled out. However, by choosing Epic Games, the creator of Unreal Engine, which powers popular video games including Fortnite Battle Royale and Gears of War, LEGO is making clear its intention to play a dominant role in shaping the future of play.

Imagine a battle between mini-figures that can be extended from the physical (brick) world into the metaverse; or a quest to collect gems in different minifigures packs that would allow you to unlock exclusive hidden worlds in the digital realm, or transport your avatar between metaverses and earn rewards on the way.

The sky—with its bits and bytes—is no longer the limit.

A CONVERSATION WITH KRIS FOK, WEB3 AND CRYPTO LEAD

While it is still a nascent space, the metaverse ecosystem is quickly developing. What geographic regions demonstrate the most potential and why?

The West undoubtedly commanded most of the market coverage a year or two previously, but the tables are starting to turn. Asia shows the most potential for metaverse development. The metaverse craze has swept over the Asia-Pacific region, especially in gaming. Asia makes up the most prominent player/user base and has the most active investors in the world.

Many Asian firms across different sectors have also started experimenting with use cases in the metaverse. From K-pop concerts to e-commerce and social media platforms, these are just the tip of the iceberg. We are also seeing giants like Tencent, Lenovo, Sony, HTC, and many more investing billions of money, fueling a new wave of technology development in the metaverse.

The awareness is high, and the adoption rate is increasing in the region.

What are some of the challenges the ecosystem will face in the next three to five years? What are the greatest opportunities?

Technically speaking, *metaverse* still doesn't exist yet. The virtual worlds we have now are just a couple of gated communities. Don't get me wrong, it is a great start, but the real metaverse is not quite there yet and probably won't be very soon. Interoperability is the key to the virtual world, as the metaverse is about building and connecting many virtual worlds together. However, now, it is difficult to connect them. The worlds are not interoperable, hindering the metaverse development's growth and creating barriers for new users.

And beyond the virtual worlds, another problem that limits the full potential of the whole development would be the infrastructure gap. Emerging markets consist of over one-third of the world's population but not everyone can afford to be "connected." The metaverse cannot be developed to its full potential if we do not address the issue of internet inclusion in emerging markets. The whole point is about interoperability, no matter if it is inside the virtual world or in real life.

But it is ok, as Rome wasn't built in a day.

There might be specific industries on which the metaverse has more impact and opportunities, like gaming. Still, the most significant opportunity is changing how businesses operate across different sectors.

The immersive experience will revolutionize what and how goods are served, no matter whether you are a bank, a luxury brand, or a conference. Yes, of course, customers still enjoy in-person service. Still, the great thing about metaverse is it can happen anywhere, anytime, with even more "wow" and personalized elements that only the 3D world can provide. Let me take the car company as an example. Customers can visit car showrooms, do simulated test drives, or even customize their dream car in the metaverse, which is nearly impossible in real life. And this whole experience creates interaction and deepens the connection to the brand.

Even more, the brand can build a community that allows its users to interact with others who share the same values and interests. And community is what makes it interesting and sticky! I am looking forward to seeing how metaverse changes customer interaction and needs in the future.

Is that the reason behind the name change, from Finnovasia to Finoverse, as well, to capitalize on the movement and opportunities?
Finnovasia was founded in 2015 and has been at the cutting edge of fintech innovation in Asia for the past seven years. However, we are at an inflection point—many of the first wave of fintech innovations are now industry standards. Today innovators are exploring AI and web3— and their building blocks from metaverse to blockchain.

To reflect this, we updated ourselves and announced a new brand: Finoverse.

Our new name reflects both the scaling up of our focus on web3 technologies and our ambition to become a company with global reach. From our headquarters in Hong Kong, we are now engaged in large-scale events in the Middle East, our home in the Greater Bay Area, and a fresh event in the Bahamas in late 2023. We are proud to call Hong Kong our home. But web3 is borderless. Our goal is to bring connectivity to the companies and individuals developing web3 solutions, bringing them into a wider conversation with established players and regulators.

We are proud of our achievements and the role we continue to play in the development of this remarkable industry. As part of this, we introduced Finoverse Impact, our ESG and community engagement program. We partner with high-profile NGOs and use our global events to raise awareness and engagement to help them achieve their ambitions.

At Finoverse we know fintech is about people: creative, curious, and passionate people. The only constant is the human factor. And the communities we have formed in the world's fintech centers of excellence—Hong Kong, Dubai, Greater Bay Area, Abu Dhabi, and beyond. Extraordinary times call for fresh thinking, new ideas, and opportunities to share and exchange. So we can build the future of finance together. As we embark on this next chapter we are excited to see what future will emerge.

The Fuel Powering Communities

Beyond having common interests (as in the case of LEGO Ideas) or as a badge of honor, what motivates and empowers the community, especially those driven by fans and their loyalty for the brand? What drives passion and engagement, and sustains growth?

Monetary Incentives

Does money make the world go round? Would incentives drive brand loyalty and innovation? Some big players certainly think so. YouTube, for example, announced a change to their Partner Program that will allow creators to earn money from ads viewed between videos in the Shorts Feed.[22]

And, as mentioned in an earlier chapter, Roblox also has a revenue-sharing model for the game developers. According to Roblox's "developer economics," 3.4 million creators and developers earned Robux during September 2022; and on average, Roblox pays developers 29 cents per in-experience dollar spent.[23] Robux are earned from each transaction in the experiences built by the developer, and via the sale of virtual avatar items in the Marketplace. There are also additional incentives based on engagement—the share of time a

Premium subscriber spends in the experience—as a way to reward engaging experiences, powered by user-generated content. With over 50 million active daily users on the platform, Roblox provides a powerful example of how a hyper focus on "creation by community" can fuel exponential growth and innovation.

Shared Passion and Professional Experiences

Another obvious example of community is one where members share common backgrounds and professional experiences.

The Mastercard Artist Accelerator, for example, is a new web3 collective designed to connect musicians, creators, and fans. The program aims to help emerging artists build and own their brand through web3 experiences, connect with mentors, and grow their music communities.[24]

Shared Purpose

Building a community that lasts takes intentional effort. A key ingredient for a successful community is something that can bind people together: A shared purpose.

As humans, we aspire to be part of something bigger than ourselves. We want to belong and we want to be accepted. Having a shared purpose can help to drive the sense of belonging and identity, and unite people from different walks of life. Volunteers, for example, gain a sense of satisfaction and belonging from connecting with other volunteers who share the same aspirations and beliefs. They are energized and motivated by the organization that they serve.

In the web3 world, DAOs are changing the way that communities operate. With no single centralized authority, members of a DAO have the right to vote on issues such as what to build and how money is spent, thereby shaping the direction of the organization that they serve. For example, the Women Build Web3 DAO is a global collective of women and non-binary developers learning and building in web3, that aims to build the next wave of web3 builders through education, opportunities, and funding.[25] According to their white paper, the Women Build Web3 DAO collaborates closely with

Developer DAO as a "sister" DAO, and the community is united in their passion to make the web more equitable, accessible, and transparent and to bring the power back to individuals.[26]

Another interesting community joined by common purpose and interest is OMA3, the Consortium DAO, a collaboration of web3 metaverse platform creators. The DAO includes notable brands such as Animoca Brands, Dapper Labs, The Sandbox, and Decentraland, with the goal of ensuring an open metaverse, where virtual land, digital assets, ideas, and services are interoperable between platforms and transparent to all communities.[27] The guiding principles of OMA3 are built around a vision of user-centricity that is the hallmark of web3 world, and include the big themes of decentralization, user ownership, and inclusivity.

A CONVERSATION WITH WINCIE WONG, HEAD OF SERVICES WORKFORCE TECHNICAL CAPABILITY, NATWEST GROUP

What are some of the biggest challenges when it comes to attracting and retaining diverse talent to the financial services industry?
One of the biggest challenges we face is that perceptions of people working in technology begin from a young age. According to a study by PWC UK, just 27 percent of the A-level and university-age females surveyed were interested in careers in technology, compared to 62 percent of males—while only 3 percent of females cited technology as their first-choice career. In a study NatWest commissioned with Code First Girls, only 9 percent of respondents said they were encouraged to go into technology because of good IT teaching and curriculum. Three-quarters of those polled weren't encouraged to pursue a career in technology at all. To overcome these perceptions, active work needs to be done to start showcasing and role modeling the huge variety of creative tech roles that are available. This is why NatWest is a strategic partner with the Tech She Can charity, which is working with over 250 member organizations to provide free learning materials to be used by teachers and parents to inspire young people about a future career in technology.

NatWest Group is a relationship bank for a digital world and we are building financial confidence for our 19 million customers across the UK.

Technology and the people behind it are crucial to help us achieve this. Recruiting and retaining staff skilled in tech and data from a diverse talent pool is an important part of delivering the technology solutions and services our customers need. In order to attract and retain diverse talent, there needs to be role modeling to show that there are successful senior leaders in the organization who embrace the diversity and differences in their workforce and demonstrate it as a critical part of its purpose and commercial strategy.

Do you think we'll face the same challenges when it comes to hiring for non-traditional roles or emerging/newer tech areas in financial services (e.g., AI, blockchain, digital assets, and metaverse)?
It becomes more difficult to hire for these new tech areas as there are even fewer people working in the space and technology that is not yet widely adopted. There are therefore fewer role models to draw on for inspiration and fewer people who can teach others about potential careers in this space. This can be overcome with access to early and continuous education to make it relatable. The focus should not just be on the tech itself but on inspiring the wider community on what the tech enables you to do day-to-day.

How do you see the future of talent evolve in the next three to five years?
There will be three million new roles in Software, Data, AI/ML, Cyber by 2025 in the UK, according to Microsoft Data Science utilizing LinkedIn Data. According to UCAS, there will only be 150,000 new skilled graduates by 2025 and only 26,000 of them will be women. This tech talent shortage will only continue to grow as these new technologies continue to advance. To fill this gap, companies will need to look at communities who haven't traditionally embraced tech as a career. At the same time, there has been a genuine shift in attitudes in the workforce to work for purpose-driven companies who are diverse and inclusive. People will look to work for companies whose values align to their own. So the only way to win is to create an environment where people from all backgrounds feel welcome and included.

Sustaining Communities

If community is our new commodity, it is even more important than ever to make sure that we find ways to sustain them. Here, we offer a few thought starters:

- Organization: At the heart of any successful community is a strong founding team, and team members with passion for the cause as well as different but complementary skills. While it may not be mandatory, having a good storyteller at the top often helps the growth of the brand and the community. Nicole Muniz was brought in as the CEO of the Bored Ape Yacht Club (BAYC) and Yuga Labs by the founder Wylie Aronow for precisely her brand-building and storytelling abilities.

- Purpose: Keeping communities engaged requires inspiration and purpose. What is the mission and why do people want to be associated with it? Do people feel a sense of belonging and ownership? Several web3 brands have also relied on cultural movements to create the sense of belonging. Be it regenerative art, psychedelics, or a fitness-focused business, having a tribe mentality can help to retain community.

- Communication: Encourage participation and make sure that the community feels heard. Be intentional in seeking outside input for critical matters that need industry buy-in (for example, when setting a new standard). Identify and invest in a set of tools that the community can use to exchange ideas and disseminate information.

- Transparency: Community governance is critical to ensure members can have a voice and are able to vote on issues. How are ideas debated and elevated? What are the guidelines and how are decisions communicated and documented?

- Tokenomics: For web3 DAOs, governance tokens can be used to reward members or provide individuals with voting power. So, before you start, it is crucial that you are clear about the purpose of your tokens and how they will be allocated. However, let's learn from the mistakes from the previous cycles, where businesses created overreliance on tokenomics to sustain their communities.

- Business model: The solution to moving away from overreliance on tokenomics is to find a scalable business model. In bull markets, as tokens keep appreciating (generally), it is easier to incentivize a user base that's growing exponentially. That is not a solution in a bear market. The only sustainable solution is to identify a business model that scales through seasons and channelize a portion of the revenue stream to community incentives.

Building communities and sustaining them takes time and resources. But having a strong community is crucial for the success of your ecosystem, regardless of use case or industry.

The Capital Ecosystem

Like any asset, trust must be earned and then preserved.

JELENA MCWILLIAMS

It typically takes several trillion dollars to establish a new asset class and web3 markets are no different. For nearly 15 years retail and institutional investors have been more than willing to fund the growing crypto and NFT space. But for the metaverse narrative to achieve its full potential, more capital would be needed. Do we have enough capital, or rather the appetite, to support this journey?

In this chapter we will go through the evolution of the crypto capital ecosystem between 2008 and 2023, the failures and the successes, and what would be needed for it to become a credible capital market for innovative projects to thrive on.

The Rise of Digital Money

It was on October 31, 2008, just about six weeks after Lehman Brothers filed for bankruptcy, when Satoshi Nakamoto published the Bitcoin white paper. He had started working on the code for Bitcoin a year earlier. Call it a coincidence, but 2008 also signaled the beginning of a shift in the balance of power from incumbent financial services players to challengers, especially as compliance and risk functions took center stage. New products and services emerged in the ever-evolving fintech and web3 ecosystems. And these were not just financial products, but new economic models based on technology innovation.

Over the course of the decade that followed, Bitcoin has been called digital money, digital gold, and store of value. The market capitalization of Bitcoin is just a few hundred billion dollars at the time of writing. However, several Bitcoin maximalists and experts expect the Bitcoin market cap to surpass that of gold, which is around $12 trillion.[1] This would take time, but an event such as that would establish Bitcoin as the apex digital asset.

The rise of Bitcoin was followed by a number of other blockchain protocols like Ethereum. If Bitcoin is digital gold, Ethereum can be termed digital oil, an analogy used in the web3 world from an economic perspective—as we are burning more Ethereum than is being created. Since the launch of Ethereum in 2015, its ecosystem has come on in leaps and bounds. There have been several application categories that have thrived on the Ethereum blockchain, namely DeFi, NFTs, gaming, and more. This subsequently inspired several blockchains to launch their infrastructure and develop their ecosystems.

Today we have a number of layer 1 blockchains, a few layer 2 blockchains that help scale layer 1 chains, and thousands of applications that are built on these blockchains. As per DappRadar, there were about 12,500 Dapps across these chains in October 2022.[2] The rise of the application tier of blockchains has brought more users to the space, which in turn creates more transaction volumes on the blockchain.

The increase in users and user-driven transaction revenue brings more developers into ecosystems, who in turn create new Dapps for users to consume. This network effect has been fascinating to watch in several blockchains, but most notably with Ethereum and Solana. And this is perhaps the litmus test to demonstrate the quality of the ecosystem and the usability of the blockchain.

Even the most experienced crypto mind would admit that it is still very early days for the ecosystem. However, the space has matured, often achieved the hard way, over the years through several Bitcoin boom and bust cycles. The growth of the crypto industry couldn't have been achieved without serious interest from retail and institutional investors.

As the web3 ecosystem has grown over the years, so has the infrastructure around capital raising and management. However, there is much that needs to be done to improve the capital ecosystem around the web3 industry. In light of the events through 2022, it is amply clear that there would need to be regulations in place to protect investors. In this chapter we will look at how a parallel capital market has developed over the years, in particular since 2017, and what more needs to be done to bring credible and large-scale institutional capital into the space.

The Initial Coin Offering (ICO) Episode of 2017/18

The rise of Bitcoin demonstrated to the world that a monetary system can be created and managed digitally and programmatically. This also gave confidence to founders and investors that a digital token could prove to be a way to raise capital for a project and create a community around the cause at the same time.

The Ethereum blockchain launched in 2015 and since then has remained a case study for different business models that have emerged from a masterpiece of engineering. Firstly, it demonstrated that, unlike Transmission Control Protocol/Internet Protocol (TCP/IP), Ethereum could be a protocol layer that could have a value attached to it. Secondly, it demonstrated scalability through different application categories such as DeFi, NFTs, and gaming built on the same protocol layer, leading to network effects and exponential growth of the Ethereum ecosystem.

Growth of the Ethereum ecosystem had its ebbs and flows through the years. Driven by demand from numerous Dapps that started to build on the Ethereum blockchain, in particular through the crypto bull market in 2017 and 2018, the price of Ethereum rose from $14 in 2016 to over $1,000 in 2018. Most of these, however, were just simple white papers published by a group of eager, often greedy, and sometimes fraudulent founders.

These white papers were funded through token events called Initial Coin Offerings (ICO), which saw a huge influx of capital as retail and institutional investors participated from across the world. A retail investor with $1,000, for example, could invest in a crypto project supporting women farmers in Brazil through their ICO event. Such mechanisms were touted to be the future of venture capital as they helped raise funds for startups around the world.

Apart from the ease with which capital could be raised, tokens were seen as liquid instruments that investors could trade, should they wish to exit their position in a crypto startup. This was quite different from traditional venture capital investments that were not readily convertible to cash. VC investors who wanted to exit their positions in a startup often had to wait for a liquidity event like a takeover, funding round, or strategic investment to sell their shares in the firm. They would often exit their positions at a discount to market price, too.

ICOs were hailed as a solution to such issues that the VC industry suffered from. However, what crypto enthusiasts and investors did not realize in 2017 was that the ICO boom really happened during a crypto bull market and was fueled by irrational exuberance. Most projects funded by ICOs do not exist anymore, and some of them were clearly scams. Cracks started to emerge in late 2018 as the crypto market came crashing down.

Unfortunately, most of these projects came crashing down with the crypto market and Bitcoin as they lacked fundamentals like product ideas, strategy, and target market to capture—beyond white papers. Yet, several projects kept their heads down and kept building. As the crypto market turned the corner in 2019 and 2020, many of these survivors who kept building great products were able to reap benefits. Their survival adds to their credibility as crypto winters are harsh but their products gain traction.

While the ICO boom and bust left a lot for the crypto industry to learn from, bear markets have often created great projects and products. The detox that happened through the ICO bust was a blessing in disguise for the entire industry.

Did the Crypto Market Learn?

The Bitcoin cycle often mirrors investor fear and greed. There is even a Bitcoin Fear and Greed Index that is derived from the sentiments around the crypto market that investors use to make macro decisions around this asset class. As Bitcoin hits record highs during a bull market, the greed readings on the index shines bright; when Bitcoin hits cycle lows, the fear is at its peak. This has been a phenomenon that has been seen repeating itself through the Bitcoin cycles.

The ICO debacle should have provided lessons learned for the web3 stakeholders, but it didn't. As the market took off post the Covid-19 crash in March 2020, DeFi grew from $600 million in January 2020 to $175 billion in November 2021, representing a 25,000 percent growth in less than two years. Such growth often breeds greed. The DeFi bull run was shortly followed by the rise of NFTs with CryptoPunks and Bored Apes leading the space. This in turn was followed by the rise of layer 1 protocols like Solana, Near, Avalanche, and Luna. As the layer 1 run started to plateau, the GameFi fever kicked in, with investors chasing projects to get allocations to invest.

As described, all these different subclusters of web3 saw growth spurts throughout 2020 and most of 2021. This time wasn't too different from the ICO boom of 2017. The new three-letter acronym was TGE, which stood for token generation event. How did this work? Let's illustrate it through a fictional scenario.

Two founders with a product idea or a product create a pitch deck describing their value proposition, growth plans, but most of all the tokenomics—which informs investors how many tokens are allocated to fundraising. Investors will look at vesting periods to ensure liquidity in the short term, and commit capital to a private fundraising process, which precedes a public token launch.

The price of the token for the private fundraising process is 30–50 percent lower compared to the price at public launch. For instance, an investor will typically deploy $100,000 into Token A, valued at 5 cents. Once the project team raises $5 million through private investors, they announce a date for the public launch of Token A. The public launch price can then go up to 8 cents, for example.

The project launch activities typically include a massive marketing campaign, "ask me anything" sessions, and influencer-backed content distribution leveraging investor capital and designed to increase visibility and hype around Token A. This often requires systematic community management through platforms like Discord, Twitter, and Telegram, and active engagement by the founders with the community to keep the momentum towards the public launch of Token A.

With the community now buying into the idea that Token A will be their "get rich quick" scheme, and eagerly waiting to buy Token A at launch, the project team then works towards listing their tokens across blue chip exchanges. The more blue chip the exchange is, the higher the expectation is of a price appreciation for Token A as larger exchanges have more users and liquidity. Token A launches on TGE day, and retail enthusiasm pushes token price from the open 8 cents to $1, often more.

At this point, the treasury management function of the project, and several investors who have participated in the private investment event before the token launch, will likely exit some of their positions. From an investor perspective, the TGE has de-risked their exposure to such tokens. From a founding team perspective, selling some tokens into the opening day exuberance extends them some capital to manage operating costs.

While some retail investors saw through these tactics, most of them fell prey to these ideas. There were several credible projects that raised capital through 2021 through TGEs and have since then done quite well. However, the large majority of projects that raised through TGEs in 2021/22 suffered the same fate that ICOs did in 2018.

Yet, 2021 felt different compared to 2018. In 2018, most participants in the exuberance were retail audience. There were very few institutional investors who contributed to the rise of ICOs. However, through 2020, institutional participation in the web3 world has been steadily on the rise, resulting in quite a good number of venture capital institutions participating in several investment opportunities through TGEs.

While the involvement of VCs added some degree of credibility to the due diligence process for projects launched before TGE, signs of trouble were brewing. Some projects were able to raise funding merely through a pitch deck, while others were shrouded in secrecy with founder identities; and a great number of commitments came through one pitching zoom session or a telegram chat. Most projects that raised through 2021 had investors practically clamoring for allocation in the funding round.

The greed index was clearly glowing bright. What could go wrong?

The Crypto Shadow Lending Economy

While the venture capital ecosystem was getting greedy with equity offerings via tokens, there was a shadow lending economy that was growing behind the scenes. Some bright minds that witnessed the ICO boom in 2018 realized that there could be a financial solution that could be built on ICOs for greater financial upside. They chose to use leverage.

As DeFi products were growing through 2020 and 2021, so were platforms that resembled banks but operated in the crypto markets. They were called centralized finance (CeFi) platforms. These platforms offered high returns to those who deposited cryptos with them. Some of these returns were so high that they couldn't have possibly offered them without using the customer funds for high-risk investments elsewhere on DeFi platforms.

The cryptocurrency that retail users deposited into the CeFi platforms resembled traditional banking experiences. However, the CeFi platforms lacked the governance and controls that main street banks had in place to be custodians of customer capital. As a result, the deposits were used for lending and investing into high-risk products, sometimes even to borrowers who had no collateral to offer in return.

Several big names like Celcius, BlockFi, Genesis, and FTX all fell from their ivory towers in 2022, creating a massive crypto contagion. The shadow lending economy was largely unknown to the outside world until some of them had exposure to Luna Terra. When Luna's stablecoin UST depegged in May 2022, it caused limitless inflation with Luna, resulting in a 99.99 percent loss of value to Luna. Retail and institutional investors lost billions of dollars in the episode as the founding team decided to pull the plug with UST and rolled out a forked version of Luna.

WHAT IS STABLECOIN DEPEGGING?

Stablecoins are cryptocurrencies that have a relatively stable price and are pegged to a fiat currency or a commodity like gold. Stablecoins must therefore reflect the price of the asset that they are pegged to. When depegging happens during a crisis, the price of the stablecoin shows higher than normal variance from the asset they are pegged to.

Many of these CeFi platforms that had used Luna's ecosystem to make high returns lost huge sums of money, often in billions of dollars. With several billions lost within days, rumors of "illiquid CeFi firms" triggered a bank run from retail investors who rushed to withdraw their crypto assets from these platforms. A lack of liquid cryptos with these institutions meant they were unable to honor their obligations to these retail investors who wanted their cryptos back. Over the course of the following weeks and months, many of these platforms filed for bankruptcy. The contagion spread to bring FTX, the poster child of crypto, down.

The founders of these organizations who followed very little corporate governance in handling retail funds now face legal repercussions, and in some cases prison time.

From ICOs to TGEs to shadow lending economies, there is no lack of bad actors within the capital ecosystem in cryptos. However, that does not necessarily make all these models inefficient, broken, unsustainable, or evil. With some regulatory and governance controls, these models can potentially benefit a large number of innovative companies and help them grow with an inclusive community as they build for our collective future.

Let us now look at what the key takeaways are and who the key actors are within the crypto capital ecosystem that can help this space in the long run.

Stakeholders Within the Crypto Capital Ecosystem

Capital flows into the crypto industry through three key gateways:

- primary issuance of tokens
- purchase of tokens from centralized and decentralized exchanges
- traditional equity and debt issuance

Primary Issuance

This is the process through which a token is created and distributed to institutional and retail investors. There are different actors who come together to make this happen and create a continuum into the token being managed and primed for further growth.

Founders

Picking the right combination of demand and supply enables the founders to leverage their ecosystem and the network effect to properly deploy tokens for their use case. They must assess the need for a token, how they would make it sustainable, and ensure investors and the ecosystem that relies on the token grow in the long run.

Such tactics help to secure a stable growth of the token's value for the ecosystem, which will in turn affect the price and liquidity increase.

Private Investors and Advisors

Once the founders have created a business case to justify the need for a token for their product and business, they typically seek advice from those who have been through this process before, or those who see primary issuance happen regularly. These stakeholders help the founders refine their token model and ensure they are thinking long term with their tokenomics and business models.

Private investors and advisors can also choose to invest in the firm once they are convinced of the merits of the business. These investors typically get a cheaper valuation before the token is launched on an exchange. While this has been a typical route to raising capital through a token, there have been some concerns raised by the ecosystem when a firm is backed by big venture capital funds. This is primarily due to the risk of centralization as these VCs may end up holding a large portion of the tokens, which doesn't bode well with an ecosystem that prefers and preaches decentralization as a way to do business.

Yet, many web2 like a16z, Sequoia, Electric capital, and Paradigm have launched sizable crypto funds and deployed through the last few years. Similarly, native web3 funds like 6thMan Ventures and Shima Capital have made strides with token and equity investing within the web3 industry. This looks like a trend that is set to continue into future cycles and hopefully we should see better due diligence frameworks used for web3 investments leading to more robust firms that can survive crypto winters.

Operational Steps to a Token Issuance

Once private investors complete their investments in the firm, they receive documentation describing their ownership of tokens and the vesting schedule of the tokens. But the investments provide the firms with the capital needed to run the next set of steps to launch the token to a retail audience.

Launching a token typically involves the following steps:

1 Onboard blockchain capability to create the code behind the token.

2 Get the smart contract audited by a credible firm.

3 Hire a legal team to assess legal and regulatory risks with the launch of the token.

4 Plan and execute marketing and promotional activities to hype up the firm, without directly promoting the token.

5 Hire a liquidity/treasury management firm.

6 Engage with a number of centralized and decentralized exchanges and shortlist a few.

7 Launch the token and manage the treasury.

Each of these operational steps needs quite a lot of attention and time from the founding team to get it right.

Create Blockchain Capability

Most firms aspiring to create a token will need a blockchain development team, which can be done in-house or outsourced to an external technology team. This step is important as the firm needs to decide on the blockchain that it will use to create its token. Dapps create their tokens on top of layer 1 (L1) and layer 2 (L2) platforms. However, L1 and L2 platforms typically use their own network to launch their token.

This process is a lot simpler if the firm is operating at the application level rather than when it is a protocol tier proposition. For a metaverse, it typically means that the token being created will sit on one of the L1 or L2 blockchains. The choice of the blockchain will depend on the use case for the token. For instance, Ethereum may not be the best choice if the token is used to conduct micro transactions across millions of users; companies prefer to use one of Ethereum's L2 platforms like Polygon or Immutable, or go to another L1 like Solana that is better at handling thousands of transactions per second at a fraction of the cost.

Having the right technical team to make the right decisions makes a difference!

Audit Smart Contract

The crypto world has been plagued by cyber attacks in recent times. Therefore a thorough smart contract audit on the token is an absolute must. Even retail investors often expect a token that they invest in to be audited and are generally aware of the usefulness of this process. If the audit fails or comes back with some key findings, exchanges will not be willing to list the token. Therefore, getting a credible smart contract audit performed is a critical prerequisite to the exchange listing process.

Legal and Regulatory Review

Most Dapps may not necessarily need to go through this step. But if the token is for a DeFi stablecoin platform that has legal and regulatory implications, it helps to conduct a legal and regulatory review. It is also important to decide on the jurisdictions where the token will be issued. Any additional legal process that the firm needs to go through before they can have investors from certain jurisdictions participate in the token sale would also be discussed and decided in this phase.

This analysis allows the founders to pick the most favorable jurisdiction for the project, depending on the token type and legal and regulatory requirements for the issuance. It protects the founders and reduces the investment risks for investors.

Marketing and Promotions

Once the token has been created, audited, and reviewed, the hype process starts. Founders engage with their communities closely through various channels and social media platforms. They conduct AMA sessions with giveaways in the end, Twitter spaces with random rewards, and Discord growth hack programs and community competitions. This creates quite a lot of excitement around the project and the community rallies behind it in a big way. With projects such as Moonbirds and Bullieverse, some community members have even tattooed the logo on themselves. The cult fever typically reaches the peak over the course of these few weeks before the token launch.

Often these activities are supported by influencers who have either bought into the vision, or are being paid by the firm to vouch for the token and the business. Influencers have been fined by the US Securities and the Exchange Commission (SEC) for promoting tokens in the past and misleading retail investors. For instance, Kim Kardashian was fined $1.26 million by the SEC for paid promotions of the EthereumMax token.[3]

In recent times, new platforms called "launchpads" have emerged that contribute to this process as well. These launchpads typically have thousands of members who have invested in their tokens. In return for this investment, launchpads create pre-launch distribution events to offer early access to their users and investors, thereby creating further demand. Firms also use other traditional marketing channels such as press releases and other events to further promote the brand.

Liquidity and Treasury Management

Launching a token can help raise millions of dollars, and when timed, planned, and executed well it can bring hundreds of millions of dollars to the firm. This provides the funding for day-to-day operations, and allows for a portion of these tokens to be allocated for the founders, team members, and advisors, with an embedded vesting schedule. That becomes another personal incentive for the stakeholders to ensure the token value stays high.

However, tokens are also a long-term solution for funding the business through efficient liquidity and treasury management. There are service providers who take up the responsibility of buying and selling tokens launched on behalf of the business launching it, thereby making profits from the market which will be sent back to the firm to fund their business. This is not a new capability and is largely inspired by traditional capital markets where market makers and brokers often do the buying, selling, and liquidity creation on behalf of their clients.

In web3, firms like GSR, Wintermute, and Acheron take that responsibility and charge either a transaction fee or a monthly fixed fee for their services. These liquidity providers are extremely important to ensure a relatively stable token price and a healthy company treasury; they are integrated to the exchanges and ensure orders placed are automated and happen at the right price points for their clients. Therefore, firms looking to launch their tokens must perform their due diligence around the various liquidity and treasury management solutions these firms offer and select the right one for their business and tokens.

Shortlist Exchanges

Exchanges are platforms that list tokens on the launch day and bring large volumes of liquidity to the token. Some of the top centralized exchanges are Binance, Coinbase, Kucoin, and Huobi. Decentralized exchanges are also known to list tokens and some of the bigger ones are Uniswap, Sushiswap, Orca, Raydium, and Quickswap. While centralized exchanges are able to bring high volumes and liquidity, decentralized exchanges offer flexibility to users who want to transact from their crypto wallets.

Most firms go for a mix of exchanges. It may be harder to list on some of the bigger exchanges as they have stricter criteria and often need blue chip investors to back the firm. Binance and Coinbase also expect buy and sell volumes as track records to demonstrate demand for a token before it is considered for listing. There have been, however, instances where new tokens get listed on these top exchanges, typically when the team behind the crypto can draw a huge crowd to these exchanges.

In essence, choosing and getting listed on credible exchanges can make or break the future of a token and hence the business backing it. Many businesses have a ramp-up plan to their listing strategy to ensure they start from a smaller exchange and slowly move up the ladder. As they constantly release news of listings on larger exchanges, the hype is kept up. It is also important to remember that tokens typically have a temporary increase in value when they announce a listing on an exchange with better volumes or larger user base. Therefore, a staggered listing schedule helps sustain token prices rather than a big bang launch across several exchanges.

Token Launch

The token launch typically happens a day or two after it has been announced to the community and retail followers. Most token launches look similar to the initial public offering (IPO) process that happens on traditional capital markets. However, the price movements are generally exaggerated with cryptos and volatility is extremely high on listing days.

This is precisely what the liquidity management platforms are looking for. They agree on the price points with their clients to buy and sell tokens and build a robust treasury for their clients. A healthy crypto market often makes this job easier. They also understand the market from demand for tokens of other clients to plan their orders. The token launch day is often an important day for the business as it helps them build their treasury and establish their brand.

It is not enough to just have a good token launch, however. It is also critical to ensure treasury management is well planned. Most web3 entrepreneurs have development backgrounds and often lack the experience needed to get this right. Some hold their treasury in their native tokens, only to see the price plummet during a bear market. There are companies who held their treasury in Luna Terra stablecoins, lost most of them during the crash, and eventually went out of business as they lacked the capital to compensate their team.

Before their historic crash, FTX were known to have invested in several firms under the condition that they would be managing the treasury of these firms. As a result, many of FTX's investee firms entrusted their tokens and capital to FTX. When FTX collapsed, these firms lost their operational capital and many of them have since gone out of business.

This goes to show that while raising capital is important, preserving capital in a cyclical crypto market is essential for survival as well. As the industry matures, better treasury management practices and audited firms that perform this task well would make it easier for inexperienced entrepreneurs to focus on their business.

As Mike Dudas, founder and General Partner of 6MV, commented to us, "Token economy is challenging to figure out. But it also offers opportunities to do things differently if we can clear the roadblocks and learn from the past."

A CONVERSATION WITH BOWIE LAU, FOUNDER, MAGE GROUP

What are some of the challenges the web3 ecosystem will face in the next three to five years?
The biggest challenge is to get people to truly realize and understand the potential of web3. In the era of fake news, phishing, hacks, and incessant scams, people are rightly concerned about the true intentions of any new model of interaction and commerce enabled by the internet like web3. It also doesn't help that centralization has produced several multi-billion and even trillion-dollar companies that feel threatened by the customer empowerment and ownership of data provided by the new decentralized web3 economic models. Such unhealthy competition from centralized industry behemoths creates fear, uncertainty, and doubt in the minds of people and slows down the adoption of a more beneficial web3. The only way to tackle this systematically is to operate web3 business models with a higher standard of conduct and active transparent involvement of the community in driving the direction of the business.

From a funding perspective, which aspects of the metaverse economy do you think will see the most traction on the horizon?

I'm seeing interesting opportunities emerge in a few areas. First, DeFi is evolving into a potential replacement for TradFi investment banking and financial market activities. The market has evolved to the next level of sophistication with the onset of DeFi Option Vaults which could soon unleash all forms of crypto structure products to become mainstream. Second, gaming is no longer a hobby and GameFi along with NFTs will be a powerful agent of social change and economic empowerment. The current generation of youth who despise the stifling corporate culture will embrace the freedom and dignity afforded by decentralized gaming, play-to-earn economies, and e-sports. Third, metaverse will take an increasing time-share in people's lives, and marketing models that are compatible with web3 and wallets will find more success in targeting their customers. Especially adtech companies that figure out ways to achieve meaningful engagement without click bait or spamming customers, and rewarding loyalty will find great success in the metaverse.

What Is in It for the Metaverse?

While the crypto capital markets are not perfect, it is important to remember that this ecosystem is still in its infancy when compared to the more matured capital markets, and some of the frameworks are native to the web3 ecosystem and still need to be proven. With more institutional capital and regulatory guidance, this could become a refreshing alternative to the traditional Wall Street experience.

Most web3 metaverses will need to leverage the capital ecosystem that we describe in this chapter. As metaverses scale and grow, there will be a need for them to support micro-ecosystems to launch their own economies and tokens. As a result, founders of metaverses will need to have a good understanding of this ecosystem, which is important not only for their own business, but also for the number of micro businesses, creator economies, and others who are dependent on them. With maturity, metaverses can turn into capital launchpads and ecosystems where microeconomies can interact with each other and interoperate.

Looking Beyond the Hype   11

We cannot predict the future. But we can play a part in creating the narrative.

In October 2008, when Lehman Brothers came crashing down, we may have seen the beginning of the end of Wall Street as it once was. Compared to spending pre-financial crisis, the cost of regulatory compliance has increased significantly. According to LexisNexis, the projected total cost of compliance across financial institutions world-wide was $274.1 billion in 2022, up from $213.9 billion in 2020.[1]

A similar moment might have come to pass for the big techs when the Cambridge Analytica scandal broke out, tainting Facebook's brand, and scrutiny towards other big tech companies and social media giants soon followed, especially when it comes to the use of data and how it feeds the exploitatory profit motives. As Tristan Harris stated in the movie *Social Dilemma*: "If you are not paying for the product, you are the product."[2]

When we knew that Wall Street dominance was starting to be challenged by regulations and a lack of customer centricity, we saw the fintech narrative emerge as an alternative. Whether fintech has lived up to its promise is a different topic for another time. However, on a similar note, as technology companies were seen to be exploiting users and creators, decentralization is perceived as the narrative that would potentially address the gaps.

In this book, we have seen several business models, technology paradigms, and alternatives that would help address the gaps in today's internet applications. Yet, the metaverse, which could potentially be a refreshing alternative, still has a long way to go to really displace the king from the throne.

In this chapter, we will review some of the key concepts that we touched on throughout the book. We will also summarize the challenges that still remain for the web3 metaverse to scale beyond its faithful few.

The Cogs

Since the second chapter of this book, you have been made aware of the ways in which various web2 and web3 paradigms could, should, or will resonate with various stakeholders to make the metaverse a reality. Let us summarize the takeaways from the different chapters so that we can address the challenges and pain points that must be considered and tackled to ensure this can make a significant impact in our lives.

Inclusive Incentives

The Silicon Valley-led models of the past where entrepreneurs, investors, and institutions owned the economic upside from a business endeavor could soon be a thing of the past. With tokenomics as a new paradigm, the community, creators, developers, users, and all other actors who contribute to an ecosystem can benefit from the growth of a business. The dimensions of inclusion are not just stakeholders, but also geographies and technology tiers from across the globe, local regulatory and legal constraints notwithstanding.

Unlike the internet of the past, the new paradigms allow the participation of stakeholders right at the protocol level, through the application tier, right up to the user tier. The protocol tier is where participants can capture value by being coders, validators, and just users of blockchains like Ethereum and Solana. Applications built on these chains can also accrue value to users. As SocialFi models and micro-economies start to emerge, we could see one more tier of activity and value creation for participants.

As a result, it is not just a privileged few who benefit financially from the growth of a business or an application.

Universal Basic Equity

While this is pretty close to the previous point, it is perhaps broader and is focused more around how citizens of the world could go about earning their livelihoods in the future. The concept of universal basic equity will also enable large organizations to establish network effects more easily and sustainably.

Token economies already allow more stakeholders in an ecosystem to hold equity and look for long-term upside. However, as these models scale, everyone, irrespective of their geographical location, professional, and social status can become part of several ecosystems. This can offer fractional equity to anyone contributing, especially if they want to scale their offering.

Imagine a model where Facebook could help users accrue points for participating on the social media platform. Users could collect points over a period of time for their content creation. Similarly, businesses could lure users to interact with their content by offering them points. These points could be exchanged for real-world value, giving users an incentive to not only stay on the social media platform, but to be more active. These incentives can be funded via an advertising revenue sharing model, thereby giving users an upside to being on the platform. They will be more likely to interact with the advertisement content as they know there is a fractional financial gain; businesses will also feel the return on investment for their retail outreach, through better user adoption and conversation. Everybody wins. And the model can be extended to other applications including social media, product or restaurant reviews, and search engine optimization. At scale, this could potentially offer a basic living wage to some people, depending on the local economy.

Identity (Self-Sovereign Identity)

We discussed identities at length in Chapter 3 where we covered NFTs. The concept of identity is nothing new to us. However, the definition and the provisioning of identities have been largely centralized, either with governments or with social media platforms. The future driven by web3 could challenge if not change the paradigm, and we have already witnessed the use of PFP NFTs as identities on social media platforms.

With cryptographic techniques like zero-knowledge proof, the identity of users can be stored in their wallets, and revealed to the application that is looking to verify them in a safe and secure way. This is already the norm with Dapps, where users sign their identities with the NFTs in their wallets. Could the same happen with real-world identities in the future?

More importantly, this can lead to a change in how identities are defined, as artists and creators build their ecosystem identity and credibility through their contributions. Frank DeGods, the founder of the DeGods NFT collection, did not reveal his real-world identity until late in 2022, when the NFT collection was easily the biggest and most coveted in the Solana ecosystem. To many, his actions and impact on to the community mattered more than his real-world identity.

As the metaverse narrative scales, there will be instances where the real world and virtual world collide and users will need to provide their real-world identities. For instance, a metaverse user could gain access to a real-world bank account as a consumer, while joining the metaverse course at the virtual University of Oxford, all without revealing their real-world identity. However, the implementation of such a process could be based on modern-day cryptographic techniques.

Credibility and Track Record

We discussed soulbound tokens (SBTs) when we explored NFTs and SocialFi models. SBT and similar constructs can drive how a stakeholder's contribution to web3 ecosystems is tracked. In today's world, credibility is managed by rating organizations both at the retail and institutional levels, and it is augmented by personal networks that often lead to privileged circles, whereas, in a trustless world, credibility is often gauged by one's contribution to the ecosystem (e.g. their GitHub profile).

SBTs draw inspiration from this model. SBTs or variations to this model will capture contributions and do NFT drops to the wallets of the contributor. An artist may get a stamp if they have had 1,000 users mint their artwork at a cost of 1 ETH each. Similarly, a gamer could get a stamp in their wallet if they win a leaderboard competition. A blogger could get a stamp if their article received 10,000 views.

Employers looking to hire could just create criteria in a trustless way; and GitHub has already proven this model for open source code contributors. Such mechanisms can help us establish our social, professional, and ecosystem credibility without barriers such as race, gender, or other biases. By now, we hope that this fundamental principle has been ingrained as we have spoken about it across multiple chapters so far in this book.

Creator Centricity

Web3's significance for the monetary framework far outweighs its significance for technology innovation, as it offers us an economic system that can be programmatically defined for a trustless network to then govern and execute, supporting creators who have been largely exploited by the previous batch of internet players.

While creators can thrive in web3, we may even potentially see a phygital world where real-world creators of value can benefit from these structures. Authors, farmers, sculptors, designers, goldsmiths, gardeners, landscape artists, builders could all benefit from web3 if they could bridge their real-world creations on-chain.

Of course, we will need to have applications that are custom built for these use cases. And while there are several applications that are purpose built for farmers to track their "farm to fork" activities, this is still early in development. Whether or not these apps can impact the ecosystem at scale and move the value chains onto the blockchain remains to be seen. From bottom-up awareness (community) to top-down regulations (state) and technology innovation (businesses), multiple factors are at play in driving change over the next few decades to make these ecosystems creator centric.

Coming back to web3, artists, coders, designers, game studios, and content creators will all thrive in the trustless economic system that keeps them at the heart of their business models. Tools like NFT, SocialFi, SBTs, and on-chain transactions, that are fundamental to the creator economy, have already seen green shoots and are starting to scale. We should see these building blocks mature over the next couple of crypto cycles, making the creator economy the de facto model of building internet businesses by the dawn of the next decade.

Value Ownership, Retention, and Interoperability

Business models serving creators are a start. But where value is being created and accrued by creators and other ecosystem participants, the right infrastructure needed to retain value created is critical. The retained value must be owned by those who have created it, rather than by the platforms where it gets created. Value once created in an ecosystem should be transferable to other ecosystems when needed.

We have touched upon these concepts alongside the use cases of NFTs and GameFi. As web3 draws inspiration from the likes of Roblox, creators must truly own their assets, instead of having their fate determined by the platforms themselves. A football field created by a Roblox creator should be readily available to list on an asset marketplace. When it is bought via the marketplace and transacted in the secondary market, the creators must be able to benefit from those transactions in the form of royalties. These asset marketplaces can be part of a Roblox-like ecosystem or operate as independent platforms that creators and others use to buy and sell digital assets.

Interoperability is another critical aspect of managing digital assets. Creators should not have to recreate their assets because the infrastructure (blockchain) layer is different across metaverses. An Arsenal football stadium created on an Ethereum blockchain-based metaverse should be available for a Solana-based metaverse. The decision to use the asset on two different metaverses should be that of the creator.

Cross-chain bridges must be capable of creating a copy of the asset onto the new metaverse. Alternatively, where the creator chooses to leave a metaverse and set up shop in a new metaverse, they should also have the option to move their assets to their new metaverse of choice and burn their assets on the original metaverse. Bridges have proven to be the Achilles' heel of the industry and much needs to be done before they can be relied upon. More on this in just a moment.

Culture and Communities

We discussed the role of communities in Chapters 8 and 9. Crypto and NFT community-building strategies are now used in case studies within business schools such as Harvard Business School. The rise of the CryptoPunks and Bored Ape Yacht Club communities has shown the world that such communities could be built around a brand even without a real underlying product. A second wave of communities came to the fore through the bear market of 2022. NFT collections like Moonbirds and DeGods are two noteworthy brands that have tremendous following to the extent that they are now more of a tribe than just a community.

We also discussed several growth hacks and community sustenance strategies in Chapter 8. There are new experiments that we see every day in this space by crypto and NFT entrepreneurs. Some are extremely successful, some are less so. For instance, when DeGods launched its NFT collection Yoots, it launched an application process where applicants had to write up justification as to why they must be part of the Yoots community. Tens of thousands of applications came in, from which 3,000 applicants were granted an opportunity to mint the NFT.

While this doesn't sound like a completely new idea, the way the team went about executing the application process, creating fear of missing out (FOMO) across the NFT world in general, they ended up drawing a lot of attention. Again, attention is the new currency and community is the new commodity. Therefore, community is just a result of the attention that the project is able to receive from its activities.

The focus on attention strategies to draw the crowd, build communities, draw larger capital from investors, and then focus on a product strategy is perhaps going to remain as we embark on the next cycle. Yet, the fact that community is a precursor to building a product allows entrepreneurs to listen to a very loyal group of people while deciding their roadmap before they scale.

NFTs have also brought people with certain allegiances together. From psychedelics and meditation to generative art or gaming, these communities are built with stakeholders who share a common passion. These advocates can also guide the founders in their journeys by becoming an insider of the tribe.

Monetizing Influence

Influencers across the world have been able to monetize their social media swag through promotional activities that they get involved in. However, most influencers that operate in the web2 world have a big real-world presence and are seldom anonymous.

Web3 is a trustless framework to do precisely that, where even an anonymous ecosystem stakeholder can monetize their influence. This is largely due to the SocialFi models that have emerged over the last couple of years. The SocialFi platforms can allow creation of micro economies through influencer tokens, where to interact with an influencer's post a person must hold the influencer's token in their wallet.

The precise economic model behind these tokens will take time to bottom out. However, while that is in progress, SBTs already allow ecosystems to identify their top performers. For instance, if a metaverse wants to launch a new game, it can collaborate with the top performers of its previous games to promote the new game. These influencers can be identified purely using on-chain activity and the following they have within the ecosystem. In return, they can receive the tokens of the gaming economy that is being launched.

In such instances, not only can these top performers monetize their place in the ecosystem through such promotional activities, they can also receive special discounts on products within the metaverse. If the metaverse is launching a bank, these performers can receive preferential interest rates for deposits and loans, or their activity may qualify them for a higher credit limit on a bank credit card.

While this may sound hypothetical, such models have been sporadically implemented. For instance, there are NFT DeFi protocols that lend to users who are willing to collateralize their NFTs. The amount they can borrow is decided by the floor price of the NFT collection. It is a process where no other aspects of the user need to be revealed.

Competitions that ecosystems conduct have monthly superstars identified and rewarded for their contribution to the community.

Over time, consistent contributors are identified as ecosystem influencers. As part of that process, they receive an NFT airdropped to them for their commitment to their communities, which offers them lower entry fees into leaderboard competitions launched by the platform. Therefore, as hypothetical as these models may sound, the building blocks are already in place, though it may require a crypto cycle or two for them to become productized into metaverse ecosystems.

Capital Ecosystems

While most outcomes from the web3 models may prove to be superior to the web2 equivalent, it must be understood that most web3 entrepreneurs have stood on the shoulders of web2 firms to get to this point. The capital ecosystem that has evolved within web3 over the years is no different. The token economy offers startups a new path to secure capital from investors from around the globe. For investors, these tokens are liquid instruments that they can exit at any point, unlike equity in traditional venture capital and private equity. In the traditional web2 models, typically only technologists and more specifically product companies can gain access to early stage capital. With web3, founders, creators, and artists have found a different way to raise capital and launch their dream projects.

In this new paradigm, web3 projects can first benefit from the community following and raise capital via NFTs, which often come earlier in the cycle before the tokens are launched. As mentioned earlier in the book, BAYC is a great example of such an approach, where several collections of NFTs were launched to get the community in motion before Apecoin came. Moonbirds is following a similar roadmap as well.

With so much going right for web3 metaverses, one might wonder, is it the perfect system we need to build as an alternative to the internet and capital markets? The fundamental building blocks are all in place, and they are maturing at a different pace. Yet, there are several challenges that need to be overcome before we see sustainable and viable metaverses to drive the Internet 2.0 narrative forward.

What Needs to Work?

Here is a wish list of pain points that need to be addressed before we can start being bullish about the metaverse narrative. Without enough regulatory controls, better user experience, technology scalability, and a stable and matured capital ecosystem, web3 and the metaverse may remain nothing more than a pipe dream.

Regulation and Governance

There are several areas that need regulating. Let us look at each of them and consider why.

Exchanges

Centralized exchanges (CEx) are often the entry point for new crypto and NFT users into the web3 ecosystem. However, in 2022 there were several issues where the CExs have proven less than reliable. This was largely due to a lack of risk management and compliance controls. Exchanges must regain their trust with retail and institutional customers and must have a clear liquidity management methodology. Regulators from across the world should provide guidelines to ensure crypto exchanges have the right governance to protect investor capital.

Stablecoins

Stablecoins have become the primary storage of value for web3 participants when they sell other forms of digital assets. Unlike in the past crypto cycles, stablecoins have held a reasonable market cap through 2022. At the time of writing, the entire crypto market capitalization is at just over $1 trillion, and the stablecoins contribute over $138 trillion, representing 12 percent of the pie. Stablecoins are second to Bitcoin and Ethereum in market capitalization, and could take the top spot in the pie in a few years.

With the pace at which stablecoins are being used by crypto natives, this is another key area that regulators must look into. Stablecoins must be backed by liquid real-world assets and there must be regular audits to ensure these assets are in good health. Real-time on-chain solvency checks would be the best future to aim for, yet, for the near and medium term, there must be sufficient stress testing performed and reported to ensure stablecoins are robust. The Luna Terra episode, for example, brought the entire market down in May 2022, resulting in tens of billions of dollars' loss to investors.

Lending and Borrowing

Bank-like services offered by both crypto banks like Celcius and BlockFi, and DeFi applications, would probably never have seen dawn if they had been through traditional regulatory reviews. Most regulators across the world consider mis-selling financial products to investors as a key regulatory breach. A loan offered at 30 percent APR may be considered as mis-sold in traditional banks, whereas there are hardly any such standards within DeFi and the crypto world.

Most lending in web3 is collateralized, yet the shadow lending economy that was created between CExs and DeFi platforms caused a contagion that could have been avoided with regulatory oversight. If web3 participants want a credible and sustainable future, they need to cleanse their capital ecosystem, and embracing regulations is the first step towards that.

Parental Controls and Content Moderation

As we have learned from past years, moderating social media content is extremely difficult. After all, it is a delicate balance between protecting freedom of expression and banning bad actors and toxic behavior.

Unsurprisingly, the metaverse is not immune to toxic behavior and content from the real world.[3] While protecting children from harmful content and predatory behavior is, and must be, a priority, doing so with anonymous actors is a difficult task to accomplish, never mind doing it well at scale.

Beyond ensuring this is top of mind for platforms, ingraining awareness with children and providing parents with the right tools to set boundaries are crucial as well. Among the many lessons learned is the need to ensure that the controls infrastructure is in place and ready before the product takes off. This also presents an excellent opportunity for a new "metaverse as a service" model.

Anti-Money Laundering

Metaverse platforms are going to have digital assets that have real-world value, and these can be excellent tools for money launderers. The ban of the crypto mixer Tornado Cash that allowed over $7 billion worth of anonymous transactions on its platform came through the second half of 2022. But money launderers have since resorted to cross-chain and cross-asset transactions to avoid being traced by on-chain analytics platforms.

Having the right regulatory controls in place is a journey rather than a destination. As regulations block one way of anonymous transactions, bad actors will find another way. More sophisticated technology capabilities will be needed in order to keep up and stay vigilant. As metaverses scale, money launderers and hackers are going to be one of the harder problems for regulatory bodies to protect retail audiences from.

Legal Frameworks

A lack of legal frameworks to guide the web3 space came to light when Alexey Pertsev, an open source code contributor to the virtual currency mixer Tornado Cash, was arrested by the Dutch authorities in August 2022. The mixer has been used to launder a substantial amount of virtual currency, including more than $96 million stolen from the Harmony Bridge heist, and at least $7.8 million from the Nomad heist.[4] After the US sanctioned the Tornado protocol, Pertsev was accused of facilitating money laundering by writing the open-source code and was arrested by the Dutch authorities.

To avoid such events, and to protect developers from being harmed by an ambiguous legal stance, frameworks must be in place for open source and decentralized platforms to draw guidance from. They need to define what the different stakeholders of a decentralized platform are liable for. Protocol layers have developers, validators, users, investors, and other actors on the transaction supply chain.

They cannot all be held responsible if a bad actor chooses to use the protocol for illicit activities. They may be accountable for certain activities and liable for others, but that needs to be clarified at the outset.

The other key area where legal clarity is needed is around intellectual property. As digital assets grow in market capitalization, legal guidance is required to ensure clear ownership rights. The year 2022 saw several NFT collections embrace Creative Commons Zero (CC0), where the NFT community relinquished intellectual property rights on the collection. However, this absolutist route may not be possible for all digital asset communities. Legal frameworks may also need to be codified to some extent to ensure any smart contract development reflects these frameworks. The legal stance behind the treatment of intellectual property around digital assets may also decide how metaverse adoption takes off in the future.

Taking our imagination further down the road, could we find utility in a legal metaverse with on-chain arbitration, where disputes are resolved on the blockchain? This is what MetaCourt, a legal tech startup, is on the quest to find out.[5]

There is no lack of areas where legal and regulatory oversight can add value to the web3 ecosystem. In order for cryptos and NFTs to go mainstream with institutional capital and adoption, regulatory clarity is a must.

User Experience

Despite some of the smartest minds contributing to the industry, the crypto user experience is arguably the worst possible digital experience that one could go through. It can be intimidating and complex to create a wallet, write down the private key, and fund the wallet, as demonstrated by the step-by-step guide provided earlier in the book on what it would take for a new user to purchase an NFT.

From creating an exchange account, to buying cryptos, creating a wallet, moving the cryptos using the long wallet address, connecting to the NFT marketplace, and buying the NFT, the journey couldn't have been more complicated, especially when compared to the web2 equivalent of online purchase experience. This must be addressed in the next few years for web3 to attract mainstream web2 digital audiences.

There are now several on-ramp solutions in place to allow users to buy cryptos from their wallets using cards and bank accounts. We also need "private keyless" wallets such as ZenGo that can make the process of creating a wallet simpler, smoother, yet secure. Web3 user journeys must become friction-free like their web2 counterparts.

In fact, behind-the-scenes technology complexities should be hidden from the user, as long as they understand that the new application would use their data more responsibly and with transparency, giving them fair compensation for their contribution to the application ecosystem. Any assets they hold in the application would be theirs, with real-world value.

On that note, while the web3 ecosystem has had excellent engineers, architects, and people with great technical knowledge, we can all benefit from outstanding narrators to help simplify the story. The consensus mechanism a protocol layer chooses to use, or the blockchain their transaction resides in, are data points that would not necessarily interest most users. To speed up user adoption and gain trust will require better storytelling.

Technology Innovation

There are several challenges within web3 that need top-notch engineering talent to address, in order to deliver the optimal experience at scale that meets the needs and use cases of the future.

The "blockchain trilemma" still remains the trillion-dollar problem that the industry grapples with, in that decentralized networks can only provide two out of three benefits at any given time: decentralization, security, and scalability. Even as new generations of blockchains emerge, scalability remains a key issue to resolve for most blockchains where transactions still take seconds and minutes. While greater scalability is possible, security, decentralization, or both, will suffer as a result.

The other scalability aspect, particularly with respect to social media, is storage costs. Blockchain can be a great transaction ledger, but it is not a big data storage layer for large data types such as images and videos. The approximate cost of on-chain storage for 1 gigabyte of data on Ethereum is approximately $390 million, whereas it is much lower on Solana at $1.3 million and even lower on the DeSo blockchain at $80.

However, spending $80 for 1 GB storage is still unsustainable for big social media sites that generate petabytes and zettabytes of data every day, and growing exponentially. According to the International Data Corporation, Global DataSphere is expected to more than double in size from 2022 to 2026, reaching more than 221,000 exabytes (an exabyte is 1,000 petabytes) by 2026.[6]

With more than 2.2 billion monthly active users, Facebook is the largest social networking site in the world, generating 4 petabytes of data on a daily basis.[7] If all this data were stored on the DeSo blockchain, it would cost $320 million per day and a cost base of around $117 billion per year. With just over $116 billion in revenue for 2022,[8] if the entire Facebook data were to go on-chain using DeSo, the business would be instantly unviable.

This is not meant to be a criticism of current blockchains; rather, it is a way to demonstrate that there is still plenty of work to be done if we want to realize the web3 internet.

Beyond Scalability

We have described immersive experiences that the metaverse could deliver using VR, AR, and extended reality (XR) headsets. However, these headsets can only offer those experiences if the environments are built with high-quality processors. Delivering the right experience will require immense processing power and storage of high-quality graphics in cloud servers and client devices alike, much more so than what we have today.

The roll-out of such an infrastructure is also reliant on availability and affordability of high-bandwidth internet. As a result, we would see a digital divide for a period of time.

While this may not be an exhaustive wish list, the need for high-quality engineering solutions to accommodate millions of simultaneous users on a metaverse experience cannot be underestimated. For fast-action multiplayer games in particular, high latency will result in sub-par experience. Capturing concurrent changes and ensuring they are reflected across thousands of participants with minimum lag is a big engineering challenge.

One of the challenges that classical computers have had is in the processing of multiple concurrent states, and this is where quantum computers can fill the gaps. But quantum computers are not mainstream yet and they have their own stability challenges to overcome before they become commercially viable.

State management in the metaverse is one of the harder problems to solve. A medium-term solution that some gaming and metaverse platforms have used is to limit the number of concurrent states by allowing only up to 100 gamers, for example, to play an instance of a game at any point. While this is a more manageable solution for the time being, it needs to be fixed in the long term.

Diversity, Equity, and Inclusion

In Chapter 9, we reviewed examples of new opportunities to drive positive impact, and how the technology behind web3 can help underrepresented communities gain better economic outcomes. In fact, web3 entrepreneur Del Titus Bawuah in an interview with Dominic-Madori Davis from Techcrunch stated optimistically: "Through the power of web3, we could be looking at an entirely new world where a lot of what is disjointed within our technological infrastructure could be completely renewed."[9]

While funding to web3 startups cooled off in 2022, falling from a record high of $29.2 billion in 2021 to $21.5 billion in 2022,[10] US Black web3 founders were able to raise $60 million, which was substantially higher than the $16 million raised in 2021. This is by no means close to the parity that we seek. But it does offer a small glimmer of hope that change is on the horizon.

To create a vibrant ecosystem that truly represents the ethos of web3 and the future of the internet, we must be more intentional in bringing diverse voices and talent to the table. And we cannot overstate the urgency. Especially if the emerging ecosystems have such transformation potential for communities worldwide, we cannot— and we must not—repeat mistakes of the past where underrepresented communities were simply forgotten, if not dismissed.

Increasing talent representation in the fast-growing ecosystem can help ensure that the technology solutions are inclusive of the needs and perspectives of those who typically are not invited to the table. Providing more targeted education programs, especially in science, technology, engineering, and math (STEM), can encourage participation and offer more opportunities and pathways for students from underserved communities, while providing a new and diverse source of talent for companies.

The new tech paradigm offers us a golden opportunity to do things differently and better. And it will be up to all of us to change the status quo for a better future. The only way we can all thrive is together.

The Capital Ecosystem

The capital ecosystem must also attract institutional players who can bring better liquidity, reduce volatility, and, more importantly, make this a more credible environment that can be sustained through business cycles. In Chapter 10 we discussed the need for a more mature capital ecosystem. While a more inclusive and innovative capital ecosystem is possible due to the web3 infrastructure, regulations are needed to ensure actors of this system are governed appropriately. Investor protection is hardly appreciated by the stakeholders of this ecosystem, and regulations would ensure that changes.

The Opening Act

In essence, we have all the building blocks that we need for Internet 2.0 to take shape. There is enough work in the pipeline for at least another decade for all of us to make this dream come true. So what can you do with what you have learned so far? And why does it matter?

To start with, all of us must keep an open mind. Web3 is not full of scammers, as it is often portrayed to be. The previous wave of innovation that happened in the 1990s and 2000s largely focused on protocols and applications that dealt with user data. With this wave of innovation, we have a chance to create a new value ecosystem.

Bugs and design flaws often lead to loss of retail and institutional capital; that is the nature of the beast. But just because we have made mistakes does not mean that we stop innovating. Rather, we need to learn from what did not work and move forward.

While governance can help to reduce damage, bringing governance to a green space too early can be counterproductive. We need to learn to appreciate the fine line that the entire ecosystem, government agencies, regulators, and capital providers have to walk. It is also helpful to remember that the concept of the new technology paradigm has been around for merely 15 years. Relative to other advanced technologies such as quantum computing, which has been in the labs for almost a century, and AI, which has had several winters and springs, web3 is still nascent; we simply cannot compare this market to the more matured mainstream capital markets. And it will take more work before it can build credibility and become less volatile.

Bear in mind that the road ahead is not without its finite disappointments and curveballs. But it is not lacking in infinite hope either. Learning by doing is one of the tried-and-true methods when it comes to innovating. There has never been a better time to start than now. We are just warming up.

NOTES

Foreword

1 Meta. Founder's letter 2021, Meta, October 28, 2021. about.fb.com/news/2021/10/founders-letter/ (archived at https://perma.cc/LQ38-NPW2)
2 J P Morgan. *Opportunities in the Metaverse*, J P Morgan, 2022. www.jpmorgan.com/content/dam/jpm/treasury-services/documents/opportunities-in-the-metaverse.pdf (archived at https://perma.cc/CY7H-G236)

Preface

1 Anon G McGovern. 99% of data has been produced in the last 10 years, CMSWire, February 10, 2023. www.cmswire.com/customer-experience/99-of-data-has-been-produced-in-the-last-10-years/ (archived at https://perma.cc/KC4S-3VUY)

1.   Background

1 M Osman. Wild and interesting Facebook statistics and facts (2023), Kinsta, December 6, 2022. kinsta.com/blog/facebook-statistics/ (archived at https://perma.cc/7ERD-FLUE)
2 Similarweb. google.com traffic and engagement analysis, Similarweb, nd. www.similarweb.com/website/google.com/#traffic (archived at https://perma.cc/VY5U-3SH6)
3 J Zote. 26 Facebook statistics marketers should know in 2023, Sproutsocial, February 14, 2023. sproutsocial.com/insights/facebook-stats-for-marketers/ (archived at https://perma.cc/8ALS-RLSU)
4 Statista. Net digital advertising revenue share of major ad-selling online companies worldwide from 2016 to 2023, March 9, 2022. www.statista.com/statistics/290629/digital-ad-revenue-share-of-major-ad-selling-companies-worldwide/ (archived at https://perma.cc/85U9-X3PR)

5 S Chevalier. Retail e-commerce sales worldwide from 2014 to 2026, Statista, September 21, 2022. www.statista.com/statistics/379046/worldwide-retail-e-commerce-sales/ (archived at https://perma.cc/6PK9-YUYA)

6 Computer History Museum. Hewlett-Packard Company (HP), Computer History Museum, nd. www.computerhistory.org/brochures/g-i/hewlettpackard-company-hp/ (archived at https://perma.cc/997H-95VK)

7 Nobel Prize. The Nobel Prize in Physics 1956, William B. Shockley biographical, Nobel Prize, nd. www.nobelprize.org/prizes/physics/1956/shockley/biographical/ (archived at https://perma.cc/7EYH-XEMD)

8 White House. Fact sheet: CHIPS and Science Act will lower costs, create jobs, strengthen supply chains, and counter China, White House, August 9, 2022. www.whitehouse.gov/briefing-room/statements-releases/2022/08/09/fact-sheet-chips-and-science-act-will-lower-costs-create-jobs-strengthen-supply-chains-and-counter-china/ (archived at https://perma.cc/B7KH-J93P)

9 PC Magazine. The biggest tech mergers and acquisitions of all time, PC Magazine, April 12, 2021. www.pcmag.com/news/the-biggest-tech-mergers-and-acquisitions-of-all-time (archived at https://perma.cc/2DS5-WYQU)

10 GDPR.EU. What is GDPR, the EU's new data protection law? GDPR. EU, nd. gdpr.eu/what-is-gdpr/

11 GDPR Enforcement Tracker. Statistics: Fines imposed over time, GDPR Enforcement Tracker, nd. www.enforcementtracker.com/?insights (archived at https://perma.cc/ENW9-4GAP)

12 European Parliament. Deal on Digital Markets Act: EU rules to ensure fair competition and more choice for users, European Parliament, July 1, 2022) www.europarl.europa.eu/news/en/press-room/20220315IPR25504/deal-on-digital-markets-act-ensuring-fair-competition-and-more-choice-for-users (archived at https://perma.cc/J8Y5-BBPY)

13 World Bank. *The Global Findex Database 2021*, World Bank, 2022, 134–35. www.worldbank.org/en/publication/globalfindex/Report (archived at https://perma.cc/JWE9-T6ZG)

14 Alliance for Affordable Internet. *The Costs of Exclusion: South Asia regional report*, Alliance for Affordable Internet, 2022, 5. webfoundation.org/docs/2022/06/EnglishReport.pdf (archived at https://perma.cc/Z972-9TUC)

15 World Bank. *The Global Findex Database 2021*, World Bank, 2022, 37. www.worldbank.org/en/publication/globalfindex/Report (archived at https://perma.cc/JWE9-T6ZG)

2. The Future is Web3

1 J Fischels. A look back at the very first website ever launched, 30 years later, NPR, August 6, 2021. www.npr.org/2021/08/06/1025554426/a-look-back-at-the-very-first-website-ever-launched-30-years-later (archived at https://perma.cc/DJ28-3KL6)

2 Statista. Advertising revenue of major digital ad-selling companies worldwide in 2022, Statista, March 22, 2022. www.statista.com/statistics/1202672/digital-ad-revenue-ad-selling-companies-worldwide/ (archived at https://perma.cc/KK7U-FXLH)

3 S Joseph and R Shields. The rundown: Google, Meta and Amazon are on track to absorb more than 50% of all ad money in 2022, Digiday, February 4, 2022. digiday.com/marketing/the-rundown-google-meta-and-amazon-are-on-track-to-absorb-more-than-50-of-all-ad-money-in-2022/ (archived at https://perma.cc/B6A2-XE9J)

4 Web3 Foundation. About, Web3 Foundation, nd. Web3.foundation/about/ (archived at https://perma.cc/7TPW-XN2X)

5 M Gottlich. NFT market cap could reach over $80B by 2025—CoinDesk, Seeking Alpha, January 20, 2022. seekingalpha.com/news/3789990-nft-market-cap-could-reach-over-80b-by-2025-analyst-says (archived at https://perma.cc/HZ4P-9HRJ)

6 PwC. Perspectives from the Global Entertainment & Media Outlook 2022–2026, PwC, nd. www.pwc.com/gx/en/industries/tmt/media/outlook/outlook-perspectives.html (archived at https://perma.cc/4ZGP-UM22)

7 History.com. This day in history: July 16, 1995—Amazon opens for business, History.com, November 4, 2015. www.history.com/this-day-in-history/amazon-opens-for-business (archived at https://perma.cc/8RQS-4A7R)

8 Slate. Amazon: Ponzi scheme or Wal-Mart of the web? Slate, December 8, 2000. slate.com/business/2000/02/amazon-ponzi-scheme-or-wal-mart-of-the-web.html (archived at https://perma.cc/84VC-YQ9J)

9 S Lebow. Gamers make up more than a third of the world's population, Insider Intelligence, October 19, 2021. www.insiderintelligence.com/content/gamers-make-up-more-than-one-third-of-world-population (archived at https://perma.cc/Y3ME-K7CH)

10 D Nelson. Solana Labs is building a Web3 mobile phone, Coindesk, June 23, 2022. www.coindesk.com/business/2022/06/23/solana-labs-is-building-a-Web3-mobile-phone/ (archived at https://perma.cc/H9W8-6RED)

11 Grand Amphi Théatre. Vitalik Buterin, YouTube, July 21, 2022. www.youtube.com/watch?v=kGjFTzRTH3Q (archived at https://perma.cc/N3GM-KHYQ)

3. Non-Fungible Tokens and the Ownership Economy

1 Duke Pratt School of Engineering. Duke Engineering's fintech program sends certificates to Coursera students as NFTs, Duke Pratt School of Engineering, January 13, 2022. pratt.duke.edu/about/news/duke-engineerings-fintech-program-sends-certificates-coursera-students-nfts (archived at https://perma.cc/4KJM-KE2A)

2 BBC News. NFT or non-fungible token is Collins Dictionary's word of the year, BBC News, November 24, 2021. www.bbc.com/news/newsbeat-59401046 (archived at https://perma.cc/QED4-WKK9)

3 Y Assia. Bitcoin 2.X (aka Colored Bitcoin)—initial specs, Yoni Assia, 27 March 2012. yoniassia.com/coloredbitcoin/ (archived at https://perma.cc/4S88-UY2B)

4 M Rosenfeld. Overview of Colored Coins, Bitcoil, December 4, 2012. bitcoil.co.il/BitcoinX.pdf (archived at https://perma.cc/EG4G-X5KR)

5 R Shelburne. Golden State Warriors become first pro team to launch NFT collection, ESPN, April 27, 2021. www.espn.com/nba/story/_/id/31344010/golden-state-warriors-become-first-pro-team-launch-nft-collection (archived at https://perma.cc/G4Q6-ZEU3)

6 Sensorium. 10 most expensive NFTs ever sold [June 2022 update], Sensorium, June 10, 2012. sensoriumxr.com/articles/most-expensive-nft-sales (archived at https://perma.cc/R5W4-BBHA)

7 Julien's Auctions, Event details: Lennon Connection—The NFT collection, Julien's Auctions, February 7, 2022. www.juliensauctions.com/about-auction?id=400 (archived at https://perma.cc/B2ZZ-KWA2)

8 Roblox. The Gucci Garden experience lands on Roblox, Roblox, May 17, 2021. blog.roblox.com/2021/05/gucci-garden-experience/ (archived at https://perma.cc/J6P6-9TWZ)

9 L Bitsky. Justin Bieber buys Bored Ape NFT for $1.29m, Page Six, January 31, 2022. pagesix.com/2022/01/31/justin-bieber-buys-bored-ape-nft-for-1-3m/ (archived at https://perma.cc/VB5E-WFHU)

4. Decentralized Finance

1 FDIC, Deposit Insurance FAQs, FDIC, December 8, 2021. www.fdic.
gov/resources/deposit-insurance/faq/ (archived at https://perma.cc/
FWN8-VZXG)

2 Federal Reserve History, Banking Act of 1933 (Glass-Steagall),
November 22, 2013. www.federalreservehistory.org/essays/glass-
steagall-act (archived at https://perma.cc/U9DY-AYCR)

3 FDIC. Letter: Potential violations of Section 18(a)(4) of the Federal
Deposit Insurance Act [FDIC issues cease and desist letters to five
companies for making crypto-related false or misleading
representations about deposit insurance], FDIC, August 18, 2022.
www.fdic.gov/news/press-releases/2022/ftx-harrison-letter.pdf
(archived at https://perma.cc/6QT5-S9BU)

4 N De. FDIC orders crypto exchange FTX US, 4 others to cease
"misleading" claims, Coindesk, August 19 2022. www.coindesk.com/
policy/2022/08/19/fdic-orders-ftx-us-4-other-companies-to-cease-and-
desist-misleading-consumers/ (archived at https://perma.cc/4M7J-PZZK)

5 P Daian. Flash Boys 2.0: Frontrunning, transaction reordering, and
consensus instability in decentralized exchanges, Cornell University,
April 10, 2019. arxiv.org/abs/1904.05234 (archived at https://perma.cc/
97K7-GYHG)

6 Ethereum. Maximal extractable value (MEV), Ethereum, August 30,
2022. ethereum.org/en/developers/docs/mev/ (archived at
https://perma.cc/BD7D-8A5S)

7 T Farren. ImmuneFi report $10B in DeFi hacks and losses across 2021,
Cointelegraph, January 7, 2022. cointelegraph.com/news/immunefi-
report-10b-in-defi-hacks-and-losses-across-2021 (archived at
https://perma.cc/PZ6E-JA56)

8 CertiK. *HACK3D: The Web3 security quarterly report—Q2 2022*,
CertiK, July 6, 2022. 4972390.fs1.hubspotusercontent-na1.net/hubfs/
4972390/Marketing/Web3%20Security%20Q2-2022-v4.pdf (archived
at https://perma.cc/CCJ6-QXCV)

9 Statistica. TVL (total value locked) in five different decentralized
finance (DeFi) segments on the Ethereum blockchain as of March 29,
2022, Statistica, March 29, 2022. www.statista.com/statistics/1263220/
defi-market-size-value-crypto-locked-usd-by-segment/ (archived at
https://perma.cc/MRT6-SY9R)

10 moreReese. What are Soulbound Tokens? Building blocks for a Web3
decentralized society, Decrypt, June 9, 2022. decrypt.co/resources/

what-are-soulbound-tokens-building-blocks-for-a-Web3-decentralized-society (archived at https://perma.cc/BAR7-AYY3)

11 Uniswap. What is Uniswap? Uniswap, nd. docs.uniswap.org/protocol/introduction (archived at https://perma.cc/TF6A-Z75L)

12 V Desai, A Diofasi, and J Lu. The global identification challenge: Who are the 1 billion people without proof of identity? World Bank, April 25, 2018. blogs.worldbank.org/voices/global-identification-challenge-who-are-1-billion-people-without-proof-identity (archived at https://perma.cc/SZU4-4VM2)

13 M Rutkowski, A Garcia Mora, G L Bull, B Guermazi, and C Grown. Responding to crisis with digital payments for social protection: Short-term measures with long-term benefits, World Bank, March 31, 2020. blogs.worldbank.org/voices/responding-crisis-digital-payments-social-protection-short-term-measures-long-term-benefits (archived at https://perma.cc/L9QT-2558)

14 Microsoft. Thousands of displaced Filipinos empowered with digital IDs from AID:Tech and Save the Children, enabling faster access to critical financial aid, Microsoft, July 9, 2021. news.microsoft.com/en-ph/2021/07/09/thousands-of-displaced-filipinos-empowered-with-digital-ids-from-aidtech-and-save-the-children-enabling-faster-access-to-critical-financial-aid/ (archived at https://perma.cc/AJ4X-D5ZJ)

15 AID:Tech. Volunteering reimagined, AID:Tech, nd. www.aid.technology/kaulana (archived at https://perma.cc/D5MC-DT5L)

16 R Wolfson. Reinventing yourself in the metaverse through digital identity, Cointelegraph, August 11, 2022. cointelegraph.com/news/reinventing-yourself-in-the-metaverse-through-digital-identity (archived at https://perma.cc/ND8Z-9Z4W)

17 S Graves and E Genc. 13 biggest DeFi hacks and heists, Decryp, April 18, 2022. decrypt.co/93874/biggest-defi-hacks-heists (archived at https://perma.cc/TK6W-9Z2Y)

18 S Graves and E Genc. 13 biggest DeFi hacks and heists, Decryp, April 18, 2022. decrypt.co/93874/biggest-defi-hacks-heists (archived at https://perma.cc/TK6W-9Z2Y)

19 S Graves and E Genc. 13 biggest DeFi hacks and heists, Decryp, April 18, 2022. decrypt.co/93874/biggest-defi-hacks-heists (archived at https://perma.cc/TK6W-9Z2Y)

20 S Graves and E Genc. 13 biggest DeFi hacks and heists, Decryp, April 18, 2022. decrypt.co/93874/biggest-defi-hacks-heists (archived at https://perma.cc/TK6W-9Z2Y)

21 S Graves and E Genc. 13 biggest DeFi hacks and heists, Decryp, April 18, 2022. decrypt.co/93874/biggest-defi-hacks-heists (archived at https://perma.cc/TK6W-9Z2Y)

22 S Graves and E Genc. 13 biggest DeFi hacks and heists, Decryp, April 18, 2022. decrypt.co/93874/biggest-defi-hacks-heists (archived at https://perma.cc/TK6W-9Z2Y)

5.   GameFi—Experiential Pillar of the Metaverse

1 National Museum of American History. The Brown Box, 1967–68, National Museum of American History, nd. americanhistory.si.edu/collections/search/object/nmah_1301997 (archived at https://perma.cc/WL97-SX7B)

2 Visual Capitalist. 50 years of gaming history, by revenue stream (1970–2020), Visual Capitalist, nd. www.visualcapitalist.com/50-years-gaming-history-revenue-stream/ (archived at https://perma.cc/8Y5W-JU4L)

3 Visual Capitalist. 50 years of gaming history, by revenue stream (1970–2020), Visual Capitalist, nd. www.visualcapitalist.com/50-years-gaming-history-revenue-stream/ (archived at https://perma.cc/8Y5W-JU4L)

4 PwC. Perspectives from the Global Entertainment and Media Outlook 2022–2026, PwC, nd. www.pwc.com/gx/en/industries/tmt/media/outlook/outlook-perspectives.html (archived at https://perma.cc/4ZGP-UM22)

5 Statista. Global games market revenue share by segment 2022, Statista, 2023. www.statista.com/statistics/298403/global-video-games-revenue-segment/ (archived at https://perma.cc/Q52J-FC5T)

6 Data.ai. Mobile gaming 2022 and beyond, Data.ai, nd. www.data.ai/en/go/mobile-gaming-2022-and-beyond-report/ (archived at https://perma.cc/9VCJ-D6RZ)

7 Guinness World Records. Most successful video game engine, Guinness World Records, July 16, 2014. www.guinnessworldrecords.com/world-records/most-successful-game-engine (archived at https://perma.cc/RG94-X3NG)

8 M Iqbal. Fortnite usage and revenue statistics (2022), Business of Apps, September 6, 2022. www.businessofapps.com/data/fortnite-statistics/ (archived at https://perma.cc/2YEF-YBSA)

9 Roblox. Roblox reports fourth quarter and full year 2022 financial results, Roblox, February 15, 2023. ir.roblox.com/news/news-details/2023/Roblox-Reports-Fourth-Quarter-and-Full-Year-2022-Financial-Results/default.aspx (archived at https://perma.cc/J4UF-BZ5C)

10 Activeplayer. Axie Infinity live player count and statistics, Activeplayer, nd. activeplayer.io/axie-infinity/ (archived at https://perma.cc/UVM5-HKLB)

11 Z Sun. Axie Infinity player count falls back to Jan 2021 levels, Cointelegraph, October 12, 2022. cointelegraph.com/news/axie-infinity-player-count-falls-back-to-jan-2021-levels (archived at https://perma.cc/C5AU-CDF9)

12 Activeplayer. PUBG live player count and statistics, Activeplayer, nd. activeplayer.io/pubg/ (archived at https://perma.cc/DQF3-7AR4)

13 D Curry. PUBG mobile revenue and usage statistics (2022), Business of Apps, September 6, 2022. www.businessofapps.com/data/pubg-mobile-statistics/ (archived at https://perma.cc/MX86-UEC7)

14 K Molenaar. 51 mobile app stats that will blow your mind, Influencer Marketing Hub, November 23, 2022. influencermarketinghub.com/mobile-app-stats/ (archived at https://perma.cc/T8VJ-MAEX)

15 W Witkowski. Videogames are a bigger industry than movies and North American sports combined, thanks to the pandemic, MarketWatch, January 2, 2021. www.marketwatch.com/story/videogames-are-a-bigger-industry-than-sports-and-movies-combined-thanks-to-the-pandemic-11608654990 (archived at https://perma.cc/QU3L-L9MV)

16 Cypherhunter. Vitalik Buterin, Cyperhunter, nd. www.cypherhunter.com/en/p/vitalik-buterin/ (archived at https://perma.cc/Z7DY-V7WY)

17 Roblox. Roblox reports fourth quarter and full year 2022 financial results, Roblox, February 15, 2023. ir.roblox.com/news/news-details/2023/Roblox-Reports-Fourth-Quarter-and-Full-Year-2022-Financial-Results/default.aspx (archived at https://perma.cc/J4UF-BZ5C)

18 T Huong Le. Mark Cuban joins Vietnamese gaming startup Sky Mavis' $7.5m series A round, Tech in Asia, May 11, 2021. www.techinasia.com/mark-cuban-libertus-capital-join-vietnamese-gaming-startup-sky-mavis-75m-series-a-round (archived at https://perma.cc/4NPR-ENA9)

19 Activeplayer. Axie Infinity live player count and statistics, Activeplayer, nd. activeplayer.io/axie-infinity/ (archived at https://perma.cc/UVM5-HKLB)

20 Activeplayer. Axie Infinity live player count and statistics, Activeplayer, nd. activeplayer.io/axie-infinity/ (archived at https://perma.cc/UVM5-HKLB)

21 J P Buntinx. Move-to-earn Darling STEPN has under 350 new users per day as GMT momentum sours further, Crypto Mode, October 11, 2022. cryptomode.com/move-to-earn-darling-stepn-has-under-350-new-users-per-day-as-gmt-momentum-sours-further/ (archived at https://perma.cc/UM8R-FWKL)

22 M K Manoylov. Users logged over 67 million miles on the move-to-earn app Stepn since launch, The Block, September 22, 2022. www.theblock.co/post/172123/users-logged-over-67-million-miles-on-the-move-to-earn-app-stepn-since-launch (archived at https://perma.cc/55LJ-2W28)

23 Google Play. Change the game, Google Play, nd. services.google.com/fh/files/misc/changethegame_white_paper.pdf (archived at https://perma.cc/RA2N-H7V5)

24 A Chen, J Lai, and J Gwertzman. Games Fund One: Building the future of games, a16z, May 18, 2022. a16z.com/2022/05/18/games-fund-one-building-the-future-of-games/ (archived at https://perma.cc/7TXX-NWJL)

6. The Metaverse

1 J Desjardins. The rising speed of technological adoption, Visual Capitalist, February 14, 2018. www.visualcapitalist.com/rising-speed-technological-adoption/ (archived at https://perma.cc/4C58-ZUBY)

2 Slate. Amazon: Ponzi scheme or Wal-Mart of the Web? Slate, February 8, 2000). slate.com/business/2000/02/amazon-ponzi-scheme-or-wal-mart-of-the-web.html (archived at https://perma.cc/84VC-YQ9J)

3 E Nix. The world's first web site, History.com, nd. www.history.com/news/the-worlds-first-web-site (archived at https://perma.cc/UT7D-6RCX)

4 Roblox. Roblox reports fourth quarter and full year 2022 financial results, Roblox, February 15, 2023. ir.roblox.com/news/news-details/2023/Roblox-Reports-Fourth-Quarter-and-Full-Year-2022-Financial-Results/default.aspx (archived at https://perma.cc/J4UF-BZ5C)

5 Roblox. Roblox reports fourth quarter and full year 2022 financial results, Roblox, February 15, 2023. ir.roblox.com/news/news-details/2023/Roblox-Reports-Fourth-Quarter-and-Full-Year-2022-Financial-Results/default.aspx (archived at https://perma.cc/J4UF-BZ5C)

6 Roblox. Homepage, Roblox, nd. corp.roblox.com/ (archived at https://perma.cc/G7XW-RTLF)

7 Roblox. Form 8-K, Roblox, February 15, 2023. s27.q4cdn. com/984876518/files/doc_downloads/2023/02/RBLX-2023.02.15-8-K-EX99.1-and-EX99.2-SEC-Filed.pdf (archived at https://perma.cc/S4VM-KEY4)

8 Roblox. Q4 2022 supplemental materials, Roblox, February 15, 2023. https://s27.q4cdn.com/984876518/files/doc_financials/2022/q4/Q4'22-Supplemental-Materials-[FINAL].pdf (archived at https://perma.cc/U9XW-U6VW)

9 T Huddleston Jr. This 21-year-old is paying for college (and more) off an amateur video game he made in high school, CNBC, September 23, 2019. www.cnbc.com/2019/09/23/college-student-video-game-creator-made-millions-from-jailbreak.html (archived at https://perma.cc/7S9Z-2ANP)

10 J Boniface. Funding the future of Roblox creations, Roblox, September 20, 2022. blog.roblox.com/2022/09/funding-future-roblox-creations/ (archived at https://perma.cc/Y8KP-U8CN)

11 Roblox. Game Fund, Roblox, nd. create.roblox.com/docs/production/monetization/game-fund (archived at https://perma.cc/C38A-RTM9)

12 S Needleman and S Donaldson. Kids don't want cash anymore—they want "Robux," *Wall Street Journal*, December2, 2022. www.wsj.com/articles/robux-kids-virtual-currency-metaverse-cryptocurrency-11669929636 (archived at https://perma.cc/96MY-KZH9)

13 A Webster. Gucci built a persistent town inside of Roblox, The Verge, May 27, 2022. www.theverge.com/2022/5/27/23143404/gucci-town-roblox (archived at https://perma.cc/CKA5-K8PR)

14 PSFK Research. Nikeland Roblox activation brings the metaverse into the store, PSFK Research, February 27, 2022. www.psfk.com/2022/02/nikeland-roblox-activation-brings-the-metaverse-into-the-store.html (archived at https://perma.cc/HNA3-5DFS)

15 C Sutcliffe. 21m people have now visited Nike's Roblox store. Here's how to do metaverse commerce right, The Drum, September 22, 2022. www.thedrum.com/news/2022/09/22/21m-people-have-now-visited-nike-s-roblox-store-here-s-how-do-metaverse-commerce (archived at https://perma.cc/67KZ-MB7B)

16 Lavazza. Lavazza enters the metaverse with Lavazza Arena! PR Newswire, September 29, 2022. www.prnewswire.com/news-releases/lavazza-enters-the-metaverse-with-lavazza-arena-301636803.html (archived at https://perma.cc/YJ5B-FRAS)

17 Walmart. Walmart jumps into Roblox with launch of Walmart Land and Walmart's Universe of Play, Walmart, September 26, 2022. corporate.walmart.com/newsroom/2022/09/26/walmart-jumps-into-roblox-with-launch-of-walmart-land-and-walmarts-universe-of-play (archived at https://perma.cc/6QXE-AAKR)

18 J Casale. Museum of Science, Boston enters metaverse with "Mission: Mars" Roblox experience, eSchool News, January 31, 2023. www.eschoolnews.com/digital-learning/2023/01/31/metaverse-mission-mars-roblox/ (archived at https://perma.cc/PV9D-S2GE)

19 M Iqbal. Fortnite usage and revenue statistics (2022), Business of Apps, September 6, 2022. www.businessofapps.com/data/fortnite-statistics/ (archived at https://perma.cc/2YEF-YBSA)

20 M Iqbal. Fortnite usage and revenue statistics (2022), Business of Apps, September 6, 2022. www.businessofapps.com/data/fortnite-statistics/ (archived at https://perma.cc/2YEF-YBSA)

21 W Ketchum III. Fortnite's Travis Scott concert was historic. But he's not the only artist getting creative, NBC News, April 30, 2020. www.nbcnews.com/think/opinion/fortnite-s-travis-scott-concert-was-historic-he-s-not-ncna1195686 (archived at https://perma.cc/GX6F-WNR6)

22 DappRadar. The Sandbox, DappRadar, nd. dappradar.com/polygon/games/the-sandbox (archived at https://perma.cc/E7D7-AUPK)

23 The Sandbox. The Sandbox Alpha Season 3 reached 17m visits, a threefold increase over Season 2, Medium, December 2, 2022. medium.com/sandbox-game/the-sandbox-alpha-season-3-reached-17m-visits-a-threefold-increase-over-season-2-5f56071455aa (archived at https://perma.cc/NHJ7-EGDK)

24 D Takahashi. The Sandbox metaverse hits 2m users and launches Alpha Sesson 2, GamesBeat, March 3, 2022. venturebeat.com/pc-gaming/the-sandbox-metaverse-hits-2m-users-and-launches-alpha-season-2/ (archived at https://perma.cc/BVG6-Y9T3)

25 The Sandbox. What is SAND used for? The Sandbox, nd. sandboxgame.gitbook.io/the-sandbox/sand/what-is-sand-used-for (archived at https://perma.cc/WSP7-WNKM)

26 Decentraland. Decentraland Public Launch (15 January 2020), Decentraland, January 15, 2020. decentraland.org/blog/announcements/decentraland-announces-publich-launch/ (archived at https://perma.cc/6GML-LZUL)

27 Samsung. What's new at Samsung 837X in Decentraland and on Discord? Find out here, Samsung, November 8, 2022. news.samsung.

com/us/samsung-whats-new-837x-decentraland-discord-metaverse (archived at https://perma.cc/X7HH-C8YG)

28 S Tse. The highs and lows of the first-ever metaverse fashion week, Elle, March 31, 2022. www.elle.com/fashion/a39589084/metaverse-fashion-week-highs-and-lows/ (archived at https://perma.cc/BVY7-3XB9)

29 C Davies and S Jung-a. Asia's largest metaverse platform ZEPETO ramps up global expansion, *Financial Times*, September 26, 2022. www.ft.com/content/14c88e84-f3c8-485e-a9df-31ead34e48f0 (archived at https://perma.cc/2Y9A-73CG)

30 C May Choon, D Dasgupta, T Tam Mei, K Wei, A Cheng Wei, et al. Metaverse craze hits Asia, with cities and companies chasing after a $1.1 trillion pie, *The Straits Times*, September 10, 2022. www. straitstimes.com/asia/metaverse-craze-hits-asia-with-cities-and-companies-chasing-after-a-11-trillion-pie (archived at https://perma.cc/7JD7-SNAM)

31 ZTX Foundation. ZTX Litepaper, ZTX Foundation, nd. www.zepetox. io/ztx-litepaper.pdf (archived at https://perma.cc/739Z-K3YQ)

32 Seoul Metropolitan Government. Seoul, first local gov't to start new-concept public service with "metaverse platform," Seoul Metropolitan Government, November 8, 2021. english.seoul.go.kr/ seoul-first-local-govt-to-start-new-concept-public-service-with-metaverse-platform/ (archived at https://perma.cc/XDV8-RAJF)

33 J Keane. South Korea is betting on the metaverse—and it could provide a blueprint for others, CNBC, 30 May 2022. www.cnbc.com/ 2022/05/30/south-koreas-investment-in-the-metaverse-could-provide-a-blueprint.html (archived at https://perma.cc/M6EE-YJMJ)

34 Mave:. Profile, Mave:, nd. www.mave-official.com/en/profile (archived at https://perma.cc/9XF2-96TA)

35 Smobler Studios. The Sandbox's first metaverse wedding set in Singapore's historic Alkaff Mansion, Smobler Studios, September 19, 2022. www.prnewswire.com/news-releases/the-sandboxs-first-metaverse-wedding-set-in-singapores-historic-alkaff-mansion-301626820.html (archived at https://perma.cc/NG42-XQ3L)

36 CNBCTV18. The world's first metaverse wedding just happened; what's next, CNBCTV18, December 17, 2021. www.cnbctv18.com/ technology/the-worlds-first-metaverse-wedding-just-happened-whats-next-11852472.htm (archived at https://perma.cc/PX9H-B7YZ)

37 A Sharma. Sheikh Hamdan approves new phase of Dubai Metaverse Strategy, The National, November 24, 2022. www.thenationalnews.com/

business/2022/11/24/sheikh-hamdan-approves-new-phase-of-dubai-metaverse-strategy/ (archived at https://perma.cc/B579-YUEE)

38 A Cabral. Dubai's virtual assets regulator becomes world's first authority to enter the metaverse, The National, May 3, 2022. www.thenationalnews.com/business/technology/2022/05/03/dubais-virtual-assets-regulator-becomes-worlds-first-authority-to-enter-the-metaverse/ (archived at https://perma.cc/C3QV-JQ5R)

39 A Thurman. Barbados to become first sovereign nation with an embassy in the metaverse, Coindesk, November 15, 2021. www.coindesk.com/business/2021/11/15/barbados-to-become-first-sovereign-nation-with-an-embassy-in-the-metaverse/ (archived at https://perma.cc/Q6GV-ZG3F)

40 C Thompson. Norway steps into the metaverse with decentraland tax office, Coindesk, October 26, 2022. www.coindesk.com/Web3/2022/10/26/norway-steps-into-metaverse-with-decentraland-tax-office/ (archived at https://perma.cc/Q6Y5-ZFYA)

41 V Vouloumanos. An island nation in the pacific is rapidly sinking, so to make people pay attention, they put forth a digitized (and devastating) plea, Buzzfeed, December 2, 2022. www.buzzfeed.com/victoriavouloumanos/tuvalu-metaverse-rising-sea (archived at https://perma.cc/LPC5-UK6B)

42 S Goschenko. Colombian court holds hearing in the metaverse, Bitcoin.com, February 17, 2023. news.bitcoin.com/colombian-court-holds-hearing-in-the-metaverse/ (archived at https://perma.cc/XH42-P5VY)

43 Revolve AI. Benefits of augmented reality in education sector—a revolution in the making, Revolve AI, April 6, 2022. revolveai.com/benefits-of-augmented-reality-in-education/ (archived at https://perma.cc/F4UZ-NTWG)

44 S Mondal. Hong Kong University to build world's first metaverse campus: MetaHKUST, Benzinga, August 1, 2022. www.benzinga.com/22/08/28296720/hong-kong-university-to-build-worlds-first-metaverse-campus-metahkust (archived at https://perma.cc/J9DD-9RM9)

45 CB Insights. *AR/VR Trends to Watch in 2022 and Beyond*, CB Insights, September 15, 2022. www.cbinsights.com/reports/CB-Insights_AR-VR-Trends.pdf (archived at https://perma.cc/FQ4U-HX5W)

46 J Teper. Microsoft and Meta partner to deliver immersive experiences for the future of work and play, Microsoft, October 11, 2022. blogs.microsoft.com/blog/2022/10/11/microsoft-and-meta-partner-to-deliver-immersive-experiences-for-the-future-of-work-and-play/ (archived at https://perma.cc/SY9Q-6VAR)

47 K M Lee. Korea ranked 3rd worldwide in metaverse-related patent applications, Korea.net, February 6, 2023. www.korea.net/NewsFocus/Sci-Tech/view?articleId=228409 (archived at https://perma.cc/RJ2A-QHPD)

48 *Korean Herald*. [Editorial] Guidelines for metaverse, *Korean Herald*, December 1, 2022. www.koreaherald.com/view.php?ud=20221130000773 (archived at https://perma.cc/X6C6-BSNV)

49 L Chan and S Woo. Hong Kong toy story: Playing the metaverse game, HKTDC, June 29, 2022. research.hktdc.com/en/article/MTA5NzM5NDg1Nw (archived at https://perma.cc/CHQ7-D2E4)

50 Animoca Brands.The Sandbox announces multiple Hong Kong partnerships to create mega city in the metaverse, Animoca Brands, January 5, 2022. www.animocabrands.com/the-sandbox-announces-multiple-hong-kong-partnerships-to-create-mega-city-in-the-metaverse (archived at https://perma.cc/W5ZH-RAWZ)

51 Technode. Cyberport community members Animoca Brands, Hepha, and EW Metaverse bring virtual Hong Kong to New York Fashion Week, Technode, February 14, 2023. technode.global/2023/02/14/cyberport-community-members-animoca-brands-hepha-and-ew-metaverse-bring-virtual-hong-kong-to-new-york-fashion-week/ (archived at https://perma.cc/TJ4G-6HUQ)

52 N Wood. SK Telecom's metaverse platform goes global, Telecoms.com, November 23, 2022. telecoms.com/518604/sk-telecoms-metaverse-platform-goes-global/ (archived at https://perma.cc/669A-F77Q)

53 Yonhap News Agency. S Korea opens metaverse platform for Korean-language learning, Yonhap News Agency, February 7, 2023. en.yna.co.kr/view/AEN20230207005900315 (archived at https://perma.cc/7R7B-5766)

54 Korean Times. Seoul gov't launches world's 1st public services platform in metaverse, *Korean Times*, January 17, 2023. www.koreatimes.co.kr/www/tech/2023/01/133_343778.html (archived at https://perma.cc/5D63-QVAS)

55 M Chang. Medical IP, KAA sign MOU to develop metaverse-based medicine, *Korea Biomedical Review*, June 21, 2022. www.koreabiomed.com/news/articleView.html?idxno=13951 (archived at https://perma.cc/3VBQ-AVAB)

56 C Davies and S Jung-a. Asia's largest metaverse platform ZEPETO ramps up global expansion, *Financial Times*, September 26, 2022.

www.ft.com/content/14c88e84-f3c8-485e-a9df-31ead34e48f0
(archived at https://perma.cc/2Y9A-73CG)

7. The Metaverse Economic Models

1 R de León. At Gary Vaynerchuk's "veeCon" in Minneapolis, the only
way in is an NFT ticket, CNBC, May 20, 2022. www.cnbc.
com/2022/05/20/at-gary-vaynerchuks-veecon-the-only-way-in-is-an-nft-
ticket.html (archived at https://perma.cc/C37L-3W35)

2 Microsoft. Microsoft to acquire Activision Blizzard to bring the joy and
community of gaming to everyone, across every device, Microsoft,
January 18, 2022. news.microsoft.com/2022/01/18/microsoft-to-
acquire-activision-blizzard-to-bring-the-joy-and-community-of-gaming-
to-everyone-across-every-device/ (archived at https://perma.cc/A57K-
XT77)

3 G Grigg. Crypto crime has hit main street. Here's how local law
enforcement can take action, Chainanalysis, G December 13, 2022.
blog.chainalysis.com/reports/crypto-main-street/ (archived at
https://perma.cc/W99L-XX8Q)

4 M Zoltan. Cryptocurrency scams in 2022—statistics and trends, Privacy
Affairs, December 18, 2022. www.privacyaffairs.com/cryptocurrency-
scams-2022/ (archived at https://perma.cc/4S8D-HGLA)

5 Fire, Fire Wallet Extension, Fire, nd. www.joinfire.xyz/ (archived at
https://perma.cc/32PZ-5AVA)

8. The Metaverse Convergence

1 S Graves. Animoca Brands CEO: "there is no metaverse without Web3,"
Yahoo News, November 5, 2022. finance.yahoo.com/news/animoca-
brands-ceo-no-metaverse-205323838.html (archived at https://perma.cc/
Z6S8-VF4M)

2 S Teixeira. Mozilla to explore healthy social media alternative, Mozilla,
December 20, 2022. blog.mozilla.org/en/mozilla/mozilla-launch-
fediverse-instance-social-media-alternative/ (archived at https://perma.cc/
TZH3-Q5LF)

3 GitHub. Farcaster protocol, GitHub, nd. github.com/farcasterxyz/
protocol (archived at https://perma.cc/26P9-R3ZH)

4 Lens. What is Lens? Lens protocol, Lens, nd. docs.lens.xyz/docs/ what-is-lens (archived at https://perma.cc/5BF4-37R5)

5 DeSo. Homepage, DeSo, nd. www.deso.com/ (archived at https://perma.cc/29GU-6DN7)

6 J Gomila. Golden raises $40m Series B led by a16z crypto to build the decentralized protocol for knowledge, Golden, October 3, 202. golden. com/blog/golden-raises-40m-series-b/ (archived at https://perma.cc/ J23Y-JZZ6)

7 Fabri.lens. Lensverse ecosystem applications, Medium, October 24, 2022. medium.com/@fabriguespe/2023-lens-protocol-application-ecosystem-update-cfa8cf283eb1 (archived at https://perma.cc/AV6G-QPUB)

8 Masa Finance. Introduction, Masa Finance, nd. developers.masa. finance/docs/masa/introduction/ (archived at https://perma.cc/M29U-MS38)

9 Stanford University. The original GOOGLE computer storage [Page and Brin] (1996), Stanford University, nd. infolab.stanford.edu/pub/ voy/museum/pictures/display/0-4-Google.htm (archived at https://perma.cc/FG3U-VA5D)

10 Google. From the garage to the Googleplex, Google, nd. about.google/ our-story/ (archived at https://perma.cc/7DPM-PUGU)

11 M Isaac. Facebook renames itself Meta, *New York Times*, November 10, 2021. www.nytimes.com/2021/10/28/technology/facebook-meta-name-change.html (archived at https://perma.cc/EL6H-M6VR)

12 Oxford University Press. Oxford word of the year 2022, Oxford University Press, nd. languages.oup.com/word-of-the-year/2022/ (archived at https://perma.cc/D3FE-TRUK)

13 A Silberling. Meta acquires Luxexcel, a smart eyewear company, Techcrunch, December 30, 2022. techcrunch.com/2022/12/30/meta-acquires-luxexcel-a-smart-eyewear-company/ (archived at https://perma.cc/KAF4-72L4)

14 J Horwitz, S Rodriguez, and M Bobrowsky. Company documents show Meta's flagship metaverse falling short, *Wall Street Journal*, October 15, 2022. www.wsj.com/articles/meta-metaverse-horizon-worlds-zuckerberg-facebook-internal-documents-11665778961 (archived at https://perma.cc/3EFE-S6HX)

15 T Cibean. Adults in the US check their phones 352 times a day on average, 4x more often than in 2019, Techspot, June 5, 2022. www. techspot.com/news/94828-adults-us-check-their-phones-352-times-day. html (archived at https://perma.cc/48SR-2FTX)

9. Community

1 E Blakemore. What was the Neolithic Revolution? *National Geographic*, April 5, 2019. www.nationalgeographic.com/culture/article/neolithic-agricultural-revolution (archived at https://perma.cc/75LC-XGNP)

2 M Iqbal. YouTube revenue and usage statistics (2022), Business of Apps, September 6, 2022. www.businessofapps.com/data/youtube-statistics/ (archived at https://perma.cc/NY35-GVMP)

3 CNBC. CNBC Disruptor 50: 13. Discord, CNBC, May 17, 2022. www.cnbc.com/2022/05/17/discord-disruptor-50.html (archived at https://perma.cc/93CP-WX5T)

4 J Stoll. Number of Netflix paid subscribers worldwide from 1st quarter 2013 to 3rd quarter 2022, Statista, October 19, 2022. www.statista.com/statistics/250934/quarterly-number-of-netflix-streaming-subscribers-worldwide/ (archived at https://perma.cc/V5F9-3UUP)

5 Social Coop. Mask Network acquires Pawoo.net, one of the largest Mastodon instances, PR Newswire, December 21, 2022. www.prnewswire.com/news-releases/mask-network-acquires-pawoonet-one-of-the-largest-mastodon-instances-301707919.html (archived at https://perma.cc/Y7DC-W8A9)

6 United Nations. The 17 goals, United Nations, nd. sdgs.un.org/goals (archived at https://perma.cc/6UYV-8DGS)

7 GoodDollar. FAQ, GoodDollar, nd. www.gooddollar.org/faq/ (archived at https://perma.cc/W74P-RVX7)

8 GoodDollar. The GoodDollar whitepaper, GoodDollar, nd. whitepaper.gooddollar.org/overview (archived at https://perma.cc/23BC-DR7Z)

9 GoodDollar. GoodDollar by the numbers, GoodDollar, nd. dashboard.gooddollar.org/ (archived at https://perma.cc/T5YA-TGCP)

10 Gitcoin, https://impact.gitcoin.co/ (archived at https://perma.cc/AA3S-8RLJ)

11 ReSeed. You've got questions, we've got answers, ReSeed, nd. www.reseed.farm/faq (archived at https://perma.cc/J2JE-E2RY)

12 ReSeed. Homepage, ResSeed, nd. www.reseed.farm (archived at https://perma.cc/ZHX7-YWXN)

13 Regen Network (18 October 2022), Unlock regenerative finance with Regen Marketplace, Medium, October 18, 2022. medium.com/regen-network/unlock-regenerative-finance-with-regen-marketplace-43745369315b (archived at https://perma.cc/T2Z4-WHGH)

14 Regen Network (18 October 2022), Unlock regenerative finance with Regen Marketplace, Medium, October 18, 2022. medium.com/regen-network/unlock-regenerative-finance-with-regen-marketplace-43745369315b (archived at https://perma.cc/T2Z4-WHGH)

15 Regen Network. Regen Ecosystem Fund, Regen Network, nd. www.regen.network/fund/ (archived at https://perma.cc/UX33-52VZ)

16 Stellar Development Foundation. UNHCR launches pilot cash-based intervention using blockchain technology for humanitarian payments to people displaced and impacted by the war in Ukraine, Stellar Development Foundation, December 15, 2002. stellar.org/press-releases/unhcr-launches-pilot-cash-based-intervention-using-blockchain-technology-for-humanitarian-payments-to-people-displaced-and-impacted-by-the-war-in-ukraine (archived at https://perma.cc/D5QP-BW3V)

17 Marketing Charts. 2022's top brands ranked by customer loyalty, Marketing Charts, September 26, 2022. www.marketingcharts.com/brand-related/brand-loyalty-227306 (archived at https://perma.cc/NNF8-CEWH)

18 Comparably. Apple is ranked #2 in top brands for Gen Z, Comparably, nd. www.comparably.com/brands/apple (archived at https://perma.cc/B9MH-96C5)

19 LEGO. About us: The LEGO history, LEGO, nd. www.lego.com/en-us/aboutus (archived at https://perma.cc/S8MY-UDD3)

20 LEGO. The LEGO history: Godtfred Kirk Christiansen, LEGO, nd. www.lego.com/en-us/history/articles/a-godtfred-kirk-christiansen (archived at https://perma.cc/EMV3-D6M7)

21 LEGO. The LEGO Group and Epic Games team up to build a place for kids to play in the metaverse, LEGO, April 7, 2022. www.lego.com/en-au/aboutus/news/2022/april/the-lego-group-and-epic-games-team-up-to-build-a-place-for-kids-to-play-in-the-metaverse (archived at https://perma.cc/J2SA-AWQ3)

22 A Malik. YouTube rolls out new Partner Program terms as Shorts revenue sharing begins on February 1, Techcrunch, January 9, 2023. techcrunch.com/2023/01/09/youtube-new-partner-program-terms-shorts-revenue-sharing-february-1/ (archived at https://perma.cc/L2UB-LLKR)

23 Roblox. Developer economics, Roblox, nd. create.roblox.com/docs/production/monetization/economics (archived at https://perma.cc/T8EM-8AET)

24 Mastercard. Mastercard announces Web3 spotlight program to develop and launch emerging musical artists in the digital economy, Mastercard, January 6, 2023. www.mastercard.com/news/press/2023/january/ mastercard-announces-Web3-spotlight-program-to-develop-launch- emerging-musical-artists-in-the-digital-economy/ (archived at https://perma.cc/3QL8-DXC5)

25 Women Build Web3. Homepage, Women Build Web3, nd. www. womenbuildWeb3.com (archived at https://perma.cc/KN3Y-968Q)

26 Women Build Web3. Women Build Web3 Whitepaper, Women Build Web3, April 15, 2022. womenbuildWeb3.hashnode.dev/whitepaper (archived at https://perma.cc/77SL-TV35)

27 OMA3. About us, OMA3, nd. www.oma3.org/#about (archived at https://perma.cc/HWE9-8QX8)

10.   The Capital Ecosystem

1 Companies Market Cap. Gold's Market Cap, Companies Market Cap, nd. companiesmarketcap.com/gold/marketcap/ (archived at https://perma.cc/32HK-JD26)

2 S Gherghelas. Dapp industry report 2022, DappRadar, December 21, 2022. dappradar.com/blog/dapp-industry-report-2022-dapp-industry- proves-resilient-in-crypto-winter (archived at https://perma.cc/WHA4- ZCMH)

3 D Chiacu, M Saini, and J Mccrank. Kim Kardashian pays $1.26 million fine for paid crypto ad, SEC says, Reuters, October 3, 2022. www. reuters.com/markets/us/sec-charges-kim-kardashian-unlawfully-touting- crypto-security-statement-2022-10-03/ (archived at https://perma.cc/ 74JC-M65G)

11.   Looking Beyond the Hype

1 LexisNexis. Explore the global cost of financial crime compliance, LexisNexis, nd. risk.lexisnexis.com/global/en/insights-resources/ research/true-cost-of-financial-crime-compliance-study-global-report (archived at https://perma.cc/54YQ-3ZQB)

2 Center for Humane Technology. Key issues overview, Center for Humane Technology, nd. www.humanetech.com/key-issues (archived at https://perma.cc/Q8FR-9VBR)

3 BBC. Metaverse app allows kids into virtual strip clubs, BBC, January 23, 2023. www.bbc.com/news/technology-60415317 (archived at https://perma.cc/L2BQ-4RS3)

4 US Department of the Treasury. US Treasury sanctions notorious virtual currency mixer Tornado Cash, US Department of the Treasury, August 8, 2022. home.treasury.gov/news/press-releases/jy0916 (archived at https://perma.cc/PX4W-4NTK)

5 MetaCourt. IBM acceleration program welcome MetaCourt in new cohort, MetaCourt, December 4, 2022. metacourt.tech/blog/IBM-Acceleration-Program (archived at https://perma.cc/UM3B-GSQF)

6 E Burgener and J Rydning. *High Data Growth and Modern Applications Drive New Storage Requirements in Digitally Transformed Enterprises*, Dell Technologies and NVIDIA, July 2022). www.delltechnologies.com/asset/en-us/products/storage/industry-market/h19267-wp-idc-storage-reqs-digital-enterprise.pdf (archived at https://perma.cc/JWE3-ZSLY)

7 M Osman. Wild and interesting Facebook statistics and facts (2023), Kinsta, December 6, 2022. kinsta.com/blog/facebook-statistics/ (archived at https://perma.cc/7ERD-FLUE)

8 Meta. Meta reports fourth quarter and full year 2022 results, Meta, February 1, 2023. investor.fb.com/investor-news/press-release-details/2023/Meta-Reports-Fourth-Quarter-and-Full-Year-2022-Results/default.aspx (archived at https://perma.cc/65TQ-HLAA)

9 D Davis. VC funding to Black Web3 founders popped last year, bucking trends, Techcrunch, January 29, 2023. techcrunch.com/2023/01/29/vc-funding-to-black-Web3-startups-popped-last-year-bucking-trends/ (archived at https://perma.cc/3MJY-9QSZ)

10 C Metinko. Funding to Web3 startups plummets 74% in Q4, Crunchbase News, January 16, 2023. news.crunchbase.com/Web3/startup-funding-q4-drop/ (archived at https://perma.cc/8PCE-7ZPA)

GLOSSARY

Airdrop: An airdrop is a mechanism where web3 projects give away their tokens to their loyal community members for free. Community members are identified through on-chain interactions with the project, and wallets that have had interactions get rewarded with airdrops.

Amazon Web Services (AWS): AWS is the cloud infrastructure provided by Amazon.

Ancillary revenues: Ancillary revenues are non-core to the primary business model of a firm and are often generated as a by-product of growth in a user base.

Anti-money laundering (AML): AML is the function/capability that helps organizations identify illicit transactions and proactively mitigate the risks.

Application programming interfaces (APIs): APIs are a set of definitions and protocols that are built to allow applications to interact and exchange information.

Art Blocks: Art Blocks is an NFT project on Ethereum platform that uses programmable and generative art for collectors.

Augmented reality (AR): AR is the modification of real-life environments with the addition of visuals and sounds.

Automated market makers (AMM): AMMs leverage smart contracts-based transactions to derive the price of digital assets and provide liquidity, eliminating the need for an intermediary to facilitate the trade.

Azure Cloud: Azure is the cloud infrastructure provided by Microsoft.

Battle pass: Battle pass is a construct that rewards gamers for completing certain in-game milestones. Battle passes have tiers or levels that users can progress in, through their gaming achievements.

Blockchain: Blockchain is an immutable ledger that records transactions and shares it across the network. A decentralized network of nodes manages the validity of these transactions through consensus mechanisms.

Bored Ape Yacht Club (BAYC): BAYC is an NFT collection that was launched in 2021 at the peak of the crypto bull market.

Boson Protocol: Boson Protocol enables web3's ecommerce through the tokenization, transfer and trade of physical goods as redeemable NFTs.

Central bank digital currency (CBDC): CBDC is a currency that is issued by a country's central bank. Implementations that are being discussed should allow central banks to see the state of transactions within their economy in near real time.

Composability: Composability is the ability that a platform offers for seamlessly combining existing applications or their code to create new products. Features such as smart contracts, APIs, and software development kit allow web3 platforms to be composable.

Consensus mechanism: A consensus mechanism is a method by which agreement, trust and governance are achieved in a decentralized network. Proof of work (PoW) and proof of stake (PoS) are the two widely known consensus mechanisms in web3. While PoW has nodes using processing power to validate transactions, PoS depends on network validators using staked tokens.

Cost of acquisition of customers (CAC): CACs refers to the overall costs involved in marketing and onboarding a user to a platform.

Cross-chain bridge: A cross-chain bridge helps transfer cryptos from one blockchain to another.

Crypto wallet: A crypto wallet is a digital location where users can store their digital assets. Most blockchains have applications that provide the wallet functionality which can support cryptos and non-fungible tokens (NFTs) that are built on the blockchain.

Crypto whale: A crypto or an NFT whale is someone who holds a large quantity of a particular crypto token or an NFT collection. The entry of a whale into an NFT community is often seen as a bullish sign for the price of the NFT. We also see the reverse when a whale leaves an NFT collection and the price drops. Therefore, whales can often make (or break) the future of an NFT collection/crypto token both by bringing a lot of attention, but also by helping the price of the asset.

Cryptocurrency: Cryptocurrency is a digital asset in which transactions are managed and recorded on a decentralized network.

CryptoPunks: CryptoPunks are one of the first NFT collections to gain the spotlight. They were launched in 2017 by Larva Labs.

Dapps (decentralized applications): Dapps is the shortened form for decentralized applications. They are applications that are built on blockchain protocols. As blockchains create a developer ecosystem, there is an increase in tools and applications for users. These Dapps include simple crypto wallets, NFT platforms, DeFi applications, and games.

Decentralized autonomous organization (DAO): A DAO is an organization governed by a community. The community typically includes the founding members of the firm, the users of the platform that the organization is working on, creators, developers, and ecosystem members who contribute to the platform, and investors who have invested in the organization.

DAOs are formalized by the launch of a token through a token generation event, and the token holding is often proportional to the voting powers that community members have on DAO resolutions. This effectively makes decisions quite decentralized, unlike traditional capital market constructs.

Decentralized exchanges (DEXs): DEXs are peer-to-peer marketplaces where transactions occur directly between crypto traders.

Decentralized finance (DeFi): DeFi is a financial system that leverages blockchain technologies. The products on DeFi are built on smart contracts and are programmed based on the supply and demand from the network of participants. There is no need for a centralized authority to govern the system.

Decentralized governance: Decentralized governance in a blockchain context refers to how validation of transactions happens using consensus mechanisms. Apart from transaction level governance, if the DAO is set up, resolutions can be voted on by the participants of the ecosystem.

Digital assets: Digital assets is a term used to refer to cryptocurrencies, NFTs, virtual lands, and any other assets that are created on a blockchain.

Discord: Discord is a social media platform that came to prominence mostly due to the crypto bull market in 2020 and 2021. It is used as a community management platform by projects.

Dogecoin: Dogecoin is a cryptocurrency that was launched in 2013. Due to the nature of the asset, it is classified as a meme-coin.

Economic actors: Economic actors in a blockchain context refers to various stakeholders that help a blockchain platform work.

Economic models: Economic models in a blockchain context refers to how the value generated by a platform is distributed across the different economic actors involved in creating the value.

Fiat currency: All forms of money that are made legal tender by a government decree are called fiat currency. In the web3 world, fiat is typically used to refer to USD, GBP, and other mainstream currencies.

GameFi: GameFi is the convergence of gaming and finance, built on blockchain using NFTs and smart contracts.

Gas fee: Gas fee is the term used to refer to the transaction fees that a blockchain network charges the user. The gas fee is used to pay the economic actors involved in conducting the transaction on the network.

Generative art: Generative art refers to the art that is created completely or partially by an autonomous system like an AI platform.

GitHub: GitHub is an online software development platform that is used by developers across the world to store, track, collaborate on, and create software products.

Graphics processing unit (GPU): GPUs are purpose-built processors for rendering images. Over time, they have evolved from graphics accelerators to much more. Their parallel processing abilities have now paved the way for better visual effects, realistic graphics, shadowing techniques, data mining, big data applications, artificial intelligence, and deep learning.

Immutable X: Immutable X is a layer 2 blockchain solution that was built to enhance the capabilities of Ethereum blockchain. It was founded by Jamie Ferguson and Robbie Ferguson in 2018.

In-game assets: In-game assets refer to the assets that gamers and creators create, buy, sell, and own within a gaming ecosystem. They could be gaming weapons, wearables, gadgets, vehicles, or other creatives that can be used within a game.

Initial coin offering (ICO): Initial coin offering was the term used to refer to the launch of a cryptocurrency to raise capital from retail investors. The term was largely used during the 2017/2018 crypto cycle.

Layer 1 (L1): L1 is the base network, such as Bitcoin or Ethereum, and its underlying infrastructure. Layer 1 blockchains can validate and finalize transactions without the need for another network.

Layer 2 (L2): L2 blockchain solutions are built on top of L1 chains to help enhance certain capabilities. This has been particularly true where L2 solutions like Immutable X and Polygon have helped improve transaction throughputs at lower costs on Ethereum blockchain.

Lifetime value (LTV): LTV is the average revenue a customer will generate throughout their lifetime in using a platform.

Market capitalization: Market capitalization of a firm/cryptocurrency/NFT collection is the value of the company derived by multiplying the unit market price of the asset to the total number of shares/tokens/units.

Maximum extractable value (MEV): MEV is defined as the maximum value that can be extracted from block production in excess of the standard block reward and gas fees by including, excluding, and changing the order of transactions in a block.

Metamask: Metamask is one of the leading wallets that supports tokens on the Ethereum blockchain and those on blockchains that are compatible with the Ethereum virtual machine.

Metaverse avatar: Metaverse avatar refers to the digital equivalent that a user poses as to traverse the metaverse.

Metaverse Standards Forum: Formed in June 2022 with 35 founding members, the Metaverse Standards Forum is open to any organization at no cost, and helps to foster interoperability standards for an open metaverse.

Mixed reality (MR): MR refers to an environment that is a combination of a computer-generated immersive environment and a real-world one.

Move to earn (M2E): M2E is a web3-based model where the users could earn cryptos to stay active and move around.

Multiplayer online role-playing game (MMORPG): MMORPG refers to a game category in which several players simultaneously play the game and enjoy features of role-playing games.

NFT marketplaces: NFT marketplaces are platforms that allow users and creators to list NFTs for sale or buy them. These marketplaces typically charge a transaction commission on every sale. Opensea, Blur, and Magic Eden are some examples of NFT marketplaces.

Non-fungible tokens (NFT): NFTs, unlike crypto currencies, are unique, have a digital signature, and can't be replaced. As a result, they have several applications to identify assets both in a virtual and physical goods context.

On-chain analytics: On-chain analytics refers to the data analysis of transactions on a blockchain network. As transactions are transparent, developers can source, analyze, and mine them to derive invaluable insights that can help drive business models and investment decisions.

Oracle: Oracle in a blockchain context refers to the data pipelines that carry information to and from the smart contracts within a blockchain network.

Peer-to-peer (P2P): P2P refers to a model where intermediaries like banks or brokers are absent, and transactions happen from one user to another in a direct fashion. P2P payments and lending are two well-known use cases in this space.

Petabyte (PB): A petabyte is 1024 terabytes, or over 1 quadrillion bytes. To store 1 PB of data will require 745 million floppy disks or 1.5 million CD-ROM discs.

Phygital NFT: Phygital NFTs allow buying and selling real-world physical goods through digital collectibles.

Play to earn (P2E): P2E refers to the economic model where gamers get paid to play and win games. Gaming applications like Axie Infinity and StepN embraced this model and saw some successes too.

Polygon: Polygon is a layer 2 solution for the Ethereum blockchain and helps enhance functionalities on Ethereum.

Private keys: Private keys are hash codes that are used to unlock a crypto wallet. When users lose their private keys, assets in the wallet are not accessible.

Profile picture NFTs (PFP NFTs): As CryptoPunks and BAYC collections grew in popularity, Twitter had many NFT stakeholders sport their punk and ape pictures as their profile picture.

Proof of stake (PoS): PoS is a more environmentally friendly alternative to proof of work. Validators use staked tokens to govern transactions on the network.

Proof of work (PoW): PoW is a consensus mechanism that the bitcoin network uses. It relies on processing power from servers to validate a transaction on the network.

Quantum computing: Quantum computing harnesses the principles of quantum mechanics to solve problems that are too complex for classical computers to handle.

Quantum proof cryptography: Quantum computers are expected to have the ability to break cryptographic techniques like RSA (Rivest–Shamir–Adleman) and elliptic curve cryptography that are mostly used for authentication. However, organizations across the world are working on cryptographic techniques that can be quantum proof or quantum resistant. Blockchains using these cryptographic techniques are expected to be a lot more secure in the long term.

Scenario modeling: Scenario modeling in a token economics (or economic model) context is the process of defining various scenarios and modeling the price of a crypto currency. This process would help assess how a crypto's price would fluctuate depending on market conditions, and what the organization must do to mitigate any risks that would arise from that volatility.

Sensitivity analysis: Sensitivity analysis in token economics is the process of understanding the variables that a token is most sensitive to. This would help assess what the risks around those variables are, and address them proactively, hence ensuring price stability of the token.

Silicon Valley ecosystem: The Silicon Valley ecosystem refers to the collaborative environment built in Silicon Valley by investors, founders, start-ups, and educational institutions like Stanford.

Smart contract: Smart contracts are programs that run on a blockchain that execute certain actions when some predefined conditions are met. In many cases these actions result in the execution of a transaction.

SocialFi: SocialFi is the intersection of social media and finance, where an economic layer is built underneath a social media user experience. The economic layer is typically governed by a decentralized entity.

Solana seed vault: The seed vault inside the Solana mobile is used to store the seed phrase/private key of a user safely.

Stablecoin: Stablecoins are cryptocurrencies that have a relatively stable price and are pegged to a fiat currency or a commodity like gold. Stablecoins must therefore reflect the price of the asset that they are pegged to.

Stablecoin depegging: When depegging happens during a crisis, the price of the stablecoin shows higher than normal variance from the asset they are pegged to.

Token economics (tokenomics): Tokenomics is a construct that defines how value created in a decentralized ecosystem is shared across various economic actors through a token management and distribution mechanism.

Token generation event (TGE): TGE is the acronym used to refer to the process of creating and launching a cryptocurrency, to raise capital from retail and institutional investors.

Transaction value locked (TVL): TVL represents the total value of assets (in $USD) deposited into the smart contracts of a DeFi application.

Transmission Control Protocol/Internet Protocol (TCP/IP): TCP/IP refers to the protocol layer that governs how the individual computers interact with each other and the internet.

Virtual currency mixer: A virtual currency mixer mixes streams of identifiable cryptocurrency transactions with a view to anonymizing these transactions.

Virtual reality: Virtual reality is a three-dimensional immersive environment that a user can interact with and navigate through using special devices.

Web3: Web3 is the term used to identify decentralized platforms and applications.

Zero-knowledge proof: A zero-knowledge proof helps to prove the truth of a statement without sharing the statement's contents or revealing how you discovered the truth. For instance, if a user wants to borrow money and the interest rates are decided by the asset he holds in his wallet, he can inform the lender that he has the necessary assets to borrow, without revealing the assets he holds in the wallet.

INDEX

Page numbers in *italic* denote information contained within a table.